Belief, Truth and Knowledge

Belief
Truth
and
Knowledge

D. M. Armstrong
Challis Professor of Philosophy
University of Sydney

CAMBRIDGE UNIVERSITY PRESS
CAMBRIDGE
LONDON   NEW YORK   NEW ROCHELLE
MELBOURNE   SYDNEY

Published by the Press Syndicate of the University of Cambridge
The Pitt Building, Trumpington Street, Cambridge CB2 1RP
32 East 57th Street, New York, NY 10022, USA
296 Beaconsfield Parade, Middle Park, Melbourne 3206, Australia

Library of Congress catalogue card number: 72–83586

ISBN 0 521 08706 6 hard covers
ISBN 0 521 09737 1 paperback

First published 1973
Reprinted 1974, 1981

First printed in Great Britain by
Western Printing Services Ltd, Bristol
Reprinted in Great Britain at the
University Press, Cambridge

For Madeleine

Acknowledgements

I am greatly indebted to Professors Max Deutscher, Douglas Gasking, J. J. C. Smart and Mr D. Stove. They read the whole or parts of various drafts of this essay, and assisted me a great deal with comments and criticisms. Further useful suggestions came from R. J. Mynott and the referee for Cambridge University Press. Mr George Molnar helped me with the very difficult topic of the nature of dispositions. I should also acknowledge the help of my graduate class at Sydney University with whom I worked through the first and third part of the book. In particular I am indebted to Christopher Murphy. I should also like to thank Mrs P. Trifonoff, who typed the manuscript.

D. M. A.

Sydney University
March 1971

Contents

Part I : Belief

Part I

□□□□□□□□□□□□

Belief

1

The Nature of Belief

The purpose of this brief chapter is to give a first view of a theory of the nature of belief, preparatory to working out the theory in later chapters.

In one of his posthumously published 'Last Papers' ('General Propositions and Causality', in Ramsey 1931) F. P. Ramsey takes as an example the belief that everybody in Cambridge voted. He says that such a belief is 'a map of neighbouring space by which we steer' (p. 238). Here he attributes two characteristics to the belief: it is a *map*, and it is something *by which we steer*. Here in miniature is the account of belief to be defended in this work.

Wittgenstein has little to say directly about belief in the *Tractatus*. But I suppose that his comparison of sentences to pictures inspired Ramsey's comparison of beliefs to maps.

If we think of beliefs as maps, then we can think of the totality of a man's beliefs at a particular time as a single great map of which the individual beliefs are sub-maps. The great map will embrace all space and all time, past, present and future, together with anything else the believer takes to exist, but it will have as its central reference point the believer's present self. But we must not think of the great map as like a modern cartographer's map of the earth's surface. Such a map is too good a map to be a suitable image. (It is not just belief, it is knowledge.) The great belief-map will be much like the maps of old, containing innumerable errors, fantasies and vast blank spaces. It may even involve contradictory representations of portions of the world. This great map, which is continually being added to and continually being taken away from as long as the believer lives, is a map within his mind. If the mind can be (contingently) identified with the brain, as I believe it should be, the map will be literally a map in the believer's head. But the correctness or otherwise of this identification will not be at issue in this book.

The belief-map will include a map of the believer's own mind, and even, as a sub-part of this sub-part, a map of the believer's

3

belief-map (that is, his beliefs that he holds certain beliefs). But this entails no vicious infinite regress. If you try to make a *complete* map of the world and therefore try to include in the map a complete map of the map itself, you will be involved in an infinite series of maps of maps. But since the belief-map is not a complete map of the world, and since the map of itself that it contains is even more incomplete, the situation is no worse than those actual pictures which contain, as part of the scene pictured, little pictures of themselves.

In the case of ordinary maps a distinction can be drawn between the map itself, and the map-reader's interpretation of the map. No such distinction can be drawn in the case of beliefs. We do not read off our interpretation of reality from the data supplied by our beliefs. Our beliefs *are* our interpretation of reality. But, despite this clear difference between beliefs and ordinary maps, the analogy, as I hope will gradually emerge, is still of the greatest value. Beliefs are to be thought of as maps which carry their interpretation of reality within themselves. Of their own nature, apart from any conventions of interpretation, they point to the existence of a certain state of affairs (though there may be no such state of affairs). They have an intrinsic power of representation.

We must distinguish between beliefs and mere thoughts: between believing that the earth is flat and merely entertaining this proposition while either disbelieving it or having no belief one way or the other. Now, if beliefs can be thought of as maps, mere thoughts – the mere entertaining of propositions – seem equally entitled to be considered maps (however wild and inaccurate) of the world. What marks off belief-maps from thought-maps? In his *Treatise* (Book I, Part III, Section 7) Hume asks what marks off believing something from merely entertaining that thought. He claims to be the first philosopher to pose the question. So we may call the problem of distinguishing belief-maps from mere thought-maps 'Hume's problem'.

Ramsey's formula gives us the solution (which was in some degree anticipated by Hume). *Beliefs* are maps *by which we steer*. Unlike entertained propositions, beliefs are action-guiding. Entertained propositions are like fanciful maps, idly scrawled out. But beliefs are maps of the world in the light of which we are prepared to act.

The task of the remaining chapters of this Part of the book will be to spell out and articulate in detail Ramsey's suggestion. The suggestion is bold and simple. But, as might be expected, its working out is laborious and complex.

It might be objected straightaway that this Ramseyan account of belief can at best give an account of beliefs concerning things at particular times and places – beliefs of a historical/geographical sort in that widest sense of 'history' and 'geography' which ranges over all time and all space. (Such beliefs will in future be referred to as 'beliefs concerning particular matters of fact'.) But what of the beliefs that arsenic is poisonous or that every even number is the sum of two primes? How can beliefs in the truth of such unrestricted universally quantified propositions be represented as maps of reality?

I think that the objection is justified, and that a different account must be given of such beliefs. Ramsey himself saw the necessity for a different account. Indeed, his solution to the problem of what it is to believe that an unrestricted universally quantified proposition is true is much more widely known than his quickly thrown-out remark about beliefs concerning particular matters of fact. He suggested that such 'general beliefs' (as we shall in future call them) were 'habits of inference' which dispose us to move from a belief about some particular matter of fact to a further belief about some particular matter of fact. General beliefs are dispositions to extend the original belief-map according to certain rules.

Ramsey was following C. S. Peirce here. (See, for instance, Peirce's essay 'The Fixation of Belief', reprinted in Peirce 1940.) But Douglas Gasking has pointed out to me that Ramsey was probably led to this view by reflecting upon the difficulties of Wittengenstein's Tractatarian view of unrestricted universally quantified propositions as infinite conjunctions of particular propositions. Any attempt to give an account of general *belief* along such lines would clearly face impossible problems.

In Chapter Six a version of this Ramseyan doctrine will be developed, and linked with the notion of a man's holding a belief *for a certain reason*. It will be found to be applicable to general beliefs in the truth of both necessary and contingent propositions.

A note on symbolism. At a number of points, formulae familiar from 'epistemic logic' will be employed. Thus, 'A believes that p' will sometimes be written 'Bap' and 'A knows that p' will be written 'Kap'. Very often, however, when I use such expressions as 'Bap' and 'Kap' reference will not be being made to some proposition but to some state of affairs or situation: A's believing or knowing that p. Thus, in the course of the argument it may be said that 'Baq is the cause of Bap'. This will mean that A's believing that q brings it about that A believes that p. Max Deutscher has suggested that on such occasions it might be better to write '^{S}Baq is the cause of ^{S}Bap' to indicate that it is situations, not propositions, that are in question. I will occasionally adopt his suggestion. But since I think that the context normally makes it clear how the formulae are to be taken, aesthetic reasons plead in favour of omitting such superscripts wherever possible.

2

Beliefs as States

I   Three Ways of Conceiving of Beliefs

Having sketched a theory of the nature of belief in the broadest outline, let us begin detailed investigation by asking under what *general category* belief falls. I think that there exist in our philosophical tradition three different answers to this question, not always explicitly spelled out. First, there is the view that beliefs are *conscious occurrences* in the believer's mind. Second, that beliefs are *dispositions* of the believer. Third, that beliefs are *states* of the believer's mind. In this section these three views are set out.

1. *Beliefs as Conscious Occurrences.* The classical instance of such a theory is Hume's account of belief (*Treatise*, Book I, Part III, Section 7) as a vivid or lively idea associated with a present impression. The 'association with a present impression' will only fit those inductively acquired beliefs concerning particular matters of fact which Hume is especially interested in at that point of the argument of the *Treatise*. Hence we may take his view of belief in general to be that A's believing that p is equivalent to A's having present to consciousness a vivid or lively idea of p.

Such a view, it is notorious, fails to do justice to the way we talk and think about belief. For it is perfectly intelligible to attribute a belief to somebody although there is no relevant vivid idea in his consciousness. We can, for instance, intelligibly attribute a current belief that the earth is round to a man who is sleeping dreamlessly or is unconscious. Hume's vivid ideas may or may not occur, and may or may not have something to do with a man's beliefs, but asserting the presence of such an idea in a man's consciousness cannot be what it means to assert that he has the corresponding belief.

The difficulty has nothing to do with the particular form which Hume's theory takes. The difficulty faces any theory which equates a man's current belief with some current content of his consciousness, whether it be a vivid idea of p, an inward motion of assent

7

to the proposition 'p', or whatever. For it always seems intelligible
to suppose that the content of consciousness should be absent and
yet that the believer held the relevant belief at that time.

2. *Beliefs as Dispositions.* At least since Ryle's *Concept of Mind*
(Ryle 1949), it has been common for philosophers to compare the
attribution of beliefs with the attribution of dispositions to objects.
The word 'disposition' is a philosopher's term of art here. In
ordinary language, dispositions such as cheerfulness and irritability
are attributed to persons and animals, not to ordinary physical
objects. But the philosopher's paradigms of a disposition are properties of physical objects such as brittleness, solubility, elasticity
and friability. It would be a matter for inquiry whether such traits
as cheerfulness and irritability, although they bear obvious analogy
to philosopher's dispositions and are the source of the term, are in
fact dispositions in the technical sense. Nevertheless, the philosopher's paradigms do seem to pick out a class of properties with
clearly marked formal similarities. So, in this book, the term 'disposition' will be used to refer to this class.

The comparison of beliefs with philosopher's dispositions certainly shows promise of illuminating the nature of belief. We
distinguish between a thing's disposition and the manifestation of
that disposition; between the brittleness of a piece of glass and its
actually breaking. We recognize further that having the disposition
does not entail manifestation of the disposition: a piece of glass may
be brittle and yet never break. In similar fashion, we distinguish
between a belief and its manifestation, or, as we also say, its expression: between A's belief that p and the speech-act and other
actions or occurrences in which the belief is manifested or expressed;
and we recognize that having the belief does not entail manifestation or expression of the belief. Such a distinction enables us to give
a plausible account of the case of the sleeping or unconscious believer. So it is certainly an hypothesis worth investigation that
beliefs stand to their manifestations or expressions just as dispositions such as brittleness stand to *their* manifestations.

Ryle's dispositional account of belief was developed as part of,
and in order to support, a Behaviourist or Behaviourist-orientated
theory of mind. It is important, therefore, to appreciate that there
is nothing in the mere *dispositional view of belief* which entails
that the manifestations or expressions of a man's belief (if they
occur at all) are all pieces of outward bodily behaviour. Unspoken

thoughts, mental images or inward motions of assent are, *prima facie*, possible manifestations of A's belief that p. Hume's 'vivid ideas' are not beliefs, but, provided there are such things, there is no reason why they should not be *manifestations* of beliefs. It is awkward to use the word 'manifestation' in connection with inner mental occurrences – an awkwardness which the word 'expression' shares – but it is no more than awkward. There may be other arguments to show that such inner occurrences cannot be manifestations of belief, but the mere demonstration that beliefs are dispositions would do nothing to support any limitation of possible manifestations to outward behaviour.

3. *Beliefs as States*. The dispositional view of belief is certainly more satisfactory than the 'conscious occurrence' view. There is, however, a third and, I believe, a still more satisfactory way of thinking about belief which is at least implicit in Western philosophical thought. According to this view, A's believing that p is a matter of A's being in a certain *continuing state*, a state which endures for the whole time that A holds the belief. In the case of beliefs which are acquired, this view thinks of A's belief that p as a matter of A's mind being *imprinted* or *stamped* in a certain way. Plato's image in the *Theaetetus* (191 C–E) is that of the imprint made by a seal on a block of wax, an imprint which then endures for a greater or lesser time. I would add to this by saying that there is no reason why this state should be something which the believer is conscious of being in. He may or he may not know that he holds a certain belief.

The notion of a *state* of an object deserves some consideration. To say that an object is in some state is to attribute a property to the object. But what sort of property? First, it is a non-relational property of the object. We distinguish a thing's state from its circumstances. Of course, the state may itself involve relation, that is to say, the state may be a structural property. Indeed, the concept of the state of an object is naturally associated with the idea of a structure of, or within, the object. (But I doubt whether the idea of a structure is part of the concept of a state. The particular temperature of an object is naturally said to be a state of the object. Yet the concept of temperature does not *entail* that the hot object is structured in any way.)

But not every non-relational property of an object defines a state of the object. A thing is a horse in virtue of a conjunction of non-relational properties, and a conjunction of properties is a property. But we could not say that last year's Melbourne Cup winner is in the state of being a horse. Consider Proteus, however, who could take on the form of any animal he pleased. If he becomes a horse, is he not in the state of being a horse?

This suggests that when we speak of states of an object we always have in mind some classification of the object relative to which the state is an accidental or changeable feature of the object. Perhaps the object always possesses the feature, but it will be an intelligible supposition that the feature should be lost. If beliefs are states, then they will be accidental and changeable features of *minds* (or, if this is objected to, of *persons*).

But our account of states is still too broad. We should not want to say that a man is in the state of running, but this is permitted by what has been said so far. How is running to be excluded? I think the answer is that the concept of running is of *necessity* the concept of a process: meaning by 'process' here something whose different phases are different in nature. (*Uniform* motion would not be an example of a process.) But a state need not involve a process. It may in fact be a process, but it is not entailed that it is a process. Beliefs might in fact be processes. For instance, if physicalism is true, beliefs might be reverberating circuits. But, unlike the concept of running, it is not part of the concept of belief that belief is, or involves, a process.

A counter-instance may be proposed to the argument of the previous paragraph. We speak of a person or a liquid as being in an agitated state. Yet does not agitation involve processes? I think, however, that what is meant by 'an agitated state' is that state, whatever it may be, which is responsible for the agitation of the person or thing. We do draw a distinction, even if a fine one, between a person's being agitated and his being in an agitated state. The latter seems to refer to some continuing condition, of unspecified nature, which produces a good deal of agitated behaviour. So perhaps the counter-instance fails.

So much by way of explicating the notion of a state. Although I think that the view that beliefs are states is to be preferred to the view that beliefs are dispositions, I think also that the dispute is a very confusing one. For it seems that (i) although not all states are dispositions, dispositions are a species of state. (ii) There is one species of belief, *viz.* general beliefs, which may be plausibly said to be dispositions. (iii) In respect of other sorts of belief, despite the undoubted important resemblances between disposition-states and belief-states, there are significant differences between them. These differences make it very misleading to say that non-general beliefs are a species of disposition. The next two sections try to substantiate these three propositions.

II Dispositions are States

The argument appears to have seven steps.

1. It seems obvious that for every true contingent proposition there must be something in the world (in the largest sense of 'something') which makes the proposition true. For consider any true contingent proposition and imagine that it is false. We must automatically imagine some difference in the world. Notice that it is not being argued here that for every different true contingent proposition there is a *different* something in the world which makes that proposition true. (I think the latter doctrine is in fact demonstrably false. See Part II.)

2. As a corollary of 1, where a predicate 'F' is not applicable to an object, a, up to the time t but is applicable to that object after t, it must be the case that a has changed in some way at t.

Dr D. H. Mellor has objected (in discussion) that this corollary is falsified by a case where a man is not a hundred years old up to t, but becomes a hundred years old at t. Previously the predicate 'a hundred years old' was not applicable to him, now it is. Yet the man himself need not have changed in any way. This objection enables me to make clear how small a claim it is that is being made at this stage of the argument. For one of the man's *relational* properties (*viz.* his relation to his birth date) has changed. And for the purpose of this argument a change in a relational property is a change in the object.

3. It follows immediately that if a dispositional predicate is not applicable to an object up to t but is applicable to the object after t then there must have been a change in the object at t. For instance, if a piece of glass cannot truly be said to be brittle up to t but can be truly said to be brittle after t then the object must have changed at t.

4. It will now be argued that the change must be a change in the *non-relational* properties of the disposed object. A disposition

entails the presence (or absence) of non-relational properties of the object.

Consider an occasion where a disposition is manifested. A brittle piece of glass is struck and, as a result, it breaks. In any causal sequence the nature of the effect depends upon three things: the nature of the cause; the nature of the circumstances it operates in; the nature of the thing the cause acts upon. The glass breaks because it is struck, it is not carefully packed around with protective material, and it is brittle. Cause of a certain nature + circumstances of a certain nature + disposition = effect of a certain nature. Now a disposition is something which the disposed thing retains in the absence both of a suitable initiating cause and of suitable circumstances for the cause to operate in. A brittle piece of glass is still brittle, even although it is not struck and is so packed around with protective material that striking would not cause breaking. But the presence or absence of the initiating cause, and the presence or absence of suitable circumstances for its operation, are the only *relational* properties of the piece of glass which are relevant to its breaking or not breaking. The possession of the disposition must therefore depend upon *non-relational* properties of the glass.

This argument might be challenged by pointing to the logical possibility of surrounding circumstances of the piece of glass, circumstances which formed a nomically indissoluble unity with the glass, and which also played an essential causal role in the glass's breaking when struck. (I would like to give an example, but the situation is so weird that I can think of no case that has the slightest intuitive appeal.) But if a piece of glass did stand in this extraordinary relation to its surrounding circumstances, then I think it could be said that the two would form a unit which we would naturally treat as a single thing. And then the disposition would be naturally redescribed as a disposition of this larger thing. Hence I do not think that we would allow such a case as a counter-instance.

5. So a disposition entails the presence (or absence) of non-relational properties of the object. It will now be argued that a disposition entails that the disposed object is in a certain *state*.

(It will be recalled that, although states of objects are non-relational properties of objects, not all non-relational properties of objects are states of these objects. It was argued that the special marks of states are these. (i) If an object of a certain sort is in a state it is always intelligible, at least, that it should cease to be in that state while remaining an object of that sort. This entails that a state is always a state relative to some prior classification of the thing. (ii) Although in fact states may involve a process, such as a reverberating circuit, the concept of the state never entails the existence of such processes.)

It seems clear that the presence (or absence) of non-relational properties entailed by possession of a disposition may properly be said to be a state of the object. For it is always intelligible to suppose that the thing which is brittle or elastic, *etc.* should cease to be brittle or elastic and yet still be the same sort of thing (still glass, rubber, a solid, *etc.*). So the first condition for a state is satisfied. And since dispositional concepts leave us in ignorance concerning the properties of the disposed object which give it that disposition, it follows that attribution of dispositions does not entail that some *process* takes place in the object. So the second condition for a state is satisfied.

6. The argument so far has purported to establish that attribution of a disposition to an object entails that the object is in a certain *state*. What is the concrete nature of this state? No apodeictic answer to this question is possible. But I suggest that the most plausible general answer is: whatever state of the object scientists find to be responsible for manifestation of the disposition when a suitable initiating cause acts upon the object. In the case of brittleness, for instance, the state will be a certain sort of bonding of the molecules of the brittle object.

However, it is important to realize that accepting this step in the argument leaves a deep question about dispositions unanswered, a question which our investigation will leave unanswered. The question may be illustrated by referring again to the state of molecular bonding which makes a brittle object brittle. To talk of molecular *bonding* is surely to talk again in terms of dispositions of the bonded things. If our argument has been correct, the attribution of this new disposition will entail that the bonded things are in some state. When the description of this state is known, it may involve further dispositions. Where will this process end? *Prima facie*, it seems that it might end in one of two ways or, perhaps, not end at all. *First*, we might come in the end to properties of the disposed thing which involve no element of dispositionality. They will be the ultimate properties on which truthful attributions of dispositions rest. *Second*, we might reach ultimate *potentialities* of the disposed thing, potentialities which do not depend upon non-dispositional properties. To adopt such a solution would involve accepting an ultimate ontological division among non-relational properties into potentialities and non-potentialities. *Finally*, there is the possibility that the process goes to infinity, dispositions resting upon states which involve further dispositions which involve further states . . . The question whether all, or only one or two, of these alternatives are genuine possibilities, it is our good fortune to be able to ignore in this essay. But it is important to realize that the argument, at least, has not foreclosed any of these options.

7. The argument so far, if successful, only shows that attribution of a disposition entails that the object so disposed is in a certain state. The state is such that a triggering cause of a suitable nature acting upon the object in that state brings it about (in suitable circumstances, at least) that the disposition is manifested.

It will now be argued further that it is linguistically proper to *identify* the disposition with this state of the disposed object. It is linguistically proper, for instance, to say that brittleness *is* a certain sort of bonding of the molecules of the brittle object. The ground for saying this is simply that scientists and others often speak in this way, and there seems to be no objection to such speech. (It is not argued that we *have* to speak in this way.)

The propriety of this identification has been challenged by Roger Squires (Squires 1968). He argues in the following way. Suppose that a disposition is identified with some state of the disposed thing. Suppose also that, at a certain time, the disposition is unmanifested. Must not the currently inactive state have a disposition to bring about the appropriate manifestation in appropriate conditions? But then, by parity of argument, this new disposition will have to be identified with some further state of the object, and so *ad infinitum*. Thus, Squires argues, the attribution of a disposition will commit us *a priori* to postulating an infinite number of states in the object which has the disposition. He rightly regards this conclusion as unacceptable.

I do not think that there is a vicious regress here. The first point to notice is that dispositions are ordinarily attributed to *things*. How can a state, which is a species of property, have a disposition? However, it seems that Squires can reconstruct his argument. Suppose, again, that a thing's disposition is a state of the thing, but the disposition is not manifested. The thing which is in that state will have a disposition to display the appropriate manifestation in appropriate conditions. Squires can argue that this new disposition will have to be identified with some further state of the object, and so *ad infinitum.*

But have we really got a *new* disposition requiring a *new* state? A piece of glass is brittle because it has molecular bonding M. The piece of glass having the M-type molecular bonding is disposed to break if it is hit. But is this not the disposition of *brittleness* all over again? And can we not say that the state of the glass which this disposition should be identified with is . . . molecular bonding M? We can allow Squires that there is a regress. But it appears to be virtuous, not vicious. It is like the expression: 'if p, then it is true that p, and then it is true that is true that p . . . and so on'. I conclude that the actual identification of dispositions with states of the disposed thing is perfectly in order.

It must be confessed, however, that while the identification can legitimately be made, there seems to be no way of arguing that it *has* to be made. While allowing that attribution of dispositions entails attribution of states of a certain sort to the objects which have the dispositions, nevertheless we can, if we want to, still make a verbal distinction between the disposition and the state. (A verbal distinction that cuts no ontological ice.) But equally there seems to be no linguistic objection to the identification, and I think that, very often at least, it is the natural way of talking. It is the way of talking which will be adopted in this work.

Our seven-stage argument is now concluded. If dispositions are states of the disposed object, they are marked off from (many) other states by the way they are *identified*. When we speak of the brittleness of an object we are identifying a state of the object by reference to what the thing which is in that state is capable of bringing about (in conjunction with some active, triggering cause), instead of identifying the state by its intrinsic nature. And this in turn is connected with the rôle that dispositional concepts play in our thinking. We introduce such a concept where, for example, it is found that an object of a certain sort, acted upon in a certain way, behaves in certain further ways of a relatively unusual sort. We assign responsibility for this behaviour to some relatively unusual state of the object. But since we normally do not know, prior to painful and extensive scientific investigation, what the nature of the state is, we name it from its effects. We thus expose ourselves to Molière's ridicule, and, if we did nothing further, we would deserve it. But we have set up the formal structure of an explanation which later research may turn into a genuinely helpful one. Dispositions, in fact, are primitive *theoretical concepts*: concepts of states specified by what the thing in that state can effect. (I assume, of course, a *Realistic* view of theoretical concepts.) Successful scientific investigation leads to a *contingent identification* of the nature of these states.

III   Differences between Beliefs and Dispositions

If the argument of the previous section has been correct, it is wrong to oppose the view that beliefs are dispositions to the view that they are states. A belief might be a disposition, and yet be an imprinting on the mind, or some other state, for all that. But, as will now be demonstrated, there are some important, even if not overwhelming, differences between dispositions and beliefs (with the exception of general beliefs).

(i) One point of distinction between dispositions such as brittleness, and beliefs, is that the concept of the former involves the notion of an initiating cause of a certain sort which triggers off the manifestation. The brittle glass is brittle because it breaks *when hit*. A piece of sugar is soluble because it dissolves *when placed in water*. But the concept of beliefs seems to involve no notion of a class of initiating causes which in turn bring about the manifestation or expression of the belief. No doubt initiating causes will always be present when the belief is manifested. But they play no special role in the concept of belief.

Chomsky has frequently called attention to the stimulus-independent nature of speech-acts (see, for instance, Chomsky 1968, p. 11). When a speaker produces a grammatical and meaningful sentence there is in general no characteristic external stimulus which has caused him to produce this sentence. What speakers say is rather determined by their interests and purposes. The manifestations or expressions of beliefs are similarly stimulus-independent. But the manifestations of dispositions like brittleness are stimulus-*dependent*.

General beliefs are a plausible exception. Consider A's belief that arsenic is poisonous. This can plausibly be treated as a disposition of A's. The initiating cause of the manifestation of the disposition is A's coming to believe that some portion of stuff is arsenic. This

belief about a particular matter of fact triggers off a certain manifestation: A's acquiring the further belief that this stuff is poisonous. (A full treatment of general beliefs is reserved for Chapter
Six.)

(ii) If brittleness is manifested, it can be manifested in only one
sort of way: by the brittle object breaking if struck. But there is no
one such way that a belief that the earth is flat must manifest itself,
if it does manifest itself. For instance, the manifestations need not
take the form of outer or inner assent.

Ryle, at least, was well aware of this difference, and tried to meet
the difficulty by distinguishing between 'single-track' and 'many-
track' dispositions (Ryle 1949, pp. 43–5). Brittleness, he said, is a
single-track disposition, and so is manifested, if it is manifested, in
only one way. But Smith's belief that the earth is flat can have
indefinitely many manifestations. It is a 'many-track' disposition.
Ryle even allowed that the set of different sorts of possible mani-
festion might be an infinite one: an 'infinite-track' disposition,
apparently.

But Ryle's distinction still has not done justice to the difference.

Anyone who understands the term 'brittle' understands what the
manifestation of brittleness is: breaking when struck. But, at the
same time, the notion of 'breaking when struck' can be understood
without making any reference to the notion of brittleness. The
notion of brittleness can be *introduced* as that state of an object
which is responsible for the manifestation of breaking when struck.

By contrast, the characteristic manifestations of a belief can only
be identified as manifestations of the belief by reference back to the
belief.

To illustrate. If A believes that the earth is flat and is an Anglo-
Saxon he may well manifest his belief, on a particular occasion, by
uttering the English sentence 'the earth is flat'. Such a manifestation must surely figure in any list of possible manifestations of A's
belief. But what makes it a manifestation of A's belief? Only the
fact that the rules of English are such that uttering these phonemes
would be a natural way *of expressing such a belief.*

The point may be put thus. If we take the, perhaps infinite, set
of possible sorts of manifestation or expression of a belief that p,
the only unifying factor we can discover in the set is that they
might all spring from, be manifestations or expressions of, the one
belief. And this, I think, shows that even if we do not think of

dispositions as actual states of the disposed thing (though I have argued that we should think of them as states), we *must* think of beliefs as actual states of the believer. For it is only if the believer is in a state which, in suitable circumstances, might *give rise to*, that is *cause*, all these manifestations, that we can understand what holds them together as a class. The situation is something like that in a house where a window has been opened, a glass of whisky drunk, cigarette ash dropped and some money taken. In themselves there is nothing which unifies this heterogeneous collection of events. But a unifying principle is at once supplied if we suppose that they were all caused by an unauthorized intruder.

The distinction between the belief which is not being manifested, and the belief which is, then becomes the distinction between a *causally quiescent* state, and the same state causally active. (A useful analogy is the 'information' inactive in the memory-banks of a computer, and the same 'information' currently playing a causal role in the computing process, and so in bringing about the computer's 'print-out'.)

Once again, general beliefs are a plausible exception to what has been said about this distinction between beliefs and dispositions. It is plausible to say that A believes that arsenic is poisonous if, and only if, acquiring the belief that a certain portion of stuff is arsenic brings it about, in normal circumstances at least, that A acquires the further belief that that portion of stuff is poisonous. There is a single, logically central, manifestation of A's belief.

(iii) In the case of beliefs, as opposed to dispositions like brittleness, it seems that the states involved must have a certain internal structure. Suppose that A believes (i) the cat is on the mat; (ii) the cat is asleep; (iii) the cat is black. These three beliefs, although all different, involve a common element. Now if we take beliefs to be states of the believer, must we not take it that these states have an internal structure such that to common elements in the things believed correspond common elements in the state which is the belief? We must, of course, distinguish between the believing and what is believed: between A's believing that p which is a state of A, and the proposition 'p' which is believed. But must not the internal structure of the belief-state reflect the structure of the proposition believed? How otherwise could beliefs with different content give rise to different manifestations or expressions? Compare this with the case of brittleness. We are (I have argued) logically committed to a state of the brittle thing. But we are not *logically* committed to any further characterization of that state.

It may be thought that the notion of the internal structure of a state is a confused one. An object, or perhaps an event, may have a structure of a certain sort, but how can a state, which is a species of property, have a structure? In answer to this objection, perhaps it is true that the notion of the structure of a state is an unusual one. Nevertheless, it seems a notion that, once explained, can be understood and applied without much difficulty. The molecules of a certain brittle piece of glass may be bonded in a certain fashion. That is a state the glass is in. Now since this state involves a certain sort of arrangement of the constituent molecules of the glass, it can be said to have a structure. The state involves elements in a relation. I am arguing that belief-states must have a structure in this sense. The belief-states involve elements in a relation.

I think it is fair to say that there is no more than a difference in the degree of theoretical commitment involved in the concept of a belief as opposed to dispositions like brittleness. It has been argued that to call something brittle involves the claim that there is some state of the brittle thing which is responsible for the thing breaking if struck. With belief we are carried a step further, and are committed to states having a structure, a structure which corresponds to the structure of the proposition believed. (*This* point of distinction between beliefs and dispositions would seem to hold as much for general as for other sorts of belief.)

Concerning this structure of the belief-state a great deal more must be said in subsequent chapters of this Part.

(iv) Finally, there is a distinction between dispositions such as brittleness on the one hand and beliefs on the other, which has seemed to many philosophers to be a far deeper and more fundamental distinction than any of the three already mentioned. However, I believe that in fact it is a relatively superficial distinction.

If we ask why we attribute particular sorts of disposition to particular objects it seems that our knowledge or belief is always based upon *evidence*. It is indirect or inferential. We do not observe the disposition, but rather its manifestation; or else, even more indirectly, we observe that things of this sort have, in the past, given rise to manifestations of this sort. Now in the attribution of beliefs to other people there is, we ordinarily assume, a similar restriction to indirect evidence. But if we take *ourselves*, then, at least in many cases, we can know what our beliefs are independent of any manifestation or expression of the belief. I know directly, without evidence, that I believe that acquired characteristics are not inherited.

A lot turns on the question of how we conceive of this knowledge of our own beliefs. If this knowledge is thought of as logically indubitable or incorrigible, or a matter of logically privileged access, then no doubt this would set a great logical gulf between beliefs and ordinary dispositions. For presumably there could be no such logically privileged knowledge of the brittleness of a solid object. But I have argued against the notion that we have any such privileged knowledge of our own mental states elsewhere (Armstrong 1968, Chapter Six, Section X). I will not repeat these arguments. But once such a special knowledge of our mental states is disavowed, it seems to be simply a contingent fact that we have direct or non-inferential knowledge of (some) of our mental states, including (some) of our belief-states, but that we lack such knowledge of the brittleness of certain pieces of glass.

Not all knowledge can be based on evidence, because that evidence itself must be something which we know, and so, on pain of vicious infinite regress, there must be some things which we know directly, that is, not on the basis of evidence. (An argument which, together with the whole topic of non-inferential knowledge, we will discuss more fully in Part III of this book.) It so happens that some of the things we know without evidence are our own current states of mind, although these are not the only particular matters of fact which we know directly. We do not in general have such direct knowledge of the dispositions of the material things in our environment (although we do seem to have direct knowledge of such states of affairs as physical pressure on our body). But it seems a perfectly intelligible concept that we should have direct knowledge of dispositions. We could imagine, for instance, that, as a causal result of bringing his fingers into contact with pieces of glass, a person should come to know whether the pieces were brittle or not, but not on the basis of any evidence. The state which is the brittleness would be acting upon his mind to produce unevidenced knowledge that the object is brittle, either *via* some established sense-organ or in some other way. Such knowledge would seem to be in no different logical position from, say, knowledge gained by touch of the thing's jaggedness or smoothness. That we have no such capacity to gain unevidenced knowledge of brittleness seems to cast no light on the concept of brittleness, and so sets up no logical distinction between dispositions like brittleness and beliefs.

But we *have* found three points of logical distinction between dispositions and beliefs. (i) Manifestations of dispositions are 'stimulus-dependent'; manifestations of belief are not. (ii) Dispositions, if manifested, are manifested in only one sort of way; beliefs, if manifested, are manifested in indefinitely many ways. (iii) While attribution of a disposition to an object attributes a state to the disposed thing, the state need be credited with no particular structure; but belief-states must be credited with a structure which corresponds to the proposition believed.

When the beliefs are restricted to beliefs about particular matters of fact, it is the collection of structured belief-states in a particular mind at a particular time which is to be thought of as that mind's map of the world at that time.

It will be argued subsequently that the first two of these distinctions between beliefs and dispositions do not hold for general beliefs.

IV   Belief and Consciousness

We have rejected the view that a current belief is necessarily something we are currently conscious of. Beliefs are states of mind which, so far from us being currently conscious of, we need not even know that we possess. (Other people, or we ourselves at a later date, may postulate their existence in order to explain some feature of our observed conduct or our mental life.) Nevertheless, a belief can be a content of consciousness. It can be 'before our mind'. And so it may be demanded of a theory of belief that it explain what it is for a belief to be before our mind.

We have already distinguished between a belief which is currently causally active in our mental workings and one which is not. It is important to see, therefore, that currently causal activity is compatible with the belief not being a content of consciousness. Many of the beliefs which guide our actions never enter consciousness while the action is being preformed, yet the belief must be causally active at that time. Sometimes a confidently held belief turns out to be false, and as a result the action based on it is unsuccessful, yet only with failure do we become conscious that we had been all along assuming the truth of that belief.

It may be suggested that having a belief currently before our mind is a matter of giving inner assent or affirmation to the proposition believed. 'Assent' or 'affirmation' are linguistic notions and 'inner' assent or affirmation is presumably an imaging or other imagining of 'outward', that is, genuine, assent or affirmation to a proposition which is believed. Now there is no doubt that such mental performances do occur. But they do not cast any light on what it is for a belief to be before our mind. For exactly the same imaginative performance can occur in the absence of belief, though it might not then be called 'inner assent' or 'inner affirmation'. And could we not have a belief, and be currently aware of having it, without going through such a performance?

The fact is that an account of having a belief before our mind, as a current content of consciousness, does not demand development of the theory of belief but rather of the quite general notion of consciousness. And an analysis of the latter notion is one of the most difficult tasks facing philosophical psychology. I have tried to develop an account of consciousness in *A Materialist Theory of the Mind*, in particular in the chapter on Introspection. I there return to Kant's idea of consciousness as 'inner sense' – as *perception* of (some of) the contents of our own mind.

On this view, for a belief to be before our mind, to be a content of consciousness, is like an object being in our field of view. We have visual perceptions of various currently existing things. These perceptions may or may not be veridical and there are always plenty of things which are never perceived at all. In the same way, we have 'introspections' of the current state of our mind, introspections which may or may not be veridical and which never extend to everything currently existing or going on in our mind. In perception the world is scanned, in introspection our own mind is scanned (including our perceptions) and the latter scanning is consciousness.

The further question then arises, also a question of the greatest difficulty, what is the nature of perception. I think it is an acquiring of knowledge or belief about the nature of our physical environment (including our own body). It is a flow of information. In some cases it may be something less than the acquiring of knowledge or belief, as in the cases where perceptions are entirely discounted or where their content has been confidently anticipated. Here the process may be compared to the acquiring of totally discounted or totally redundant information. It is like acquiring knowledge or belief, but it is less than the acquiring of knowledge or belief. If this account of perception is on the right lines it can then be applied to introspection. Introspection will be the acquiring of knowledge or beliefs (in many cases quickly lost again) concerning our own current mental state.

This brief sketch of a doctrine that is developed in detail elsewhere is simply meant to indicate how difficult it would be to solve all the problems which can be raised about *consciousness of* beliefs within the present work. But, as indicated, I think that the problems which arise are not peculiar to the topic of belief.

3

Belief and Language

I   Manifestations and Expressions

In the previous chapter the notorious *multiform* nature of the possible manifestations or expressions of beliefs was mentioned. There is no single sort of manifestation or expression which stands to a particular belief as breaking on being struck stands to brittleness. Nevertheless, the question arises whether there may not be a class of manifestations or expressions which stand in a peculiarly intimate relation to a belief *viz.* expressing it verbally.

It is convenient to introduce a terminological convention here, and make 'expression' a narrower term than 'manifestation'. Some of the things which occur (if anything occurs) because somebody has a certain belief will be *actions* of that person: things which spring from his will. Other effects of a belief, while still something which the believer does in the widest sense of 'does', will not be things which spring from his will. Let us restrict the term 'expressions' to those manifestations of beliefs which spring from the believer's will. Thus, my belief that p may bring it about that on a certain occasion I blush. In the terminology now to be adopted this will be a manifestation of the belief that p, but it will not be an expression of that belief because blushing is not something we do at will.

The manifestations of mental states that are important in explicating the *concept* of the mental state in question are, in general, expressions of that mental state, not mere manifestations. It would seem that beliefs are no exception to this rule. We can further distinguish between linguistic and non-linguistic expressions of belief: between saying, and doing which is not saying. Now many philosophers, particularly in recent years, have been inclined to think that the linguistic expressions of belief are their logically primary manifestations. The thought has been vague, yet it has been pervasive. In opposition to this, I will argue that there is no special logical or conceptual connection between beliefs and their linguistic expression.

24

II   Belief without Language

The first, and obvious, point is that we constantly attribute beliefs to beings such as animals and very small children who lack any capacity to speak (and, it may be added, have small capacity to understand what is said to them). The dog digs frantically at the place where he buried a bone, or rushes to the door on hearing his master's voice. It is natural to think of his actions as expressions of a *belief* that he has a bone buried there, or that his master is at the door. If the bone has been secretly removed, or the 'voice' is simply a tape-recording, then the dog's belief is false.

It is entirely natural to explain the dog's actions by attributing certain beliefs to him. And if the explanation is so natural, that is already some argument for thinking it an intelligible explanation (whether or not it is a true explanation). Against this, however, it is argued that this 'natural' explanation of the observed facts becomes suspect when it is asked exactly what it is that the dog believes. Has the dog got concepts of 'burying', of 'bone', of 'his master', of 'the door'? It is sufficiently obvious that he does not have *our* concepts of these things. But if he lacks our concepts, what can it mean to say that 'he believes that he has a bone buried there', or that 'he believes that his master is at the door'? We want to say that the dog believes something – but we do not seem able to say what! Is our attribution of beliefs to the dog really intelligible after all? Perhaps it is concealed nonsense.

Here, however, we can take advantage of a distinction which Quine has made familiar between 'referentially opaque' and 'referentially transparent' propositions about beliefs. (See his essay 'Reference and Modality' in Quine 1961.) Suppose that I point to a man across the room and say 'Smith believes that the chap over there is the villain of the piece.' Suppose also that Smith believes that Robinson is the villain of the piece and believes that Robinson is at present in Madagascar. Suppose, finally, that Robinson is not in Madagascar but is the chap over there. Did I say something false? It depends on how I meant the sentence to be taken. If I meant it to be taken in a 'referentially opaque' way then what I asserted was false. In this way of taking my sentence, Smith does not believe that the chap over there is the villain of the piece. But if I meant my sentence to be taken in a referentially transparent way we can substitute co-designating expressions ('that chap over there' for

'Robinson') without loss of truth. If I happen to know that Smith believes that Robinson is in Madagascar I may even make it quite explicit that my sentence is to be taken in the 'transparent' way by adding 'of course, Smith believes the man is in Madagascar'.

There are these two ways of talking about beliefs, but it is clear that the referentially opaque construction is the more fundamental. For it tells us the actual content of the belief which is in the believer's mind. The referentially transparent mode of speech is a way of talking about beliefs without actually saying what their content is. Such a glancing or indirect style of reference has obvious utility in discourse. It is particularly useful where the exact content of the belief is not known. And this, I suggest, is what is happening in our reference to animals' beliefs. We do not know the exact content of their beliefs and our attributions of belief to them have no more than a referentially transparent force.

Let us return to the dog. To say that the actual content of the animal's belief is that he has a bone buried in that place or that his master is at the door is almost certainly incorrect for the reasons already given. Yet on the evidence of the dog's behaviour it is a natural hypothesis to attribute *some such* belief to him. The existence of a loose or referentially transparent way of talking about beliefs enables us to resolve the dilemma. In saying that the dog believes that his master is at the door we are, or we should be, attributing to the dog a belief whose exact content we do not know but which can be obtained by substituting *salva veritate* in the proposition 'that his master is at the door'.

Our assertion about the dog makes a claim of the following sort. The dog has a belief of the form R(a, b). 'a' is a canine 'individual concept' which picks out the very same individual as our individual concept that we express by the words 'the dog's master'. 'b' is a canine individual concept which picks out the very same individual as our individual concept that we express by the words 'the door'. 'R' is a canine concept that is applicable to the same class of ordered pairs (or much the same class) as our spatial concept that is expressed by the word 'at' in sentences like 'the dog's master is at the door'. Our characterization of the dog's belief does not render the exact content of his belief. But, then, neither does the remark 'Smith believes that chap over there is the villain of the piece' in our previous example. Both characterizations are referentially transparent.

We may happen to know the exact content of Smith's belief. In the case of the dog we do not. Generations of work by animal psychologists may be necessary before the exact content is known. (Piaget, of course, has already begun the work in the case of children who have not yet learnt to talk.) Other species of animal are beings who both lack language and are very different from ourselves. It is not surprising that, although we can recognize that they hold a belief of a certain general sort on a certain occasion, yet we cannot delineate the exact contours of the belief.

The argument, of course, does not show that dogs or other animals have beliefs, or even that it is intelligible to say that they have beliefs. It simply shows that we need not give up our natural inclination to attribute beliefs to animals just because the descriptions we give of the beliefs almost certainly do not fit the beliefs' actual content. So the question still remains whether there is any further argument for animal-belief beyond what we are naturally disposed to say when we observe their behaviour.

The following argument seems to have weight. It is obvious that animals perceive. Now there is some very close connection between perceiving, on the one hand, and acquiring knowledge or beliefs about the environment, on the other. The connection is differently construed by different theorists, but acknowledged by all. The senses inform us about what is going on in our environment (that is the evolutionary reason for their existence) and, sometimes, deceive us. But to be informed and to be deceived is to acquire knowledge and/or belief.

We distinguish between perceiving things, events and occurrences on the one hand, and perceiving that something is the case on the other. The logical connections between A's perceiving an X and the knowledge and/or belief that A acquires are somewhat complex. But if A perceives that something is the case (sees that the cube is larger, although more distant, than the sphere), then it is entailed that A knows that that thing is the case. And 'A knows that p' entails 'A believes that p.' (This entailment has been questioned. It will be argued for in Chapter Ten.) Now it seems obvious that the dog perceives that a cat is streaking across the lawn in front of him, or that his dinner has been put on his plate. (Allowing, of course, that what he is here said to perceive may not be the exact content of his perception.) So the dog acquires knowledge and, if he acquires knowledge, acquires beliefs.

But if animals have beliefs, then there is no necessary connection between having beliefs and having the capacity to express them linguistically.

The absence of this necessary connection is often admitted, but it is admitted in a very grudging fashion.

It is often said, or hinted, that those who lack linguistic competence have beliefs, but have them in some 'logically secondary' sense only. The question then arises what this phrase 'logically secondary' means. I can think of three reasonably precise meanings for the phrase. (I would rather have been able to quote some other philosopher's account(s) of the phrase 'logically secondary'. But, to use F. H. Bradley's phrase, here I have been forced to do my scepticism for myself.) In what follows I try to show that animal beliefs are certainly not logically secondary cases of belief in the first of these meanings; that *some* animal beliefs may be logically secondary cases in the second sense; and that it is quite unproven that they are logically secondary in the third sense.

The first meaning that might be attached to 'logically secondary' is this. Let it be given that there is a class of things of the sort X, and a sub-class of X: the class of things of the sort Y. Y's are then logically secondary instances of X if, and only if, (i) it is logically possible that there should be no Y's and yet there still be X's; but (ii) it is logically impossible that Y's should be the only X's which exist. For instance, a distant relative might be said to be a member of a certain family, but it might also be said that the relative was a member of the family in a logically secondary sense only. For if there were no members of the inner family circle, logically there could be no distant relatives. Yet there could be no distant relatives and still the inner family circle would exist.

But it is completely implausible to say that if there were no beings with beliefs which they could express linguistically, then it would be impossible for a dog to believe that he had a bone buried at a certain place. (That there would be nobody to *assert* the belief is neither here nor there.) If the dog believes, then what makes his belief a belief is something which pertains to the *dog*, and has nothing to do with human beings and their speech. This is utterly different from the case of the distant relative, where what makes him or her a distant relative is (distant) relationship to members of the inner family circle.

There is a second, related, but more subtle, sense which can be given to the phrase 'logically secondary'. Y's might be said to be logically secondary cases of X's without it being entailed that other X's, of a logically primary sort, exist. It is necessary only that the description 'X' makes essential reference to (possible) X's which are not Y's, but that, in applying to X's which are not Y's, the description 'X' makes no essential reference to X's which are Y's. (It will be seen that our first sense of 'logically secondary' is a special, stronger, case of this second sense.)

For instance, it is ordinarily said of brittle things that, if they are struck, they shatter. Yet, as we have had occasion to notice, a brittle thing may be struck and fail to shatter, because of the nature of the circumstances in which the brittle thing is placed. (The glass was packed around with protective material.) Further, it is conceivable that the only occasions when brittle things are struck are occasions where the circumstances are unpropitious for the manifestation of the disposition. If this was the history of the world, it is unlikely that anyone would ever form the *concept* of brittleness. But lack of the concept would not mean that there were no brittle things.

Faced with this rather complicated situation, it seems possible to say that there are certain 'logically primary' cases of brittle things: those things that are so circumstanced that, if hit, they shatter. In calling something brittle we make essential reference to cases of this sort. Brittle things that are so circumstanced that, when hit, they fail to shatter may therefore be said to be 'logically secondary' cases of brittleness. Yet there might be no logically primary cases.

It is clear that this sense of 'logically secondary' is weaker than the first sense. Does it provide a sense in which animals' beliefs are secondary to verbally expressible beliefs?

Beliefs may or may not be expressed, and among those which are not expressed there may be those which the believer is incapable of expressing. The capacity to express a belief is similar in many ways to the capacity to manifest a disposition. So it might be argued that beliefs that cannot be expressed are logically secondary cases of belief.

But this argument would only give a certain logical primacy to expressible beliefs. There is nothing here, short of begging the question, to give *linguistic* expressibility any special place. The best thing that can be said in favour of a special place for linguistic expressibility is this. There may be certain beliefs which, if they are expressed, can be given nothing but linguistic expression. (An issue to be discussed in Section Three.) If there are such beliefs, and if they can be attributed to animals, then such animal beliefs will be logically secondary cases of belief. But there is nothing in the argument to show that animal beliefs *generally* are logically secondary in this sense.

The third meaning for 'logically secondary' finds application in situations where there is a scale of some quantity or a scale of complexity. In such cases the term 'X' may have clear application to instances at one end of the scale, may clearly lack application to instances at the other end, but may be said to apply to instances falling into a twilight zone between in a logically secondary way only. (This third meaning may be another special case of the second.)

It is clear that men with language, on the one hand, and animals, on the other, lie along a certain scale or continuum. Consider the declension: men, apes, dogs, lizards, ants, earthworms and amoebae. It seems quite clear that amoebae lack beliefs, and only a few would want to argue a case for earthworms. But above that point it is not so clear. We then climb up a scale until we come to the one clear or paradigm set of cases: men with language. Now, it may be suggested, must we not treat the intermediate cases as, at best, logically secondary cases of belief?

Such a conclusion does not follow. Such a line of argument would licence us to say that, although a man with a somewhat sparse head of hair was not bald, nevertheless he was, of necessity, a logically secondary case of a man with a head of hair. But this is false. He has a head of hair and so he is not bald. He would be a logically secondary case of a man with a head of hair if it was so sparse that he had entered the zone where we had begun to be undecided whether it might not be appropriate to use the word 'bald'. But if he is clear of that zone, then he is just as much a man with a head of hair as a man with the bushiest mop imaginable.

By parity, in order to show that animals have beliefs in this secondary sense only, it would be necessary to show that animals stand in a borderline zone between cases where the term 'belief' is definitely applicable and cases where it is definitely not. It is *not* enough to point out that animals are nearer on a scale of complexity and sophistication to amoebae (who do not have beliefs) than men are (who have beliefs). For animals might still be clear-cut cases of believers for all that. Now how is it to be shown that animals' beliefs are of this twilight sort? By comparison with men, animals lack one important means of expressing their beliefs: language. But it would be begging the question to argue that lack of this important means of expression entails that we are dealing with logically secondary cases of belief.

Admittedly, it is not clear how it is to be proved that animal beliefs are not, in this sense, logically secondary cases. But is not the onus of proof on the other side? As already emphasized, ordinary thought and language quite readily attribute beliefs to those who are incapable of using, or even understanding, language. Why should we not take such attributions at face value? Future scientific information about non-human animals and the springs of their behaviour might just possibly be forthcoming, information which would persuade us that animals do not have beliefs or have them only in some secondary or dubious sense. Their inability to talk should not persuade us of this.

Notice that whatever we say of beliefs must also be said of the concepts which are involved in those beliefs. So animals have concepts as well as beliefs.

III   Sophisticated Belief and Language

But even if it is admitted that animals have beliefs in a quite straightforward sense, it may still be pointed out that their beliefs are simple and unsophisticated things. If we consider beliefs with a more complex content, it may be said, these *are* logically linked to the requisite linguistic competence because without language the beliefs could not be expressed. Wittgenstein's remark that a dog cannot believe his master will come the day after tomorrow (Wittgenstein 1953, p. 174) was, I suppose, intended to support some such view. And even if the example is incorrect, we can substitute a belief of a much more abstract sort. Could a dog believe in the truth of Goldbach's conjecture (that every even number is the sum of two primes)? How could we suppose this without endowing the dog with a sophisticated linguistic competence?

It is important to realize that there are two questions to be decided here. First, are there beliefs which can be given none but linguistic expression? Second, if there are such beliefs, is it possible for a being without the necessary linguistic competence to hold such a belief despite the fact that he cannot express it?

In answer to the first question: I think that there are some beliefs which can only be expressed linguistically, by bringing into existence some sort of symbolic entity either in the believer's mind or in the world. A class of such beliefs will be mentioned in Chapter Seven (unrestricted existentially quantified beliefs about contingent existences). But the class of beliefs which can only be expressed linguistically is very much smaller than is often assumed. A little ingenuity can often produce descriptions of behaviour which are plausible candidates for non-linguistic expressions of quite sophisticated beliefs. Suppose one dog's master is accustomed to leave the dog for a full day, while another regularly leaves his dog for two days. If the first dog appears alert for his master's return the very next day, but the second dog lets a day pass before appearing restless and expectant, it would not be unreasonable to suggest, on the basis of their behaviour, that the first dog expected his master to return tomorrow, but that the second dog expected there to be a day's interval before *his* master got back. Admittedly, the belief involved is still quite simple. It is hardly comparable with a dog's believing the truth of Goldbach's conjecture. But it may be that one could work up through a series of ever more complex cases culminating in the providing of behavioural but non-linguistic expressions of beliefs in the truth of abstruse mathematical hypotheses.

For the sake of argument, however, let it be admitted that there are beliefs which can be expressed in a linguistic way only. It is a further step to argue that a being which lacks linguistic competence cannot *hold* such a belief. And in fact it seems to be an incorrect step.

At this point we should recall the following facts. We speak of groping successfully or *unsuccessfully* for the words which express our belief. We say that the words which we do utter quite fail to capture what it is that we believe, yet we may not know what better words to utter. We speak of our never having put certain beliefs into words, even although they belong to that class of beliefs which have no natural expression except a linguistic one. There seems no reason to discount such ways of talking. But if they are not discounted, then there is a gap between (i) holding a belief and (ii) knowing how to express the belief linguistically. So why should it not be possible to hold sophisticated beliefs in the complete absence of the linguistic capacity to express them?

It may be replied that the sort of talk about beliefs just mentioned cannot be taken to support any *radical* distinction between sophisticated belief and the competence to express it. When I struggle to express my belief in words, I do not lack linguistic competence entirely. I can indicate in words the general area with which my belief is concerned. I can recognize that some verbal formulations are more appropriate than others. Perhaps there exists a verbal formulation which, if it occurred to me, I would recognize as rendering my belief *exactly*. So, it might be argued, even in the difficult cases, belief and its linguistic expression are linked in some loose, admittedly hard to formulate, but nevertheless logical relation.

At this point in the argument it seems appropriate to appeal to empirical data of a relatively recondite sort. Certain persons have claimed to hold beliefs of a quite abstract and sophisticated sort when quite unable to express such beliefs verbally or understand a verbal formulation of them. A famous case is reported by William James (James 1950, Vol. 1, pp. 266–9).

A deaf-mute, Mr Ballard, lost his hearing as a child. He said of himself:

I could convey my thoughts and feelings to my parents and brothers by natural signs or pantomime and I could understand what they said to me by the same medium; our intercourse being, however, confined to the daily routine of home affairs and hardly going beyond the circle of my own observation . . .

Nevertheless, Ballard records that during that time he

gained ideas of the descent from parent to child, of the propagation of animals, and the production of plants from seeds.

He says that at that time

I believed that man would be annihilated and there was no resurrection beyond the grave . . .

He also entertained various views about the earth, sun and moon. Besides holding such beliefs, he records that he struggled with such questions as 'the source from which the universe came'.

The case is discussed by Wittgenstein in the *Philosophical Investigations* (Section 342). Wittgenstein's direct concern is with wordless thought rather than wordless belief, but it seems clear that what he says about thought he would also have said about belief.

Wittgenstein is rather tentative, but he raises the sceptical question how Ballard can be sure that he has correctly translated his thought into language, and suggests that these recollections may be a 'queer memory phenomenon'. This latter remark seems to link up with what he says elsewhere in the book about dreaming (p. 184) and 'calculating in the head' (Section 364), where it is hinted that all that occurs is that the waking man has the impression of certain things having happened which never did happen or the 'calculator' has the (incorrect) impression of having (overtly) calculated.

But why should we say that Ballard's recollections are a queer memory phenomenon? Why might they not be a correct report of what he believed and thought? (Allowing, of course, for the *empirical* fallibility of memories of childhood.) The chief obstacle seems to be the *a priori* conviction that there is a logical link between belief and thought on the one hand, and linguistic competence on the other. But to use this as an argument is to beg the question at issue.

One problem which obviously worries many philosophers here, including, I think, Wittgenstein, is the problem of verification. How could we ever have any independent check on reports such as that of Ballard? But I think that these philosophers have failed to see (despite their frequent references to such possible evidence) that neurophysiological evidence could, in principle at least, provide the independent check required.

It may be helpful to consider first the parallel question concerning mental images. We know that others besides ourselves have mental images because they tell us so. Nothing else in their behaviour gives us any clue. Do animals and small children have mental images? We can at least conceive of the issue being settled fairly conclusively by physiological evidence. Suppose that we discovered, by interrogating human subjects, that in the case of those interrogated, certain idiosyncratic neurophysiological processes were necessary and sufficient for the occurrence of mental images. This correlation would have to be established by reference to introspective reports. But we regularly accept as true, generalizations whose scope is far wider than the evidential base on which they rest. So there would be no bar to extending the scope of the generalization to include animals and small children. If the idiosyncratic processes occurred in their central nervous systems, this would be compelling evidence (not, of course, logically conclusive evidence) that they too had mental images.

Now, in just the same fashion, it seems perfectly possible that neurophysiological evidence should bear on the question whether a deaf-mute did or did not have beliefs or thoughts which he was unable to express. The identification of the nature of these beliefs from mere neurophysiological evidence is, no doubt, a piece of science-fiction in the present state of neurophysiology. But it does show the logical possibility of an independent check upon claims like that of Ballard. This should be sufficient to remove the suspicion that such claims are a legitimate target for *philosophical* scepticism.

Returning to the particular case of the dog who believes Goldbach's conjecture to be true, it might be objected that it is impossible to hold such a belief *by itself*. A belief of this sort presupposes the possession of a whole set of other mathematical beliefs and concepts. Such a belief can only exist as a member of a system of beliefs.

Whether or not this contention is true, it clearly has a good deal of plausibility. Let us grant it for the sake of argument. But it seems to have no force against the supposition of our mathematical but inarticulate dog. For, although the objection forces us to endow the dog with a whole complex of beliefs and concepts all of which he is unable to express, there seems to be no greater difficulty in this than in the original supposition.

Of course, none of what has been said rules out the view that development of a sophisticated linguistic competence is empirically essential for the development of very abstract beliefs. It seems to be a matter of fact that systems of abstract belief (and thought) and the attempt to express such beliefs (and thoughts) linguistically, develop hand in hand. (A development which is, perhaps, a matter of mutual causal interaction, belief leading to expression of belief, and the expression leading in turn to the forming of more sophisticated beliefs. The process is one of 'positive feedback'.) There may be deep psychological reasons why it is impossible for a belief in the correctness of Goldbach's conjecture to develop except in association with the development of appropriate linguistic skills. All that has been argued for is that there is no *logical* link between possessing such beliefs and having the corresponding linguistic competence.

It has, however, been admitted that in one rather weak sense of 'logically secondary' such beliefs might be said to be logically secondary cases of beliefs.

IV   Thought and Language

It seems clear, and it has already been implied in passing, that if belief is not logically dependent upon the competence to express the belief verbally, then the same will apply to thoughts.

For each possible belief whose content is p, there is a thought with the same content. Someone who does not believe that p may nevertheless have the thought that p. We will restrict discussion of 'thoughts' in this essay to this sub-class of thoughts, thoughts in the absence of the corresponding belief, since our concern is with belief, and it is thoughts in this restricted sense which it is natural to contrast with beliefs. (It is such thoughts which bring up 'Hume's problem' of the distinction between belief and thought.)

Now it seems obvious that there are such thoughts, and that they are mental occurrences that can be dated. It would seem further that they endure for a certain time (often a very short time), and that they are entire for the whole time that they endure. The argument for the latter is that it seems to make no sense to speak of being, say, half-way through having a certain thought. One can be half-way through a certain *train* of thought, or half-way through expressing the thought in words, but the thought itself is just there, or it is not. In this, thoughts resemble beliefs. Unlike beliefs, thoughts may be acts, may be things which the speaker does, which spring from his will, although they may also be 'unbidden'.

Like beliefs, thoughts may or may not be expressed in outward action. In the case of thoughts, this outward action would seem to be simply a matter of putting the thought into words (or other symbols). Just as in the case of mental images, there seems to be no other form of outward behaviour which constitutes a natural manifestation of a thought.

But it cannot be concluded that thought is impossible without the corresponding capacity to express it, or without any capacity to express it at all. Nothing in the behaviour of dogs points to their ever having thoughts, in the way that it does point to their having beliefs. Since dogs have no language it is difficult to see how anything in their behaviour should so point. But it is not logically impossible that they should *have* thoughts. Furthermore, *physiological* evidence can be easily conceived which would convince us that they did have thoughts.

We have already noted that we can be under the impression that certain beliefs are temporarily or permanently beyond our powers of linguistic expression. Exactly the same is true of thoughts. And while in most cases language can at least skirt around our thought, Ballard reports that he had thoughts, as well as beliefs, of considerable sophistication while quite unable to use or understand language beyond the most elementary gestures. He may have been deceiving himself when he made these reports in later life. But it is mere dogmatism to say that he was *necessarily* deceiving himself.

Belief and thought appear to introspection as somewhat impalpable things, things hard to grasp. The positivistic and/or behaviouristic spirit that is even now still abroad in philosophers' thinking about the mind, seizes with relief on the concrete, observable, *outward* phenomenon of linguistic utterance. So philosophers wrongly try to give an account of belief and thought in terms of their (possible) linguistic expression.

A final observation.

Under the influence of Chomsky, modern theoretical linguistics is taking a less behaviouristic view of language. Behind the 'surface structure' of the sentence we are asked to postulate a 'deep structure' which carries, or is paired with, the semantic content of the sentence. This 'deep structure' is seen as, or as corresponding to, a psychological reality which the speaker transforms into a surface structure and the hearer recovers from the surface structure.

One hypothesis which might be considered, therefore, is that the 'deep structure' is not a specifically linguistic entity at all, but is simply the belief or thought (or other mental state such as intention or desire) which is to be expressed in words. Such a view would have to allow that there could be 'deep structures' within an individual mind which were quite beyond the linguistic competence of that mind to express perhaps because, as in the case of Ballard, that person lacked any linguistic competence. But I do not see why linguistics should not accept such a view of 'deep structure'. In particular, it seems to be at least consilient with the positions of those who now call themselves 'generative semanticists'.

4

Propositions

I   The Notion of a Proposition

It was argued in the third section of Chapter Two that belief-states must be assumed to have an internal complexity, a complexity corresponding to the content of the proposition believed. Thoughts, at least in the narrow sense which we have given to the term, also involve propositions, and so must also be credited with an internal complexity. Hence, if we wish to cast light on the nature of belief (and thought), it seems important to understand what propositions are, and in what way they enter beliefs and thoughts.

The notion of a proposition seems forced upon us when we consider beliefs, thoughts and also assertions.

It is clear that different people may all believe the same thing. Suppose, for instance, that nine men believe that the earth is flat. We have nine different beliefs. There is A's belief, B's belief, C's belief... If what we have said about belief already is correct, then there are nine numerically different *states*. (Whether these states are to be conceived of as purely physical states of the brain, or as states of a spiritual substance, or in some other way, is not at issue here.)

However, we distinguish between a man's belief-state and the thing he believes: between the believing and what is believed: between the state of affairs Bap and p. In the case of the nine men, what is believed is the same thing in each case: that the earth is flat. It is just such a case that philosophers, at any rate, describe by saying that the nine men all believe the same *proposition*. So it is sometimes true that people believe the same proposition. Whether, or in what sense, we are thereby committed to the existence of entities called propositions, is a further question that will have to be considered. But, to repeat, it is sometimes true that people believe the same proposition.

Different people may all think the same thought. Suppose that nine persons entertain the possibility that the earth is flat. (If we place them in the past, they might plausibly have done this without having any belief about the matter one way or the other.) There is A's entertaining . . ., B's entertaining . . . If beliefs are properly construed as belief-states, then the corresponding thought (the thought that the earth is flat as opposed to the belief that it is flat) will presumably be a state which endures for as long as the thought is present in the mind. At any rate, there will be nine numerically different things, thought-states or thought-episodes, however they are best conceived.

But we distinguish between the thinkings and what is thought. In the case of the nine men, what is thought is the same thing in each case (and the same as the thing believed in the previous case): that the earth is flat. It is just such a case that philosophers, at any rate, describe by saying that what the nine men think or entertain is the same proposition. So it is sometimes true that people entertain the same proposition.

Different people may all assert the same thing, even although they assert it at different times and places, in different words and even using a different language. Nine different men may all assert that the earth is flat, not necessarily using the same words or even the same language, and not necessarily believing nor even, conceivably, having what they assert before their minds. (They had all been ordered to make that assertion, or they made *that* assertion by accident.) There is A's asserting something . . ., B's asserting something . . . Here we have nine numerically different events (nine numerically different speech-acts).

However, we distinguish between a man's asserting and what he asserts. In the case considered, what is asserted is the same thing in each case (and the same as the thing believed in the first case and the possibility entertained in the second case). It is just such a case that philosophers, at any rate, describe by saying that what the nine men all assert is the same proposition. So it is sometimes true that people assert the same proposition.

Instead of speaking of 'propositions' in connection with assertions, some philosophers talk of 'statements': statements in the sense of *what is stated* rather than the stating of it. In this sense of the word, the nine men all made the same statement. But it seems better to use the term 'proposition', because this term brings out clearly that what is stated can be exactly the same as that which is believed or entertained but never expressed verbally (perhaps because of lack of linguistic competence). To use the term 'statement' ties us too closely to language.

Under what conditions do we say that what is believed, thought or asserted is 'the same proposition' and when do we say it is 'not the same proposition'? What are the conditions of identity for propositions? It seems that the smallest difference in what is believed, thought or asserted is sufficient to make us speak of difference in propositions. If A believes that the morning-star is a planet, while B believes this of the evening-star, then there is a sense in which what they each believe comes to the same thing (whether or not they realize this). But they do not believe the same proposition, because it is clear that what they believe is not *exactly* the same thing.

In some cases it is harder to discern whether what is believed, thought or asserted is exactly the same. If A says 'C is here today' *today*, while B says 'C was here yesterday' *tomorrow*, it is often uncritically assumed that they assert exactly the same thing. But, it seems, A asserts that C was here during the same day that A uttered the token 'today', while B asserts that C was here the day before the day that B uttered the token 'yesterday'. And so it is at least dubious whether A and B asserted *exactly* the same thing.

Again, there are troubles about logically equivalent propositions. If the equivalence is not perceived, then it seems correct to speak of different things being believed, thought or asserted. If A believes that p is true, but has no opinion about q; while B believes that q is true, but has no opinion about p; and p is in fact logically equivalent to q, then it seems wrong to say that what they believe is exactly the same. For Bap and Bbq are true, but Baq and Bbp are false. (Assuming referential opacity.) It would follow that different propositions are believed. But in the case of the simpler logical equivalences the situation is much less clear. If I see clearly that a proposition of the form $(x)(Fx \supset Gx)$ is equivalent to $(x)(\sim Gx \supset \sim Fx)$, and I believe the former, and so believe the latter, is what I believe exactly the same in each case? The matter can be argued. (A little more will be said about this in Chapter Six, Section Five.)

So there are difficult cases where it is unclear (or, it may turn out, just linguistically undecided) whether we should or should not speak of the same proposition being believed, contemplated or asserted. But I do not think that the uncertainties are any greater than those arising in the case of any other of the concepts which we investigate in philosophy. The term 'proposition' is, perhaps, a philosopher's term of art. But the notion of believing, thinking and asserting the same thing, and exactly the same thing, is a notion already present in ordinary thought and speech. It can be investigated by philosophers, and questions can be raised about its exact extension or denotation, in the same sort of way in which such investigations are made into other concepts.

I am arguing, then, that whether they like it or not, philosophers are landed with propositions. Or, rather, that they are landed with talk about propositions. It may be that we can give an account of such talk without being forced to postulate such *entities* as propositions. We may not have to 'quantify over propositions', as Quine would put it. But we must give an account of talk in which the term 'proposition', or some equivalent, appears. No positivistic or behaviouristic shrinking from such 'abstractions', or fear of having to admit 'intensional entities', can get rid of the notion of 'what is believed, or entertained, or asserted'. For instance, to talk about utterances and sentences instead of propositions is to change the subject. It is to turn away from a nettle that has to be grasped.

The vital importance of the notion of propositions, and the impossibility of turning our backs on the notion in philosophy, comes out when we consider that it is what is believed, entertained or asserted (and only these things) that ordinary thought takes to be *capable of truth and falsity*. Some modern philosophers have sought to give an account of truth and falsity as predicates of sentences. But in ordinary discourse we attribute truth or falsity to what X believes, Y entertains, or Z asserts, *viz.* propositions. To predicate truth and falsity of sentences is to start an inquiry into the nature of truth and falsity off on the wrong track, further confusing an already confusing problem. It is possible, of course, to introduce and define new notions of truth and falsity. But if we seek to give an account of the *ordinary* sense of these words, we must work with the notion of the proposition.

Notice, by the way, that I have only said that propositions are *capable* of truth and falsity. Some propositions are true and some are false. But is every proposition true or false? What of the proposition that the present King of France is bald or that unicorns would beat centaurs over seven furlongs? These propositions are certainly *not true*, but it is philosophically controversial whether they should be said to be false. I wish to avoid this controversy, which seems remote from the concerns of this essay, and so will say only that propositions are capable of truth and falsity. They are the sort of thing which could be intelligibly said to be true or false. It may be that whatever is capable of truth or falsity is acutally true or false. It may be not. It may even be that the question is unimportantly verbal. The formula 'capable of being true or false' is intended to dodge these issues.

II   Propositions and Language

The important question arises whether the conception of the proposition as something believed or thought is more fundamental than the conception of the proposition as something asserted, or whether the situation is the other way round, or whether neither conception is more fundamental than the other. The etymology of 'proposition' suggests that it is fundamentally a linguistic notion. It is something proposed, something put forward, and so something asserted.

But if the argument of the previous chapter was correct, this view must be incorrect. It was argued there that beliefs and thoughts are logically independent of the words they would be expressed in, if they were expressed. This holds, it was argued, even where the beliefs permit of nothing but linguistic expression, a situation which holds for all *thoughts*. But since a belief is a belief that something is the case (and, in discussing thoughts, we are restricting ourselves to thoughts that something is the case) it follows that propositions are not fundamentally linguistic in nature.

Indeed, perhaps the situation is exactly the reverse. The uttering of certain words in certain situations counts as the assertion of a certain proposition. That is the meaning which these uttered words bear. Now it is plausible to hold that these words bear this meaning only because they are a conventional device (which can be misused) for indicating to an auditor that the speaker believes or is entertaining a certain proposition. (Or perhaps something more complicated than this. See Armstrong 1971.) If so, an account of the asserted proposition can be given in terms of the proposition which is believed or thought. The 'mental proposition' will be logically prior to the 'linguistic proposition'.

But whether this suggestion about the theory of meaning is correct or not, it is at least clear, given our previous argument, that the linguistic proposition is not logically prior to the mental proposition. And since our concern is with belief it is the mental proposition that primarily concerns us.

III   Two Unsatisfactory Accounts of Propositions

But now we must ask ourselves what account we are to give of talk about propositions. What is it for people to believe, think or assert something? We have noticed that propositions are the things capable of truth and falsity. But although truth and falsity are familiar and commonplace concepts, they are wrapped in philosophical obscurity, so that observing this connection does not greatly assist us here.

If two men make advances to the same woman, it is one and the same woman they make advances to. They enter into a relationship to what is numerically the same thing. But, by contrast, if two women wear the same dress it is only the same sort of dress that they wear. Or if two persons dance the same dance, it is only the same sort of thing that they do. We must distinguish between identity of number and identity of kind (identity of token and identity of type).

This suggests two distinct accounts of the nature of propositions: (1) that when two or more people believe, think or assert exactly the same thing, they are all related to the same individual object or objects; (2) that when two or more people believe, think or assert exactly the same thing, they all have some common property, a property which is *not* a common relation to the same individual object or objects. Let us investigate these two accounts.

(1) To avoid boring repetition, let us restrict ourselves to the case of belief. In the past, many philosophers have given the first sort of account of 'believing the same thing'. If both A and B believe that p then, these philosophers have assumed, both A and B must stand in generically identical relations – the believing relation – to the numerically identical object, p. Since both A and B are identically related to this object, it cannot be in the mind of either. One philosopher who followed out this line of thought was the Scottish-Australian philosopher, John Anderson (Anderson 1962). He was led to identify true propositions with situations in the world. If you and I believe that the cat is on the mat, then the proposition to which we both have the belief-relationship is just this situation in the world: the cat's being on the mat.

But the difficulty for such a view is that propositions can be false as well as true. If you and I falsely believe that the cat is on the mat, what are we related to? Under the influence of the numerical identity model, Meinong and others provided false propositions in the world to be the objects of such things as false beliefs. Nobody with a 'robust sense of reality' (Bertrand Russell) can accept such a solution. In *The Problems of Philosophy* (Russell 1912, Chapters Twelve and Thirteen) Russell attempted a solution at once more realistic and more ingenious. He argued that when Othello falsely believed that Desdemona loved Cassio this entailed a complex relation holding between Othello, Desdemona, the relation of loving, and Cassio. All these things actually exist (or so we must suppose for the sake of the argument) but that 'portion' of the complex relation which holds between the last three entities (Desdemona, loving and Cassio) fails to correspond to the facts of the case. In order to preserve the symmetry between true and false propositions a parallel account is then given of *true* belief, except that in that case the whole of the complex relation corresponds to the facts of the case.

(Anderson, by the way, was inclined to accept Russell's account of false belief, but, in order to save the identification of true propositions with situations, went on to deny that we have to give a parallel account of true and false belief. In true belief, he held, the believer was directly related to a situation. In false belief the believer was related to the scattered 'constituents' of the thing believed. This asymmetry seems utterly implausible. Surely the essential difference between true and false beliefs must lie outside the beliefs? Russell's own solution respects this condition of adequacy.)

Despite its ingenuity, Russell's solution seems unworkable. It is criticized in detail by Peter Geach in *Mental Acts* (Geach 1957, Sections Twelve and Thirteen), in such a way that it would be wasted labour to go over the ground again. To mention just one difficulty. What is the relation which holds between Othello, Desdemona and Cassio, who are particulars, and the relation of loving which will have to be a universal? At the time that he propounded this analysis Russell still lacked a completely robust sense of reality, and he believed in the existence of a realm of universals, lying beyond particulars, in which realm the relational universal of loving was to be found. So for him loving was a strange kind of particular. But if, as is the case, there is no loving except where individuals love, then it seems impossible to give any concrete account of the required link between loving and the three particulars.

(2) Let us now consider the view that A's and B's believing the same thing is a matter of A and B being affected in the same sort of way, where 'same sort' is not to be explicated in terms of the same sort of relation to numerically the same object or objects. It has already been argued that beliefs are *states* of the believer. According to the view that we are now considering, when A and B believe the same thing, p, they both have a p-type belief-state. They both believe p-ishly. We might call this an *adverbial* account of propositions.

In the same way, when two people think the same thought, p, there are two thought-states, or at any rate two mental occurrences of some sort, which have the further similarity that they are p-type thought-states or thought-occurrences. Again, when two people assert the same thing, then there are two speech-acts of the asserting sort, which have the further similarity that they are both p-ish assertings.

A useful model, suggested to me by Philip Jacklin, is that of two persons dancing the same dance. Dancing is not a relation which holds between a person and the dance he dances. Rather, to say that a man is dancing a certain sort of dance is to characterize his dancing further. If two people dance the same dance, p, then they both dance in the p-ish way. A second advantage of the model is that a dance is a complex structure, and is thus suited to model the internal complexity of propositions (a topic we have not yet discussed). On one important point there is a disanalogy. Dancing is an action, springing from the dancer's will, while beliefs are not actions and thoughts need not be. Even here, however, the model of dancing fits asserting, which is an action.

This account of the nature of propositions seems to me to be much more attractive than the Russellian or, in general, the numerical-identity view. But it cannot be accepted as it stands. Michael McDermott (graduate student, Sydney University) has put the difficulty very simply. We believe propositions, but we do not believe features of our believings. *Therefore* believed propositions are not features of believings. Or again, we assert propositions, but we do not assert features of our assertings. *So* asserted propositions are not features of assertings. What we believe is, in general at least, something which lies beyond the belief-state itself. What we assert is, in general at least, something which lies beyond the asserting itself. If Othello believes or asserts something about Desdemona, the belief or assertion concerns *Desdemona*. If what he believes or asserts is that she loves Cassio, it is about her and her relations to that man that Othello has a belief or makes an assertion. It is at this point that the attractions of a theory like Russell's or Anderson's are again felt, but again must be resisted.

IV   An Account of Propositions Sketched

But if propositions are not objects to which those who believe, entertain or assert them are all related, nor are they features of belief-states, thought-episodes or assertings, what can they be? The only possible answer, I think, is that propositions themselves are nothing. All that can be done is to give an account of certain sorts of situation, for example, the situation when A believes that p is true, or where B entertains just the propositions that C asserts, without seeking to make the word 'proposition' stand for some thing or some feature of things. (The word functions neither referringly nor predicatively.)

Russell has familiarized us with the notion of 'definition in use' and Quine with 'contextual definition'. In the sentence 'The average family in Australia has 4.2 members' the phrase 'The average family in Australia' does not refer to any object, nor does the adjectival phrase 'has 4.2 members' predicate any property of any object. This makes an orthodox definition of 'the average family in Australia' out of place. But if we take whole sentences which have 'the average family in Australia' as grammatical subject, such as the sentence above, then these sentences can be paraphrased into a much larger and more cumbrous sentence, or set of sentences, in which the original subject and predicate phrases do not occur and whose parts function in a more orthodox semantic manner.

Now it would be an exceedingly ambitious, difficult and perhaps impossible enterprise to provide a formal 'definition in use' of the word 'proposition'. It will not be attempted here. Nevertheless, Russell's technique points the way to what we must try to do. We must try to give a philosophical account of those situations where, for example, A and B are truly said both to believe the same proposition, without conceding that propositions are things or features of things. If an account can be found which seems to give a satisfactory analysis of the situation as a whole, then the account will be an informal equivalent of a 'definition in use' of the word 'proposition'.

But once we attempt such an account, it seems clear that it is the second of the two rejected accounts of propositions that should be our inspiration. Suppose that A and B both believe that p. What is the ontology of the situation? There are two persons, and each has a belief. These beliefs are 'the same in content'. Over and above the two beliefs there is simply the world, which may or may not be such that they are true. Now beliefs, we have argued, are actual states of the believer, having a complexity of structure that corresponds to the proposition believed. Since in this case the beliefs are the same, the structures of the two belief-states which correspond to the proposition believed must be the same (however abstract this sameness may be). Now, although for the reasons given in the previous section, propositions cannot be identified with this common structure, nevertheless, given our account of beliefs, *the structure determines what it is that is believed.* Suppose, then, that we could give a satisfactory account of the structure of belief-states. (The next chapter will be an attempt to provide such an account.) We would then be in a position to *replace* talk about (believed) propositions by an account of the corresponding belief-states and their structure. This would show what was right in the (strictly incorrect) suggestion that (believed) propositions were simply features of belief-states.

In the same way, talk about entertained propositions would be replaced by an account of thought-states or thought-episodes and their structure. And talk of asserted propositions would be replaced by an account of whatever complex of psychological states and phonetic acts, and the structure of both, that are required for the 'assertion of a proposition'.

Here, then, is a schema for an answer to the philosophical question 'What are propositions?' What must now be done, and what will be the business of the next chapter, is to fill out the schema by showing in detail what must be the nature of a belief-state or thought-episode in order for it to be the belief or thought that a particular proposition is true. (Assertions involve problems of linguistic theory, problems which will not be discussed in this book.)

It may be worth anticipating here, and indicating briefly, the account of the concept of *truth* to which our account of propositions naturally leads. 'True' and 'false' are, in their ordinary meaning, predicates that apply to propositions, and only to propositions. It is natural, therefore, to think of truth as some relation of 'correspondence' between certain propositions and extra-propositional reality: 'facts' or 'states of affairs'. But a relation of 'correspondence' demands that the two terms of the relation be distinct from each other, and 'true propositions' and 'the facts' or 'states of affairs' which make them true seem to collapse into each other. To say that p is true is simply to say that a certain state of affairs obtains. (This was the strength of Anderson's identification of true propositions with states of affairs.)

But if instead we consider belief-states, thought-episodes and assertions, we may well find that it is possible to develop an account of the correspondence or non-correspondence of their structure to portions of the world. Given, for example, that a certain belief-state of A's is as it is, and certain portions of the world are as they are, then we can say that p is the case or is true. Propositions cannot correspond to reality, but belief-state, thought-episode or the speech-act of assertion, whose natures determine what proposition is believed, thought or asserted, may well correspond to reality. We can even reintroduce the word 'true' to describe this correspondence *provided we are clear that the word is not receiving its ordinary employment.*

But this is matter for the second Part of the book.

This account of talk about propositions in terms of features of believings, thoughts and assertings has to encounter an obvious objection. If it were correct, then every proposition would either be believed, thought or asserted. Propositions would be ineluctably tied to the proposing of them. But when philosophers, at any rate, talk about propositions they commonly say that there are propositions which never have been, and never will be, asserted or entertained, much less believed.

The trouble might be said to lie with the sentence 'There exist propositions that are not believed, thought or asserted.' But might we not replace this sentence, which apparently asserts the existence of propositions, with another which only speaks about *possible* belief-states, *etc.*? Suppose we say 'The actual sorts of structure found among belief-states, thought-episodes and assertions are not all that are possible'? Provided that an account can be given of the 'propositional structure' of belief-states, *etc.* – which is the task that lies immediately ahead of us – will not this second sentence say all that we want to say by means of the first sentence? We give an account of unproposed propositions in terms of *possible* proposals. We have to employ the notion of possibility, but this is hardly an objection because any philosophy must *employ* the notion, regardless of what particular account is given of it.

There remains a residual difficulty which has been pointed out to me by George Molnar. Suppose that nothing exists. This appears to be an intelligible, although false, supposition. In such a universe, the proposition 'nothing exists' will be true. By hypothesis, there will be in this universe no belief-state, thought-episodes or assertions. So, on the analysis given, the truth of the proposition will have to be constituted by the correspondence to reality of a *possible* belief-state, thought-episode or assertion. *If* there were such a belief-state, *etc.*, then this state would correspond to reality. But now the difficulty is revealed. For if there were such a belief-state, then it would be *false* that nothing exists. So it seems that our analysis is unable to give an account of what it would be like for the proposition 'nothing exists' to be true.

Notice, however, that this difficulty appears to affect all accounts of propositions equally. Suppose propositions are identified with sentences, in particular with synonymous sentences, or with possible sentences. Molnar's difficulty remains. Suppose propositions are declared to be 'abstract entities', entities which exist but not in space or time. The difficulty is in no way diminished. Now what is a difficulty for all theories is no particular difficulty for one of them.

The problem itself appears to be a problem of self-reference. The difficulty is caused by the fact that the proposition 'nothing exists' includes within its scope the 'bearer' of the proposition. I do not know how to solve it. But, for the reason given in the previous paragraph, I do not think that this is a serious flaw in the account of propositions given in this chapter.

5

Concepts and Ideas

I   The Distinction between Concepts and Ideas

Propositions have an inner complexity. If a proposition is believed
(restricting ourselves to beliefs for the present) then the belief-
state will have to have an inner complexity which mirrors the
complexity of the proposition.

How is this complexity of the belief-state to be conceived? The
analogy of a map seems useful. Suppose that what is believed is
that Perth is to the west of Sydney. In a map, this putative state
of affairs would be represented by two marks on the map, one
labelled 'Perth', the other 'Sydney', the former being to the left
of the latter. These marks, thus labelled and thus related, represent
a state of affairs. Let us think of the belief-state as a sort of map.
It will contain elements, like the map-marks labelled 'Perth' and
'Sydney', which have a certain interpretation. These elements will
be related in certain ways, just as the map-marks are related in a
certain way in the map, and the relations of the elements will also
have a certain interpretation. Given this interpretation of the
elements and the relations, the elements-in-relation to be found in
a particular belief-state determine *what it is that is believed*. (The
elements may themselves be complex, involving further elements-in-
relation, but, since the human mind is finite, we must in the end
come to elements whose *parts* do not represent.) In general, at least,
the relations in the belief-state will represent relations in the world,
and the elements in the belief-state the terms of relations in the
world. In this way, just as the claim made by a map can be 'read
off' from the map, so the content of the proposition believed could
be 'recovered' from the belief-state.

Our first question is this. Psychologists and philosophers often
talk about people coming to possess, possessing or losing *concepts*.
They are thinking of concepts as some sort of psychological entity.
Should the elements and relations which make a belief-state the
belief that it is, be identified with such concepts?

I think these elements and relations stand in close logical relations to, but are not identical with, concepts. In *Mental Acts* Geach advances a theory of what he calls 'judgements', and, although his judgements cannot be identified with our belief-states, what he says about judgements can be applied with advantage to the analysis of belief-states. Like our analysis of belief-states, Geach sees judgements (the judging, not what is judged, which is simply a proposition) as complex things involving elements in relation. The elements he calls Ideas, and since his terminology seems quite convenient it will be appropriated for our elements. Notice, however, that where the content of the judgement is that one thing is related in a certain way to another, Geach does *not* call the corresponding relation in the mental act of judging an Idea. I see no reason to follow him in this, and will call *both* the representing elements and the representing relations involved in belief-states 'Ideas'. My use of 'Idea' is therefore wider than his. I do not think that this will otherwise affect my taking over of his account of the relation of concepts and Ideas.

Why must we distinguish between concepts and Ideas? For the following simple reason. Suppose we hold two beliefs simultaneously which differ in content but which involve a common concept. One belief may be that this F is G, the other that this F is H. Since we have two distinct beliefs, then there will be, or at any rate there may be, two distinct states of mind that constitute the two beliefs. If there are two distinct states, they will have to contain two numerically distinct F-representing elements. But the F-representing elements cannot be identified with our concept of F. For we have just *one* concept of F. One may lack a concept, have an imperfect or partial grasp of a concept, or have a perfect grasp of it. But one cannot have two of the same concept. There is nothing mysterious about this. One cannot have two of the same skill, and in this concepts are like skills. But we do need to provide for more than one F-representing element in distinct belief-states. The F-representing elements are what, following Geach, I call 'Ideas of F'.

It will be noticed that I said only that the two distinct beliefs *may* be distinct states of mind. They might overlap in such a way that the *one* F-representing element served for both belief-states. This situation actually occurs in maps. It is the very same Adelaide-representing element that helps to represent in the one map that Adelaide is to the east of Perth and that Adelaide is to the west of

Sydney. But there is nothing in the concept of an Idea of F that ensures that a person at a time has at most one Idea of F. The concept of the concept of F, however, is such that a person at a time has at most one concept of F.

Geach's view is that Ideas are 'exercises' of concepts. Still better, I think, we should say that the concept of X is a *capacity* to have Ideas of the sort X.

Suppose I have the concept of X. This entails that I have a certain capacity. This capacity is a necessary (although insufficient) condition for having belief-states, or thoughts, in which the Idea representing or 'mapping' X figures. Put another way, the capacity is a necessary condition for having belief-states, or thoughts, involving propositions in which X figures. (It will be seen that 'capacity' is not to be restricted to 'capacity for *doing* something', because every belief and many thoughts are not directly 'subject to the will'. In any case, inanimate as well as animate things can have capacities.) Thus, if a child has the concept of 'dog' he is capable (given that other conditions are also satisfied) of forming beliefs and having thoughts in which dogs figure. Contrariwise, if he can form beliefs and have thoughts in which dogs figure, then it is entailed that he has the concept of dog. Each such belief-state or thought-episode will have a structure, one element of which will be an Idea of dog.

The notion of a capacity is related to, but is not the same as, the notion of a disposition in the philosopher's sense of the word 'disposition'. The great similarity is this: capacities, like dispositions, may or may not be *manifested*. And given the capacity, or given the disposition, the nature of the manifestation that may or may not occur is determined. But in the case of dispositions, such as brittleness, the nature of the initiating circumstances which bring about the manifestation is also determined. Brittle things are things which shatter *when struck*. By contrast, to say that a thing has the capacity to do something does not by itself tell us what circumstances will cause this capacity to be manifested. Manifestations of dispositions are *stimulus-dependent*. Manifestations of capacities may be, but need not be, stimulus-dependent.

The same sort of arguments which showed that dispositions are states of the disposed thing (Chapter Two, Section Two) also, I think, show that capacities are states of the thing which has the capacity. So, at any rate, I will assume. There is, of course, much more to be said about capacities, but I hope that the brief remarks here, together with our pre-philosophic understanding of the term, suffice for the present discussion.

So when A has the concept of X he is in a certain state which is a necessary condition for his coming to have a certain range of beliefs and thoughts (those in which X figures). But notice that it is logically possible that A should have the concept of X, but never have any beliefs and thoughts in which X figures. A capacity can be, and remain, latent. So the concept of X does not entail the existence of Ideas of X, although the reverse entailment holds.

A useful, if obviously oversimplified, model for the relation of concept to its Ideas is that of a metal seal to the imprints which the seal is capable of making in pieces of wax. The seal is a necessary condition for the coming into existence of an imprint, and the existence of one or more imprints of that particular sort is a sufficient condition for the existence of the seal. But the relation between seal and imprint must not be confused with the familiar philosopher's distinction between type and token: between universal and particular. The distinction between type and token cuts across the distinction between concept and Idea. We can speak of the concept of horse as a type, or we can speak of a token of that type: the concept of horse which is part of the furniture of A's mind. We can speak of the Idea of a horse as a type, or we can speak of a token of that type: the Idea of a horse which is an element in the belief that A acquired at 10.13 a.m. today that a horse had escaped from the paddock.

A second model for the distinction between concepts and Ideas which comes still closer to the distinction it models is the distinction between the capacity to use a certain word and the words which are constituents of actually produced sentences. The distinction between type and token cuts across this distinction also. If A and B can both use the word 'disinterested' then we can speak of the capacity which each has as one, because the capacities are of the same type, or as two, because the capacities are different tokens of that type. And if A uses the word 'disinterested' twice we can say that he only used the one word, taking the words as types, or that he used two words, taking the words as tokens.

Notice that there are concepts and Ideas of particulars (Julius Caesar, the Industrial Revolution) just as much as concepts and Ideas of things of a certain sort. There are also abstract and formal concepts and Ideas, such as those of non-exclusive disjunction.

Two historical notes. (1) Locke's 'way of ideas' fails to make the distinction between concepts and Ideas. When Locke uses the term 'idea' he is usually referring to concepts, but sometimes to what we, with Geach, are calling Ideas. (If a propositional view of *perception* is correct, as I believe it to be, then Locke's 'sensations' may be said to be structures of Ideas.) (2) Kant held that concepts are possible predicates of judgements. If it is assumed that 'predicate' is not here a *linguistic* term, but stands for some feature of mental judgements, then it seems that Kant also fails to distinguish between concepts and Ideas.

II Simple and Complex Concepts and Ideas

It is suggested that a belief-state may be compared to a map (correct or incorrect) of some portion of the world. But how can it be a map? An ordinary map is a map because it has been deliberately so manufactured, and certain 'mapping conventions' are understood to apply to it. It maps in virtue of these conventions. But nothing of this sort can be said of our belief-states. If belief-states are 'maps' then they are maps in their own nature. Nothing outside themselves, and in particular not conventions, make them into maps. Let us speak of this feature of belief-states as their 'self-directedness'. Our question is: how is such self-directedness possible?

One important answer to this question is that given by Brentano (Brentano 1960). According to this view beliefs (and thoughts) are states of mind which, in common with other mental states such as purposes, have an irreducible characteristic which physical states of physical things lack. They have the unique, irreducible characteristic of *intentionality*. It is in virtue of this characteristic that belief-states are self-directed.

This answer must command respect. But it is also exposed to the suspicion which attends every attempt to solve a metaphysical problem by postulating some unique and irreducible entity or property. A lot of honest toil with the object of giving an *analysis* of the self-directedness of belief- and thought-states seems in order first. What follows is an attempt to provide such an analysis.

The first step in the argument will be to draw a distinction between *simple* and *complex* concepts and Ideas, and show in what way complex concepts and Ideas are nothing but complexes of simple concepts and Ideas. This will be the business of the present Section.

It then becomes clear, I hope, that the self-directedness of beliefs (and thoughts) can be explained if we can explain the self-directedness of our *simple* concepts and Ideas. The latter task is attempted in Section Three. It is suggested there, in particular, that the self-directedness of our simple concepts is nothing more than this: they are selective capacities that the believer has with respect to things of a certain sort.

The two steps in my argument might be said to be a way of spelling out two successive propositions in Wittgenstein's *Tractatus*. (I am greatly indebted to Douglas Gasking for drawing the point to my attention.)

> 2.1514 The pictorial relationship consists of the correlations of the picture's *elements* [my emphasis] with things.
> 2.1515 These correlations are, as it were, the feelers of the picture's elements, with which the picture touches reality.

It is the second proposition that is the mysterious one. The argument of Section Three, with its appeal to the notion of a selective capacity, is my attempt to dispel the mystery. But first let us spell out the distinction between simple and complex in the field of concepts and Ideas.

A map involves certain non-relational elements related in certain ways. (The elements are certain sorts of marks on a surface, and the relations are two-dimensional spatial relations which hold between the elements on that surface.) These related elements represent (correctly or incorrectly) outstanding features in a certain region of space, and the spatial relations which hold between these features. It is clear that there must be a set of *primitive* or *fundamental* elements and relations. Given the interpretation of the whole set, then it will be determined 'what the map asserts'.

Now if our beliefs are to be conceived of as like maps of the world, they must also involve such *fundamental* 'representing' elements and relations. Such fundamental features will be called '*simple* Ideas'. Corresponding to simple Ideas there will automatically be simple concepts: capacities for having such Ideas.

The phrase 'simple Ideas' recalls, as it is meant to recall, Locke. But even after the distinction has been made between Ideas and concepts, a distinction which Locke fails to make, there are five other points of difference between my simple Ideas and Locke's 'simple ideas'.

First, it is not involved in the concept of a simple Idea that it itself be a simple thing. At times, at any rate, Locke speaks as if a
simple idea is itself an uncompounded object in a man's mind. I
disclaim any such implication for my 'simple Ideas'. If simple
Ideas can be contingently identified with physiological features of
states of the brain, as I believe they can be (although such a thesis
is not argued for in this work), then it is clear that simple Ideas will,
as a matter of fact, be enormously complex entities. A useful model
here is an elementary feature of a map. The symbol ⚲ on a particular map may represent a church. The symbol itself is complex in
nature. But in terms of the mapping conventions it is an elementary
feature or simple Idea because those conventions only provide for
the interpretation of the symbol as a whole. There is no correlation
of the related parts of the symbol with the related parts of the
church signified.

Second, it should be even more obvious that there is no necessary
resemblance between simple Ideas and the supposed features of the
world that they are Ideas of. Locke speaks as if ideas (including
simple ideas) in many cases stand in an iconic relation to the things
they represent. But this, I think, is at best a scientific hypothesis,
and, moreover, a very primitive one which there is no reason to
think true. Semi-iconic elements and relations are used in maps,
but there is no reason to think that our mind-maps of the world
are of this nature.

Third, it is not necessary that the supposed things, or supposed
features of things, which the simple Ideas are Ideas *of*, be simple
themselves. They may be, but they need not be. Locke often seems
to take it that what simple ideas are ideas of are bedrock features of
the world which have no further complexity of nature. For him,
the 'objects' of simple ideas seem to be *ontologically simple*. (But
see Book II, Chapter 21, Section 73, where he appears to take the
other position.)

But, against Locke's usual view, the simplicity of the things or
features of things represented by our simple Ideas is epistemological
only. Locke moves illegitimately from the nature of our conceptual
scheme to the nature of reality. If all we have is a simple Idea of a
certain feature, then we can give that feature *no further logical
analysis*. The feature is 'simple for us'. ('Logical analysis' here, of
course, is not confined to the explicit, self-conscious analyses which
we find in philosophy and elsewhere. Ideas which we cannot

explicitly analyse may still be complex.) Whether the feature represented by a simple Idea is in fact a simple or basic feature of the world will, in general, be a matter for scientific investigation.

A simple concept or simple Idea is therefore a concept or Idea of a thing or feature which is simple for the possessor of the concept or Idea. He cannot analyse the feature. The feature itself need not be simple. And notice further that even this epistemological simplicity is compatible with the recognition on the part of the possessor of such concepts/Ideas that there are all sorts of logical relation between different 'simple' features.

This last point is important, if only to forestall misunderstanding, and so deserves development. It is very plausible to say that the human concepts and Ideas of *red* are concepts and Ideas of an epistemologically simple feature. It is notorious that we can give no logical analysis of what redness is. (It may be possible, indeed I hold that it is correct, to identify redness *contingently* with some set of physical or physiological properties. But the legitimacy of such contingent identification is not relevant here.) It is also plausible to say that *colour* is an epistemologically simple feature. Colour is what all the hues have in common, but (it seems) what they have in common is something which we can apprehend without being able to analyse. Further, it is generally held that being red *entails* being coloured, although the reverse entailment obviously does not hold. But, and this is the point here, this entailment does not make the concept and Ideas of redness into a *complex* concept and Ideas. For no logical analysis of redness in terms of colour can be given. 'A father is a male parent' could be called a logical analysis of the concept of father. But there is no parallel necessary truth 'Redness is a colour of the sort X' which is a logical analysis of the concept of red.

(It is interesting to notice that Hume in effect made the point that epistemologically simple features can stand in all sorts of logical relation to each other. See the footnote to the *Treatise*, Book 1, Part 1, Section 7, where he writes:

It is evident, that even different simple ideas [read 'simple ideas' as 'epistemologically simple features'] may have a similarity or resemblance to each other; nor is it necessary, that the point or circumstance of resemblance should be distinct or separable from that in which they differ. *Blue* and *green* are different simple ideas, but are more resembling than *blue* and *scarlet*; though their perfect simplicity excludes all possibility of separation or distinction. It is the same case with particular sounds, and tastes, and smells. These admit of infinite resemblances upon the general appearance and comparison, without having any common circumstance the same.)

The point that the features picked out by simple concepts and Ideas are simple, if only epistemologically simple, is a little obscured by the analogy of an ordinary map. The fundamental elements and relations which go to make up a map stand for things and features of things which are complex in nature *and of which we have complex, analysable, concepts*. So although, relative to the mapping conventions, the fundamental elements and relations can be called the map's 'simple Ideas', these elements and relations are not simple Ideas *for us*, who read the map. We can supply, *just from our concepts of the thing mapped*, further complexities which the map cannot give. But it is self-contradictory to say that we can give any logical analysis of one of our simple concepts or Ideas.

Fourth, and linking up with a number of the points just made, it is not a matter to be settled *off-hand* just what a man's simple concepts are. Locke's acceptance of the Cartesian principle of the indubitability of consciousness misled him into thinking that the identification of our simple ideas is unproblematic. In fact, such identification would seem to be a major research task in psychology. The evidence of introspection is certainly useful, but it is not indubitable nor is it exhaustive. It is a starting-point for research, not an end-point. It is not possible, as Locke thought it was possible, to point to logically indubitable examples of simple concepts. With Locke, we may suspect that the number of simple concepts is relatively small compared to the number of concepts we actually have. Our concepts may all be variations on a quite small number of themes. But this awaits the validation of psychological research.

Fifth, there is no logical necessity that our simple concepts be 'derived from experience'. They need not be brought into existence by instances which fall under the concept in question acting upon our mind, *via* the senses or by any other way. That is to say, we need not accept Locke's Empiricist doctrine of ideas, at any rate as a necessary truth. A's possession of certain simple concepts will be a matter of A's being in certain internal states. How these states are brought into existence is a contingent question, to be settled by psychologists or neurophysiologists, not philosophers.

Having attempted to clarify the notion of a simple concept/Idea we are now in a position to give an account of complex concepts/ Ideas.

Complex Ideas are simply complexes of simple Ideas. (And, similarly, complex concepts are complexes of simple concepts.) They are built up out of simple Ideas in the same way that, in a map, complex representations are built up out of primitive or 'simple' representative features. Consider, for instance, the symbolization of an interchange at the meeting of motor-ways. This might require no new principle of symbolization because it can be represented simply by mapping the individual roads *etc.*, which make up the interchange, by means of the already existing conventions for mapping roads. The representation of the interchange would then be a complex representation. And it serves as a model for the way complex Ideas (and complex concepts) are to be thought of. Of course, in a map, the simple representations which make up complex representations are actually *parts* of the complex representation, a relation that is reproduced in the things represented. We certainly must not think that the relations between complex Ideas, on the one hand, and the simple Ideas of which they are complexes, on the other, will always be as straightforward as this. But, like the complex representations of a map, complex Ideas can be analysed *without remainder* in terms of simple Ideas (which, it will be remembered, include Ideas of relation). The logical analyses of concepts produced by philosophers (including the logical analyses of this essay) would seem to be attempts to lay bare to reflective consciousness the structure of our complex concepts. As we know, the task is one of the utmost difficulty.

So, given the interpretation of the *simple* Ideas – all the elements and their relations that make up a belief-state or a thought-state – the interpretation of the proposition believed or thought is fixed. The self-directedness of beliefs and thoughts is therefore explained by reference to the still-to-be-explained self-directedness of the constituents: the simple Ideas.

Despite the many aspects of Locke's doctrine of simple and complex ideas that have been criticized in the course of this section, I think enough remains to make the view put forward here a recognizable descendant of Locke's. Indeed, it may be hoped that his central contention, which he regarded as the great prop of his Empiricism, that complex ideas are complexes of simple ideas, has been illuminated and made more precise by using the analogy of the map.

III The Self-directedness of Simple
Concepts and Ideas

So at this point it seems that the problem of the self-directedness of
belief reduces to the problem of the self-directedness of our simple
concepts and simple Ideas. In the case of a map, once the 'interpretation' of the simple mapping features is fixed, the 'interpretation'
of the map is fixed. That is to say, if we know how to interpret
these simple features, we can read the whole map. The 'interpretation' of the simple mapping-features is in turn fixed by the
semi-iconic mapping conventions. But this brings us face to face
with our problem. For the interpretation of our simple concepts
and Ideas is not conventionally fixed. They have an intrinsic interpretation. Of their own nature, they point in a certain direction.
How is this to be explained without falling back into Brentano's
hypothesis?

I will proceed by giving an account of simple *concepts*. My contention is that these concepts are certain sorts of selective capacity
towards things that fall under the concept in question. And this, I
suggest further, *constitutes their self-directedness.*

In Section One of this chapter it was said that a concept of X was
a capacity for having Ideas of X. There is no contradiction between
this assertion and the contention that *simple* concepts, at least, are
selective capacities. For, as will be seen, the corresponding Ideas
play an essential role in the selective behaviour.

Although not all the concepts that people possess are selective
capacities, many are, including many that are not simple concepts.
But, my contention is, simple concepts *must* be selective capacities.
And, *qua* simple concepts, they are nothing but such selective
capacities. Of course, these capacities must be conceived of as *states*
of the thing that has the capacity.

For the sake of an example, let us assume that the concept of red
is a simple concept. This would be false if redness could be analysed
as 'property of a material surface apt to cause sensations of a certain
unique sort in normal perceivers', as many philosophers believe it
can be analysed. But let us assume that accounts of this sort are
false, and that redness is a property of material things, a property
of which no conceptual analysis can be given.

Suppose, now, that a red object acts, in suitable circumstances,
upon the mind of an individual, A. As a result, A's mind comes to

be in a certain state. This state is a capacity of A's which he can exercise if he so desires, to act in a selective fashion towards the red object. He is now capable of reacting towards this red object, of coming into some relation to it. Furthermore, this capacity to react towards the object is a capacity to react towards it *as* a red thing. A can distinguish the object as a red thing from things that are not red. He is capable, if he so desires, of reacting in that particular way to any red thing that may act upon him in this way, while refraining from so reacting to things which are not red.

Suppose, for instance, that A is rewarded if and only if he *points* to something red, and that he will be punished if and only if he points to something that is not red. Suppose that A is aware of this policy, desires the reward, fears the punishment, and is currently capable of pointing. The red object acts upon his sense-organs in a suitable way. As a result, A is now capable of reacting towards that object as a member of the class of red things. So A is in a position to maximize his satisfactions.

Notice very carefully, however, that the capacity which A's mind acquires as a result of the red object acting upon it is *not* to be identified with A's concept of red. A's concept of red is a *second-order* capacity – a capacity to acquire the capacity to react towards the red object when the latter acts upon A's mind. As will emerge in a moment, the *first-order* capacity is rather to be identified with a certain elementary type of *belief*.

A sorting-machine, say a machine that sorts apples by their sizes, does not exhibit these two orders of capacity. It has the capacity, when a certain apple acts upon it, to react according to the size of the apple. This means that it *must* react when the apple acts upon it. But when the red object acts upon A, A does no more than acquire a capacity to react.

Now, if the red object is to bestow on A a capacity to react to the object as a red object, if A should desire to react, then it must register its presence in A's mind. It must create a map in A's mind. This map must register the *redness* of the object, that is, the map must contain a feature which gives a capacity for selective behaviour towards the thing *qua* red thing. But, equally, the map must contain something which will register *where* the object is, relative to A. For if this is lacking, A will not be able to come into relation to the red object. (For instance, he will not be able to point in the right direction.)

But if the object does create this 'map' in A's mind, have we not now got a *belief* in A's mind: the belief that 'this thing here is red'? The feature in the 'map' which maps the redness of the object will be an instance of the Idea of red, while the feature which gives the place of the object relative to A will be the referential component (the Idea of 'this thing here'). Here, by the way, we have the basic notion of reference, which shows that reference is not fundamentally a *linguistic* notion.

Notice that, since A's possession of the concept of red is a mere capacity for coming to have 'maps' (beliefs) of a suitable sort when red objects act upon A's mind, it is logically possible that A should have the concept of red *before* anything red had ever acted upon his mind in the appropriate way. That is to say, it is intelligible to assert that the concept of red is an 'innate idea' for A.

Again, A may come to have false beliefs that things are red. Such beliefs – such inaccurate 'maps' – will not in general be brought into existence by red things. It is conceivable that A's very first belief that something is red should be false, and indeed, that all such subsequent beliefs should be false. Nevertheless, I suggest, where A falsely believes that something is red, the Idea of red which appears as an element in his inaccurate 'map' is identified as an *Idea of red* by reference to the causal role which this sort of map-feature plays in *accurate* 'maps'. There must be empirically repeatable circumstances in which red objects acting upon A's mind would create a 'map' of the situation containing *that* sort of map-element, and in which that map-element would enable A to react back to the object as a red object.

Notice that we have spoken about things (or situations, occurrences, *etc.*) in the environment acting upon A's mind and creating a *belief*-state. The normal process by which this occurs will be the object acting upon A's sense-organs and producing a perception of something red in A. Whether this perception should be identified with A's acquiring of the belief, or whether the perception should be thought of as a further causal intermediary which precedes the acquiring of the beliefs, is a matter which is important for the theory of perception. But I hope we can leave it aside here.

It will be seen that discrimination-experiments, beloved of animal-psychologists, are logically well-fitted to elucidate the possession or lack of possession of *simple* concepts. (They would not be well-fitted to elucidate possession of a concept like, say, 'bachelor'.)

If things of the sort X act upon an animal's sense-organs, and, as a result, the animal proves able to act in a discriminating way towards the object which acted upon it, differentiating it from something which is not X, the animal can be credited with at least a *simple* concept of X. Of course, there are all sorts of difficulties. The animal could have the concept of X, and also form the belief that there was an X before it, and still fail to respond. (It might simply not be interested!) And where it does respond, it is notoriously difficult to establish that it was the feature X which was responsible for the animal being affected, and that it responded with behaviour which treated the object as an X. But perhaps we can treat such problems as 'not difficulties of principle'.

It should be noticed that I said that such discrimination-experiments will indicate that the organism has *at least* a simple concept of X. There are many things which are capable of acting on our mind in such a way that we form beliefs that a thing of that sort is present, and so are capable of discriminatory activity towards that thing *qua* that sort of thing, but of which our concept, and so our Ideas, are complex. Such concepts will give extra, cross-referencing, potential links with the world, over and above the potential links which simple concepts *must* have. This extra cross-referencing also helps to explain the self-directedness of our belief-map.

It is worth noticing also that, in theory at least, discrimination-experiments could elicit the possession of quite sophisticated and abstract concepts, including even the concepts of logic. Among other things, this will strengthen the position argued for in Chapter Three that belief and thought are possible in the absence of relevant linguistic capacity.

As an example, which could easily be multipled, the discriminatory behaviour that would betoken possession of the abstract concept of 'all' may be briefly indicated. Let us first grant an organism possession of the concepts of various sorts of individual material objects: say marbles, billiard-balls, cubes, prisms, rubber balls, *etc.* The organism is allowed to manipulate specimens of all these sorts of object, and then exhibits the capacity to sort them: perhaps putting all the billiard-balls in one box, all the prisms in another and so on. Suppose the organism is now presented with a great number of boxes containing collections of these objects. Some of the collections contain nothing but objects of the same sort, but other collections are mixed. Suppose that the organism then exhibits the further capacity to *sort the boxes*, placing to one side those and only those boxes whose contents are things of the same sort. An organism that can do this (perhaps none but human beings actually could) would appear to have exhibited a (non-linguistic) grasp of what the boxes placed on one side had in common: *viz.* that *each* or *all* the objects in such a box were of the same sort. Perhaps such sorting behaviour could not be unambiguously interpreted, but we could imagine further sets of experiments whose successful negotiation by the organism would convince us that it had the abstract notion of 'all'. Similar scenarios can be written for other logical and mathematical concepts and for other quite sophisticated and/or abstract concepts.

Behaviour can even be envisaged which would seem to exhibit some non-linguistic grasp of the logical relations between simple concepts. Suppose, for instance, that an organism has exhibited an ability to discriminate the various hues which humans discriminate. Suppose it goes on to sort spontaneously pieces of material according to whether they are coloured (hued) or are simply black, white or grey. This would seem to involve awareness that the hues all have something in common which is lacking in the case of black, white and grey. Such an interpretation would be strengthened if, prior to gathering the experimental evidence, the organism had not been allowed to perceive any instances of some particular hue – green, say. If it was then shown green material, and spontaneously sorted it with the other material which had a hue, we should certainly think that it had grasped that 'green is a colour'.

Consider, again, our awareness that orange resembles yellow more than red resembles yellow, or that purple resembles blue more than red resembles blue. We could imagine an organism which has colour perception of the human type, presented first with a paradigm object of some sort and then with a further pair of objects. It is rewarded if it chooses from the pair the object which most closely resembles the paradigm. This is done with all sorts of different sorts of objects, so that the organism understands the abstract nature of its task. The organism, we may suppose, passes all these tests. The paradigm object is then made a yellow piece of material, and the two further objects are made orange and red pieces of material. If the organism spontaneously chooses the orange object, it would seem to have grasped the fact that orange is more like yellow than red is. A similar successful experiment with blue, purple and red material would show that it has grasped that purple resembles blue more than red resembles blue.

To return to the main line of argument.

It has been argued that A has the concept of X if it is the case that instances of X, acting upon A's mind, bring it about, in suitable circumstances, that a certain sort of state comes to be in A's mind. This state, which is identified with a belief on the part of A that there is something of the sort X in some environmental relation to A, enables A to act towards the X in a discriminatory way, distinguishing it from things that are not X. It may be thought of as a 'map' of the A–X situation: a 'map' in A's mind. But it seems to be a self-directed map.

But we must now consider the problems involved in the phrase 'in suitable circumstances'. It is clear in the first place that, on some occasions, things of the sort X act upon A's mind without producing a suitable state. For instance, an unsuitable state might be produced where A believed that the X was not an X at all, but something else. Furthermore, not every case where an X acted upon A's mind and produced a state which enabled A to act towards the X in the proper discriminatory way entails that A has the concept of X. Suppose that the set of circumstances in which A could be acted upon by an object of the sort X, and, as a result, acquire a belief that there was an X in his environment, were so special that there was no likelihood that the circumstances would ever be instantiated on more than this one occasion. Would we be prepared to say that A had the concept of X? I do not think so. Possession of a simple concept rather demands that A have the capacity to acquire beliefs of the suitable sort in a set of circumstances which are *genuinely repeatable*. And 'genuinely repeatable' here means not merely that it is logically possible that they should be repeated, or even that repetition is empirically possible, but that the repetition of the circumstances is empirically more or less likely. 'More or less likely' is a vague phrase, of course, but I do not see how to be more precise. There seems to be a continuum of cases starting from the cases where repetition is logically possible or barely empirically possible, up to cases where the circumstances regularly recur. In order to speak of A's possessing the concept of X, the circumstances under which A is capable of being acted upon by an X and, as a result, acquiring X-maps (X-beliefs) of the correct sort, must be 'more or less likely circumstances', that is, reasonably far up the continuum.

We have been trying to give an account of simple concepts as certain sorts of selective capacity. It is suggested that this account explains the 'self-directedness' of simple concepts. It has already been argued in the previous Section that if we can explain the self-directedness of simple concepts, then we have explained the self-directedness of our beliefs and thoughts. If the argument has been successful, at no point do we need to explain the self-directedness of our belief-maps by attributing some irreducibly non-physical property to our beliefs and thoughts.

But now it may be objected that the account given of the simple concepts has a serious defect. In giving the analysis of simple concepts and Ideas it was necessary to appeal to purposes. A simple concept of X is a capacity for acquiring states which in turn permit selective *action* towards objects of the sort X. Now by action is meant 'action' in the fullest sense: purposive action. And such action is only undertaken *if A desires to undertake it*. But this means that our account of the self-directedness of the simple concepts and Ideas, and so of belief and thought, has been given only at the cost of accepting as undefined a similar notion of the self-directedness of the *will*. And what assurance is there that a reductive account is available for the latter? The bulge in the carpet has reappeared somewhere else.

This difficulty requires an extended answer which I have tried to provide in *A Materialist Theory of the Mind* (Chapters Seven and Eleven). (The latter chapter should also serve to supplement the whole of the argument of this section.) But I will sketch my reply here.

In that book I argue for a traditional conception of purposes as causes within the mind (material causes, I take them to be, although that is scientific speculation and not part of our concept of purpose), causes which initiate and sustain trains of action by the organism. The special mark of the operation of these causes (and the criterion for calling their effects 'actions') is that they are *information-sensitive*. The behaviour of the organism is determined by beliefs about the nature of the world and beliefs about the developing situation as the train of action advances. The inner cause ceases to operate if (it cannot be said only if) it is believed by the organism that a certain situation has come to be. This (believed to obtain) situation is the objective of that purpose. A useful if obviously oversimplified model is any mechanism that operates to bring about and/or maintain a certain state of affairs by means of 'negative feedback' administered by 'information' received about the developing situation. Thermostats and homing rockets are stock examples.

This account of purpose may appear only to make the problem worse. It has just been said in the previous paragraph that an account of purposive action can be given only if we have the concept of belief. But before that we argued that the concept of belief cannot be explicated without introducing the notion of purpose!

But this circularity is not vicious. It simply points to the fact that purpose and belief are 'package-deal' concepts, concepts, that is to say, which must be introduced together or not at all. (A simple example of such a concept-pair is the concepts of husband and wife.) Suppose that an organism has within itself a model or map of its environment, created by that environment acting upon the organism. Suppose that this continuously updated map is used, or can be used, by the organism in the course of a variety of selective reactions to that environment. Provided that the model is a sufficiently complex affair, and the sorts of reactions which the organism is capable of are sufficiently varied and complex, then we can speak of the map as the organism's *beliefs* about the environment. We can further speak of the reactions as the carrying out, or attempted carrying out, of the organism's *purposes*, the final states on which the reactions 'home' being the things purposed.

Soldiers are soldiers only when joined in an organized way with other soldiers. Then they constitute an army. In the same way, beliefs and purposes are beliefs and purposes only when joined in an organized way with other beliefs and purposes. Then they constitute a mind. At *exactly* what stage the situation is sufficiently complex to introduce the concepts of belief and purpose would seem to be a rather arbitrary affair. It is a rather arbitrary affair how many men are necessary, and how much organization, before we have *soldiers* in an *army*.

If all this is on the right track, then I think it serves to answer our present problem about the self-directedness of simple concepts and Ideas. The fact that the concepts of 'soldier' and 'army' presuppose each other, is obviously no bar to giving a reductive account of the two concepts. Simple concepts are selective capacities, the notion of a selective capacity involves the notion of purpose, which in turn involves the notion of belief, beliefs involve concepts which involve simple concepts. However, if the sketch given in the previous paragraph but one is correct, then a reductive account is possible of all those concepts *together*. The self-directedness of purposes will then be just as much reducible as the self-directedness of simple concepts. And so, although our account of simple concepts presupposes the notion of purpose, this account does not covertly appeal to a notion of purpose which involves the very characteristic to be explained.

Perhaps, then, the self-directedness of belief and purpose can be explained without following Brentano in postulating that belief-states have a unique, irreducible, non-physical property. The account permits (although of course it does not entail) the contingent identification of beliefs (and purposes) with neurophysiological states of the brain.

Now to consider a final objection to our account of simple concepts and Ideas. Though the objection is considered last, many will think it not least. The concept of red is said to be a certain sort of selective capacity towards members of the class of red things. But are there not *other* possible concepts under which all and only members of the class of red things fall? And how would we distinguish possession of the concept of red from possession of one of these other concepts? If the class of red things is co-extensive with the class of X's, then a selective capacity towards red things is a selective capacity towards things of the sort X. How, then, could we distinguish between the concept of red and the concept of X?

This is a familiar problem in a different setting. In contemporary philosophy, the problem comes up as a problem about meaning. 'Creature with a heart' does not mean the same as 'creature with lungs'. But the two phrases apply to exactly the same class of things. What account can be given of this difference in meaning?

Our problem about concepts (and their associated Ideas) is, however, simpler because more circumscribed. Our concern is with *simple* concepts together with any other concepts which function for their possessor as *selective* capacities. Now in the case of selective capacities we have *causal* action of the object selected upon the selector. I think it is this causal action which solves our circumscribed problem. (Perhaps it indirectly solves the more general problem of meaning, but I say no more about the wider problem here.)

It seems pretty obvious that things have the causal powers that they have in virtue of the properties which they possess. If a man is poisoned by a dose of liquid, then there will be innumerable properties of the dose which have absolutely no causal role in poisoning the man. But the stuff has property P and it is in virtue of its being an instance of P that the man dies. This points to the solution of our problem. The concept of red is the concept of *red* because the red object that activates this concept (by producing an appropriate 'map' of the object involving the Idea of red) has this effect *in virtue of the object's redness*. The poison poisons *qua* stuff with property P. The red object activates the concept of red *qua* red thing. And that is the criterion for calling it the concept of red.

Thus, consider the co-extensive properties *being a creature with a heart* and *being a creature with lungs*. It is clear that one might recognize that a certain thing was a creature, and had a heart, but fail to recognize that it had lungs. Or we might recognize that it was a creature and had lungs, but fail to recognize that it had a heart. And it might be the creatureliness of the thing together with its heartedness that directly brought about the first recognition, while the creatureliness of the thing together with its lunged character directly brought about the second. (I do not think it is relevant that in the first case the lungedness is in the causal *background*, while in the second case the heartedness is also in the causal background.) Here two properties are co-extensive, but they are not both causally operative in the same way in the two situations. In the same way, I suggest, even if redness is co-extensive with property X, it may still be the case that the redness of the object turns the man on while the X-ness of the object does not. So the concept activated is the concept of *red*.

Such an account, of course, demands an objective or Realistic account of properties. If the object is to cause a certain effect in virtue of certain of its properties, it must have these properties. I argue for a Realistic (but not a Platonistic) theory of properties in Part II of this book, where I try to show the importance of this thesis for a new version of the correspondence theory of truth.

A difficulty that may be suggested for this solution to the problem of what makes the concept of red the concept of *red* lies in the possibility of co-extensive properties which do *not* endow the objects that have the properties with different causal powers in relation to men's minds.

I have just spoken of 'different causal powers in relation to men's minds'. But it seems likely that such co-extensive properties could not involve different causal powers in relation to *anything at all.* Suppose a class of objects has the co-extensive properties P and Q. If one of these objects brings about one set of changes in some portion of its environment in virtue of its possession of P, and another set of changes in virtue of its possession of Q, then these changes may in turn register upon a mind. And so, even if the *direct* action of the objects upon minds involved no possibility of distinguishing the effect on the mind due to P and the effect on the mind due to Q, still the distinction could be made in situations where the causal chain between object and mind was less direct.

The problem case, therefore, seems to be that of co-extensive properties where there is no way *at all* of distinguishing the properties in terms of the causal powers they give to the objects that they qualify.

But how serious is this case? The properties of objects are made known to us by the objects acting upon us. If the object has two properties, but affects us, directly or indirectly, in exactly the same way in virtue of both these properties, then *we will be unable to make any distinction between the properties.* So there will be no question of us having two concepts to correspond to the two properties.

This concludes my attempt to explain the self-directedness of simple concepts and Ideas.

IV   Hume's Problem

But there is still a distinction to be accounted for before our analysis of belief can stand by itself: the distinction between a belief and a 'mere thought'. The problem about the distinction is formulated by Hume in Book I, Part III, Section 7 of the *Treatise.* For Hume belief is an occurrence, a content of consciousness, so he is able to contrast directly the occurrence of a belief in the mind and the same proposition entertained without belief, and then ask what is the difference between them. But although the problem should not be stated quite in Hume's terms, substantially the same problem re-appears for us. A belief-state involves certain elements-in-relation (certain Ideas) and this organization corresponds to the content of the proposition believed. But suppose, instead, that we entertain exactly this proposition without according it belief. Must we not allow that this thought-state or thought-episode involves exactly the same Ideas organized in exactly the same fashion? In terms of the analogy of a map, it will be as much a map of the world (correct or incorrect) as the belief-state. What, then, is the essential difference between the belief and the thought?

Hume himself found the problem, which he claimed he was the first to have posed, a hard one. He wavers between looking for an internal difference between the two, such as the superior 'vivacity' of the idea that is the belief; and a difference in characteristic effects, as when he says that beliefs are, and mere thoughts are not, 'the governing principles of all our actions'. His philosophical approach inclines him to look for the internal difference, his acumen to look for the effect of beliefs upon behaviour.

At this point we recall Ramsey's suggestion. He described the belief that everybody in Cambridge voted as 'a map . . . by which we steer'. The difference between a belief and a mere thought is that the former is, while the latter is not, something 'by which we steer'. Given suitable dominant desires (which are also to be looked upon as causal factors), then the belief-state will co-operate with the desire so that they are jointly responsible for the subject's acting in a certain way.

In the course of trying to explain the directedness of simple concepts and Ideas, we have in effect already accepted this solution in the case of beliefs like 'There is a red thing over there'. We believe this proposition if, and only if, we are prepared to act towards the thing, or supposed thing, in a 'red-selective' way, if we should desire so to act. The mere *thought* that there is a red thing over there would be something in our mind which had the same structure (involved the same Ideas), but which was not, even in conjunction with suitable dominant desires, a cause of such selective behaviour.

It is an essential mark of beliefs, then, as opposed to mere thoughts, that, if suitable dominant desires are also present, the believer is moved to action: action having as its objective the satisfaction of the desire. This does *not* mean that an account can be given of beliefs as being nothing but causal factors in the believer which initiate and sustain certain courses of action in certain circumstances. Still less are beliefs dispositions to behave, where dispositions are *not* conceived of as actual causal factors. Quasi-behaviourist views of this sort (for instance, the account of belief given by R. B. Braithwaite (Braithwaite 1933 and 1946)) have simply grasped one aspect of the complex concept of belief. They have then tried to present that aspect as if it were the complete phenomenon. Our argument, on the other hand, has been that a belief is a map-like state in the believer's mind, having a complex structure. But this state with its complex structure is marked off from a 'mere thought' having the same complex structure (and so the same propositional content) by the fact that the belief-state is, and the thought is not, a potential cause or inhibitor of action. Belief that this glass of water just drawn from the tap is poisonous will make me refrain from drinking it, despite thirst. Merely entertaining the proposition that it is poisonous will have no such effect.

Notice, however, that the belief may still fail to operate causally *on a particular occasion*. It is possible to believe that p, for the belief to have the most painful relevance to current purposes, yet for the proposition believed to 'slip one's mind'. The analogy already previously mentioned, between 'information' causally idle in the memory-banks of a computer and the same 'information' playing a causal role in producing a certain print-out, is useful here. A belief which is relevant to current desires or purposes can be causally quiescent. Nevertheless, it is of the essence of belief that it can move to action in the service of our purposes and desires. (As we may put the point, beliefs are, and thoughts are not, potential premisses in our 'practical syllogisms'. This links with the point made in the previous section, that purposes and desires are 'information-sensitive' causes.)

It is being argued that beliefs are thoughts *plus*. The plus is the causal role which beliefs play in behaviour. It has been noted that this thesis is very close to one view of the matter taken by Hume. So it is all the more important to stress one great difference which divides my view from Hume's. It has been argued in this essay that *simple* concepts, at least, are fixed as the concepts that they are by the fact that they involve capacities to form *true beliefs*, in suitable circumstances, about things in the believer's environment which fall under the concept. Similarly, simple Ideas are fixed as the Ideas that they are, by the role that they play in such beliefs. Therefore, the simple concepts and Ideas which are involved in mere thoughts are fixed as the concepts and Ideas they are by reference to the role of these entities in *beliefs*. So the explication of the notion of a thought makes essential reference, *via* the concepts and Ideas it contains, to the notion of belief. But an explication of the notion of belief involves no such reference to the notion of mere thought. No such logical dependence of thought on belief is envisaged by Hume.

Let us spell out this dependence more carefully, and in order to do so begin by considering the case of *false* belief. Suppose we falsely believe that something in our environment is red, and suppose that we act upon this belief. Perhaps we put the object in the box reserved for red objects, or attempt to obey the command 'Give me a red one' by handing over *this* object. It is clear that our mind-map of the situation contains an Idea that causes us to act towards the object exactly as if the object were red. The Idea has the same causal power as the Idea that we acquire in the situation where we respond correctly to red objects. It is this sameness of causal power that makes *both* Ideas Ideas of something red.

But now let us consider the mere entertaining of the proposition that there is something red over there. We are in a state of mind which does not move to action at all. Such a state of mind must involve the Idea of red. What makes it that Idea? By hypothesis, it lacks the power to move to behaviour which Ideas of red possess when they occur in beliefs. So the Idea of red which figures in the mere thought has some other resemblance to the causally efficacious Ideas of red. What is the nature of this resemblance?

I do not think that logical analysis can answer this question. We simply find ourselves classifying a certain mental episode as involving elements which we spontaneously identify with the (causally efficacious) elements in a certain belief. A model might be our natural classification of a few rough lines on paper with *human faces*. We see that the lines have a resemblance to faces. An empirical inquiry would be necessary to discover the common characteristics on which that resemblance depends. In the case of Ideas, direct awareness leaves us still more completely in the dark. We are simply aware of 'something which resembles a (causally efficacious) Idea'. (My hypothesis is that Ideas are in fact physiological entities, and the resemblance is in fact a resemblance in physiological properties.)

It may be noticed that Ideas of red which figure in mere thoughts are 'logically secondary' cases of Ideas of red in the *second*, not very strong, sense of 'logically secondary' which was distinguished in Chapter Three, Section Two. It was said there that Y's were logically secondary cases of X's if, and only if, the description 'X' makes essential reference to (possible) X's which are not Y's, but that, in applying to X's which are not Y's, the description 'X' makes no essential reference to X's which are Y's.

We must now consider objections to this account of the distinction between a belief and the corresponding mere thought.

First, it might be objected that mere thoughts, for instance, might move to lustful actions, although the thoughts were the mere entertaining of propositions. A novelist entertains thoughts and, as a result, is moved to write.

The point, however, is that thoughts do not have the logical connection with action which beliefs have. Examples were given of mere thoughts which caused actions, but it is not part of what makes them the thoughts which they are, that they bring about action. If, however, I desire food and believe that there is food before me, then I am moved to attempt to eat it. The connection between belief and action has, of course, been stated in too crude a way here. I may have other stronger desires, for instance, the desire to be polite. I may have other beliefs, for instance, the belief that the food is poisonous, a belief which, in conjunction with the desire not to die, will inhibit action. I may believe that the attempt to eat the food is bound to fail, and so I may not make the attempt. I may believe that there is food before me, but my belief may have slipped my mind for the present. But in the absence of such countervailing conditions (and I think that I have stated most of the possibilities here) the belief and the desire *must* initiate the attempt to eat.

The belief just mentioned as an example is a simple one, and so it is easy to see the conceptual link between belief and action (although even here hard to spell it out in detail). But such a link is present in the case of all beliefs, and absent in the case of 'mere thoughts'. I suggest as a general characterization of the link: *beliefs are, mere thoughts are not, premisses in our practical reasonings*.

As for an account of the nature of practical reasoning, an explicit account will not be given in this book. But in the next chapter an account of theoretical reasoning will be suggested, in particular an account of inference. It is a matter of certain rather complex causal relations between beliefs in the mind of the reasoner. If this account is on the right track, it would be a matter of industry rather than inspiration to extend the account to cover practical reasoning.

But now for a *second* objection. It is possible to act *as if* a certain proposition is true. People used to be advised to act as if it were true that God existed. Such action, it was hoped, would eventually produce the belief that God existed, but the action was supposed to precede the belief. Again, people frequently act as if they believed that p with the object of making others believe that the actor believes that p. In general, how do we distinguish between the apparently different cases of (i) A who believes that p; (ii) A who is disposed to act exactly as if he believed that p? (This difficulty has been posed, for instance, by D. J. O'Connor (O'Connor 1968).)

It is important to notice that, in all psychologically natural cases of somebody who acts as if he believed that p, the actions are not done for their own sake. Rather, they are done because the actions are believed to be a means to some further end. A certain man would rather believe in God than not, and hopes that going through the motions of belief will produce that belief in himself. The hypocrite desires that others should believe that he believes that p, and hopes that going through the motions of belief will produce that belief in others. If we perform a thought-experiment, and subtract either the desire or the belief about the relation of means to ends which these cases involve, then it can be seen that under these changed circumstances the 'actor as if p is true' would stop acting as if p is true. But the same subtraction need have no effect upon the conduct of one who genuinely believes that p. In the case of the actor, there is a potential difference in his conduct if *other* of his desires and/or beliefs change. This potential difference enables us to distinguish between merely acting as if p is true and actually believing that p.

It seems, then, that the only case which need concern us is the extreme one. Suppose that somebody acts exactly as if he believes that p and does this for no further end at all. How is he to be distinguished from one who really believes that p?

But I wonder if we have really got two cases here. Perhaps the answer is that this actor actually believes that p. Consider a parallel case. A man may simulate a desire for X for many reasons. But suppose he has no reasons at all. Suppose he simply sets himself to act as if he desired X, and suppose, as a result, that all his actions (including his mental actions) are exactly the same as those physical and mental acts which would be performed by one who really desired X. Does not this 'actor' *actually* desire X? In just the same way, I suggest, our actor who acts exactly as if he believed that p, but not for any ulterior reason, *actually* believes that p.

A *third* and final difficulty. If we consider unsophisticated beliefs about our current environment, then it is quite plausible to say that the distinction between belief and the corresponding thought is the action-guiding potential of the belief. But in the case of more abstract beliefs, or beliefs about matters distant from us in space and time, the point is less obvious. In part, this is nothing more than lack of obviousness. The circumstances in which these beliefs would become relevant to desires and purposes are simply less likely to occur. The circumstances may be no more than barely empirically possible. In some cases, however, we cannot escape the impression that the belief in question is not linked to conduct even potentially. This has often been remarked in the case of beliefs by philosophers about matters of philosophy! A philosopher's views about some abstract point of theory may, apparently, fail to mesh with his conduct at all, even potentially. His philosophical views on one question may make a difference to other philosophical beliefs that he holds, but these other beliefs may be also entirely divorced from possible action.

If there are such cases, and it seems quite plausible to say that there are, then I think it must be said that they are beliefs in some parasitic or secondary sense. They are accounted beliefs, perhaps, because we go through or are disposed to go through, all the linguistic motions which are associated with paradigm cases of beliefs, and we do this without any insincerity. We give verbal expression and assent to certain propositions, and we call them our beliefs.

And, indeed, I do not think that we have quite the same attitude to a man's 'beliefs' upon very abstract matters far removed from practice or possible practice than to his beliefs of a more mundane sort. We readily treat the beliefs about abstract matters simply as a set of propositions which the 'believer' is prepared to express and assent to verbally, to defend verbally, to explore the connection between these propositions and other propositions with a view to extending the class of propositions to be expressed, and so on. In so doing, perhaps, we acknowledge in an unexplicit way that there is a conceptual connection between belief and action which does not exist in the case of mere thoughts. Where that conceptual connection is broken or weakened, it becomes correspondingly harder to make a clear distinction between a man's beliefs, on the one hand, and the propositions which he is accustomed to express and to assent to, on the other.

6

General Beliefs

I Having a Reason for Believing Something

The account of belief given in the last chapter is an account of beliefs concerning particular matters of fact. We have still to give an account of beliefs that unrestricted universally quantified propositions are true ('general beliefs'), and beliefs that unrestricted existentially quantified propositions are true ('existential beliefs', as we will call them). The present chapter is concerned with general beliefs. But the topic of general belief is, I believe, inextricably bound up with that of having a reason for believing something, and it will be convenient to start by considering the latter notion.

It is perfectly possible to hold a belief without the holder having any reason for it. Such a belief will be called a 'non-inferential' belief. (That a belief is non-inferential does not entail that it is unreasonable or irrational. See Part III.) But a man has reasons for at least many of the beliefs which he holds. These reasons may be good or they may be bad. Good or bad, they are still the man's reasons. They are at work in his mind. Let us speak of the reasons which a man actually has for his beliefs as 'operative' reasons. A main task of this chapter is to give an account of operative reasons.

A may take his reason for believing that p to be a *conclusive* reason or he may not. That is to say, the reason may operate in A's mind as a conclusive reason, or it may not. If the reason is not taken to be conclusive then there seem to be two possibilities. In the first place, the reason may be taken to be a conclusive reason for believing that p is in some degree probable (in some sense of 'probable'). In the second place, the reason may operate only as a reason for according p some *degree of belief*. (We have not yet discussed the notion of degrees of belief, but will do so briefly in Chapter Eight.)

In what follows, however, I will restrict the discussion to what a person takes to be *conclusive* reasons for believing that p. (Which, of course, must not be identified with what a person takes to be *deductively* conclusive reasons.) My justification is that it will simplify the discussion if the restriction is made. At the same time, I think that everything said about putatively conclusive reasons will apply to other operative reasons *mutatis mutandis*.

What is it for A to have a reason for believing that p? It seems clear, in the first place, that the existence of such operative reasons has little or nothing to do with the speech-act of *offering* reasons. A may have reasons for his belief which he does not offer, and offer reasons for his belief which are not his reasons.

But there does seem to be one positive conclusion which we can come to immediately. If A has a reason for believing that p is true then it is entailed that he holds some further *belief*, a belief which stands in some relation to the belief that p. Call this further belief the belief that q. The problem of giving an account of operative reasons is a matter of elucidating the nature of the relationship which holds between belief-states Bap and Baq.

Does this mean that A's reason for believing that p is his belief that q? Is my reason for believing Jim is dead my belief that he has been decapitated? It seems that we sometimes speak in this way, but certainly we do not always do so. Very often, at least, what is called my reason is not my belief-state, but what I believe: the proposition 'that Jim has been decapitated'. The proposition is called my reason because I believe it but, very often, it is the proposition to which the word 'reason' attaches.

The situation is the same as with the word 'father'. A father is called a father in virtue of a certain causal relation that he has to a woman and a child. In the absence of this relation he would not be called a father. Nevertheless, the word 'father' does not refer to this whole situation: male related in a certain fashion to mother and child. The word simply refers to the man. In the same way, a reason, the proposition that q, which a man has for believing that p, is called 'a reason' because (i) the man believes that q; and (ii) this whole situation Baq stands in a certain relation to his belief that p. (It will be our task to elucidate the nature of the relation.) Nevertheless, the word 'reason' need not refer to this whole complex situation. It may refer simply to the proposition 'q'.

The following is an argument for saying that reasons are, sometimes at least, propositions. A man offers his reasons (if he does offer them) in support of his conclusions. Now what is he offering except premisses of an argument which he claims has those conclusions? But the premisses and conclusions of arguments, traditionally at any rate, are held to be propositions. They are certainly not believings.

It seems, indeed, that the word 'reason' has the same convenient ambiguity as the word 'belief'. The latter may refer to a belief-state or to what is believed. In the same way, to talk of a man's reason may be to refer to a (certain sort of) belief-state of his, or it may be to refer to the proposition believed.

In so far as reasons are propositions, it is logically impossible that they should be causes. For a proposition cannot be a cause. A proposition has as much capacity (or incapacity) to cause anything as the number 2. The notion of a proposition being a cause is not an intelligible one.

This proof that reasons cannot be causes in this sense of the word 'reason', is, of course, a pretty trivial affair. For although a man's reason 'q' is a proposition, it is a proposition that he believes. Now this state of affairs Baq could act as a cause. And for anything that the argument has so far shown, it could be that causal relations of Baq to Bap that make us say that 'q' is (one of) A's reason(s) for believing that p. It will be argued in what follows that this is indeed the case.

But, anticipating this argument, it will be seen that this conclusion requires that we admit a further lack of analogy between the collection of A's belief-states at any one time and a map of the world. The parts of a map do not stand in any causal relation to each other. One part of a map can be changed without affecting another part. A map is not a dynamic unity. But if A's having certain reasons for believing that p is a matter of causal relations holding between belief-states, then, in so far as A has reasons for the belief he holds, the different parts of the 'belief-map' will be dynamically united.

II   Efficient and Sustaining Causes

No analysis of the notion of cause will be given in this work. But it is important to realize that we have a very good pre-philosophical understanding of the notion. We can point to clear instances falling under the notion (which does not, of course, mean instances beyond the logical possibility of controversy) both in the physical and mental sphere. Consider, for instance, the stone's impact which breaks the window and the face's appearing at the window which makes me start. We know how to decide, very often, whether a suggested causal connection does or does not hold. Nor, I think, have we any good reason to think that causation in the physical sphere and causation in the mental sphere are two different sorts of thing. Even if the physical and the mental were very different sorts of thing, this would not show that physical causality and mental causality were different sorts of causality.

But although no analysis will be given of causality, we must take notice of a distinction between two different sorts of causal connection to be found in the world. We must distinguish between *efficient* and *sustaining* causes. In efficient causation one alteration brings about another. The stone comes into contact with the glass and, *as a result*, the glass shatters. The face appears at the window, and, *as a result*, I start. In sustaining causation, however, one state of affairs simply maintains another state of affairs in existence. Sustaining causation does not entail that anything changes. Pillars may sustain a roof. The pillars' presence underneath the roof is one state of affairs. It sustains, that is, maintains in existence, another state of affairs: the roof's staying up. Nothing need be *happening*.

Now if we are seeking for the causal analysis of the relations between the belief-states Baq and Bap which make 'q' (one of) A's reason(s) for believing that p, it seems natural to look first to sustaining rather than efficient causes. (In the end, we shall see, they must both be introduced.) For reasons, or at least the beliefs they are associated with, are naturally thought of as underpropping and maintaining the beliefs which they are reasons for. They may or may not be concerned in the *generation* of the beliefs they are reasons for, but they do sustain them.

Our preliminary suggestion then is: 'q' functions as (one of) A's reason(s) for believing that p if, and only if, Baq causally sustains Bap.

This is certainly unsatisfactory as it stands. If the pillars are removed, the roof will fall. If this model is to be applied to the formula above, then, if it ceases to be the case that A believes that q, then he will cease to believe that p. Yet A might have other, quite independent, reasons for believing that p, so that loss of belief that q would leave his belief that p unaffected.

We seem to require a weaker condition. Let us introduce the notion of a *weak sustaining cause*. A weak sustaining cause is sufficient to maintain a certain further state of affairs. It may or it may not be necessary. An object might be suspended from ropes and supported by pillars. Remove the ropes and the object will remain in place, supported by the pillars. Remove the pillars and the object will equally remain in place, suspended from the ropes. Both presence of the ropes and presence of the pillars are weak, but not strong, sustaining causes of the objects remaining in position. Ropes and pillars can each take the weight by themselves if they have to.

The suggestion therefore becomes: 'q' functions as (one of) A's reason(s) for believing that p if, and only if, Baq is a weak sustaining cause of Bap.

Presumably any belief-state will have its sustaining causes, weak and strong, while it endures. Mental organization is a very delicate thing. But a belief-state may well lack any other *belief*-states among its sustaining causes, weak or strong. On the analysis suggested, this would be the case where something was believed for no *reason* at all. It would be a case of *non-inferential* belief.

It may be necessary to weaken our formula still further. Suppose that Smith is widely believed to be trustworthy. It may then be said, by myself and others, that my reason for believing that p is that Smith reported it. But the belief that Smith said the words 'p' may not, by itself, be a weak sustaining cause of the situation Bap. The belief-state which is a weak sustaining cause of Bap is rather the *complex* belief-state 'that Smith said the words "p" and that Smith is trustworthy'. But since the second conjunct is something which everybody takes for granted, and so is in the background, we *speak* of my reason as simply being 'that Smith reported it'.

To deal with this we could say: 'q' functions as (one of) A's reason(s) for believing that p if, and only if, Baq is, *or is the conspicuous part of*, a belief-state which is a weak sustaining cause of Bap. But perhaps this is the sort of difficulty which, having noted and having noted its solution, we can largely ignore in the subsequent discussion.

I will now try to make it plausible that our formula, or something like it, is at least a *necessary* condition for 'q' being (one of) A's reason(s) for believing that p. Let us apply what may be called 'the method of subtraction'. The method of subtraction is simply a useful dodge to use when attempting logical analysis. In order to see whether a certain condition c is, or is not, a necessary condition for the occurrence of a certain sort of situation s, try conceiving of cases of s where it is given that c does not hold. It may turn out to be fairly clear that the notion of s without c is an incoherent conception, and so fairly clear that c is necessary for s. This simple technique, which resembles the method of *reductio ad absurdum* in mathematics and logic, and the 'method of difference' in empirical research, can be astonishingly fruitful. The neglect to apply it can lead to a lot of unnecessary beating about the bush.

Let us therefore suppose an A who believes that q and believes that p, but for whom it is false that Baq is even a weak sustaining cause (or the conspicuous part of a belief-state that is a weak sustaining cause) of Bap. What could we then make of the claim that 'q' is actually one of A's reasons for believing that p? 'q' might be a proposition that A offered or *put forward* as a reason for believing that p. It might even be the case that A *believed* that q was one of his reasons for believing that p. (A case of the latter would be a man who believed that he believed in the racial inferiority of Negroes solely on the grounds of a genetic theory. Yet, when he was forced to see that the genetic theory was false, he *still* believed Negroes to be racially inferior.) But if Baq did no work in A's mind to support Bap, how could 'q' be one of A's reasons for believing that p?

III   Difficulties for the 'Sustaining Cause' Analysis

But the argument just considered shows at best that a causal relation between the belief-states is a necessary condition for one belief to be a man's reason for holding another belief. There are a number of objections against taking the causal relation to be also sufficient. And there is one important objection against even taking it to be necessary.

Objection 1. If we give an account of a man's reasons for believing something solely in terms of causal relations between belief-states, then this would commit us to saying that, because of his ignorance of the causal connections involved, a man might be totally ignorant of what his reasons are for believing something. He might even totally repudiate such alleged reasons with his conscious mind. But this, it may be argued, is an unacceptable conclusion.

I think the reply to this objection is that the conclusion is acceptable. That a causal analysis should have this consequence is a virtue in it, not a defect. Psychoanalysis (whatever we think of much of the *detail* of psychoanalysis) and modern cognitive psychology (for instance, Chomsky's work in psycholinguistics) have shown that the intellectual operations we are aware of are only a small part of the workings of the mind. And, as psychoanalysis has shown, some of those workings are profoundly irrational, and, if exposed, are consciously judged to be irrational.

A general comment seems in order. In recent years philosophers have largely managed to get clear of phenomenalistic views of physical objects and their sub-microscopic constituents. It remains to get clear of a phenomenalistic view of the mind: *viz.* an account of the mind in terms of those mental states which we are directly conscious of. In this, Descartes' doctrine that the essence of mind is consciousness (a distinct doctrine from his Dualism, even if in some degree linked) is to the theory of mind what Berkeley's *esse est percipi* is to the theory of matter: an enemy of intellectual progress.

Objection 2. The next two difficulties spring from consideration of more or less peculiar cases where Baq causally sustains Bap, but nobody would want to say that 'q' is A's reason for believing that p.

Suppose, first, that A believes that q and believes that p. Baq and Bap are causally connected in the following extraordinary manner. If it ceased to be the case that A believed that q, then this would have the effect of activating a probe in A's brain (we can imagine some ingenious electro-chemical mechanism) which would have the further effect that it ceased to be the case that A believed that p. Here Baq causally sustains Bap, but we would not want to say that 'q' was therefore A's reason for believing that p.

The trouble here seems to be that the suggested causal connection involves events which, if they took place, would occur outside A's mind. It seems, therefore, that the difficulty can be met by modifying our thesis yet again. Now we say: 'q' is (one of) A's reason(s) for believing that p if, and only if, Baq is a weak sustaining cause, *operating wholly within A's mind*, of Bap.

Objection 3. The case to be considered here is based upon one suggested to me by John Watling. A believes that q and believes that p. 'p' is actually rather dubious, and if A were to scrutinize it at all carefully he would soon cease to believe it. What is more, A *would* scrutinize it carefully, and so reject it, but for the fact that he is totally preoccupied with 'q'. 'q' is a very exciting proposition for A, and while A believes it he is busy with its implications and has no time for 'p'. So Baq sustains Bap, but 'q' is not A's reason for believing that p.

How might we set about amending our formula to exclude

Watling's case? Now seems the moment to reintroduce the notion of *efficient* causality. Suppose 'q' is, in my estimation, a conclusive reason for believing that p but that I believed that p before I came to believe that q. My belief that q was not the efficient cause of my belief that p. But suppose, counter-factually, that my belief that q had been acquired before my belief that p. What would have happened? If I am not rationalizing in thinking 'q' to be a conclusive reason for believing that p (rationalization will be discussed in Section Eight), then must I not think that Baq would have had a tendency to bring Bap into existence? It would be implausible to think that Baq would *infallibly* have brought Bap into existence. But it would be natural to expect Baq to bring about Bap.

This factor is clearly absent in Watling's case. Suppose that A had not believed the dubious but unscrutinized proposition 'p'. A's belief that q would have had no tendency to bring Bap into existence.

For the moment I will not propose an actual amendment. Let us simply note that our final account of reasons will apparently have to involve the power of beliefs to create as well as to sustain further beliefs.

Objection 4. But even if Watling's case can be dealt with, our troubles are by no means over. Suppose A believes two propositions which, as we would ordinarily say, have no connection with each other at all, for instance, that Socrates was snub-nosed and that there is water on the surface of Mars. It might be the case that, owing to some obscure cause, the first belief-state both created and causally sustained the second belief-state. (A brain-circuit might generate and sustain another circuit in some accidental manner.) We would be forced to conclude that the first proposition was (one of) A's reason(s) for believing the second. We could just accept this conclusion, but it is somewhat counter-intuitive.

I will defer for the moment any attempt to answer this objection.

Objection 5. But, finally, it may be objected that our causal condition is not even a *necessary* condition for A's taking 'q' to be a reason for believing that p.

Consider the situation where Baq in no way creates or causally sustains Bap. Is it not possible that A should believe 'q' is a sufficient ground for 'p'? He does not merely believe that he believes this, he actually believes it. This seems to be a third belief, distinct from Baq and Bap, so why should not A hold it? What can it have to do with a mere causal connection *between* beliefs? But, if A holds this belief, is not 'q' A's reason for believing that p? It is certainly peculiar that A's belief that p is not even potentially affected by possible fluctuations in his belief that q. There would seem to be something irrational in the workings of A's mind. But is not 'q' (one of) A's reason(s) for believing that p?

IV Principles of Inference

I will now propose a condition to be added to the causal condition which, I hope, plugs the gap created by Objections 3 and 4, and, after a further identification has been made, answers the still more thoroughgoing Objection 5.

Let us start with the following considerations. The notion of a reason is, surely, closely connected with the notion of *reasoning*. Now in reasoning we proceed according to general principles, according to some general pattern. So, I suggest, if 'q' is to be (one of) A's reason(s) for believing that p, there must be some general principle operating in A's mind according to which it is possible for A to move from the first proposition to the second. The general principle need not be true, nor have any plausibility to anybody but A. Nor need A be aware that the principle operates in his mind. But the principle must *be* operative in A's mind.

To turn this into a more precise proposal. For 'q' to be (one of) A's reason(s) for believing that p, not only must Baq weakly sustain Bap, but this sustaining must be the *manifestation* of a certain *disposition* that A has.

'q' is (one of) A's putatively conclusive reason(s) for believing that p if, and only if:

The dispositional condition
  (i) There exists some general proposition (x)(if Fx, then Gx), such that q has the form Fb, and p has the form Gb, and such that A is disposed so that: if A believes something of the form Fx, then this belief-state will both create (if necessary) and weakly causally sustain within A's mind the belief that the corresponding proposition of the form Gx is true.

The manifestation condition
  (ii) Baq both creates (if necessary) and weakly causally sustains Bap within A's mind.

Before showing how this new formula answers the outstanding objections a number of points of explication are in order.

(i) One particularly important case falling under this formula will be that where Baq is the efficient as well as the sustaining cause of Bap. In this case, Baq brings Bap into existence and then conserves what it has created. I think that this is the psychological process of *inferring*. It will be discussed in detail in Section Six. Where it is not the case that Baq brings Bap into existence then Bap will already have some sustainer, though this sustainer will not necessarily be another *belief*. Baq will then become a further weak sustainer for Bap.

(ii) The proposition (x)(if Fx, then Gx) need not be true, nor need it even be plausible. But it must be the sort of proposition which is capable of sustaining counter-factuals. It must assert the existence of a law-like connection in nature.

(iii) I do not think, however, that the class of propositions in question must be restricted to universally quantified propositions which are unrestricted to any particular time and place. The proposition 'Whenever Sally gets angry, she throws the crockery around' would seem to be possible 'general principle'. It can sustain counter-factuals according to which A's mind might work. Presumably one who has this proposition as a general principle will think that there *is* an unrestricted universally quantified proposition which, as it were, lies behind the proposition about Sally. For they will think that Sally has some nature, X, such that anybody of nature X, in the same sort of circumstances as Sally, and who gets angry, will proceed to throw the crockery around. But it is likely that they will have no opinion as to the nature of X, and so that they will be unable to specify this unrestricted universal proposition. (Some amendment of our formula may be necessary to cover such cases, but the amendment will not be attempted here.)

(iv) I have assumed that all well-formed assertions of law-like connection can be brought under the simple formula (x)(if Fx, then Gx). And certainly most such assertions can be brought under this formula by a little judicious torture. But it may be that there are well-formed law-like propositions which cannot be rendered in this way. Something a little more complex, such as (x)(if Fx, then (∃ y) Gy) may be required. I do not think that this affects the argument. Our definition of what it is to believe on the basis of a reason could easily be extended to cover further types of proposition.

(v) As we have stated it, condition (i) of our formula involves a quantification of the form (x)(BaFx ⊃ BaGx). (Writing ' ⊃ ' for the complex causal relationship which is actually asserted to hold between the belief-states.) But, as is well-known, such attempted quantification raises great problems. What, for example, is the quantifier supposed to range over? A may believe that something of the form Fb is true, but the putative object b may not exist.

I present the condition in this unsatisfactory form for simplicity's sake. But I think it is possible to see in principle how it should be re-stated. The condition asserts a hypothetical causal connection between mental states. A's believing that Fb is a mental state. It is a mental state involving a certain ordering of the Idea-of-F and the Idea-of-a-certain-individual. (The hyphens indicate that here we have wholes which, pending further analysis – attempted in the previous chapter – are treated as unities.) A's believing that Gb is analysed in the same way.

It appears, then, that in a proper re-statement of our condition the variable will have as its values *tokens of Ideas of individuals.* If such an Idea is suitably embedded in a belief-state of A's, then this belief-state is disposed to create and/or sustain a further belief-state which suitably embeds a further token of that very same Idea. Of course, there is the difficult question of what constitutes the principle of individuation for different Ideas-of-individuals. That is to say, there is the problem of what makes the Idea-of-b a different Idea from the Idea-of-c. The problem is a particularly difficult one when it is considered that there may be no such individuals b and c. But I have nothing to contribute to this problem of analysing the notion of reference beyond the brief remarks in Section Three of the previous chapter.

(vi) In discussing dispositions in Chapter Two we noticed that an object can have a certain disposition, the efficient cause which characteristically brings about its manifestation be present, and yet the manifestation fail to occur, because the circumstances are not propitious. Matches are inflammable, but a match struck in a vacuum will not light. Applying this point to our dispositions for belief to sustain belief, there is the possibility, if circumstances are unfavourable, of A's having the requisite disposition, and believing that q, but the causal connection with Bap failing to occur. This possibility will prove very important to our argument. I am assuming, of course, that the disposition, like all dispositions, can be

identified with some underlying, categorical, *state* of A's mind, a
state whose nature further psychological or physiological investigation may ultimately reveal.

We proceed now to see how our amended and somewhat complex account of what it is for 'q' to be (one of) A's (putatively conclusive) reason(s) for believing p, rules out the objections 3, 4 and 5
that were made to the previous account.

Objection 3 was Watling's case. Baq sustains Bap only because
believing q causes A's mind to be engaged so fully that he never
gets around to doing what he would otherwise do: examining and
rejecting 'p'.

It is clear that this case is no difficulty for our amended analysis.
As already pointed out, in Watling's case Baq is not a potential
creator of belief-state Bap. Suppose A had believed that q but did
not believe that p. It is not the case that Baq would have brought
Bap into existence. Watling's case may be a difficulty for an analysis
which proceeds purely in terms of sustaining causes. But our
amended account involves *both* sustaining and efficient causes.

Objection 4 was the objection that the belief that Socrates was
snub-nosed might, by some obscure causal mechanism, create and/
or sustain the belief that there is water on Mars, and yet we would
be reluctant to say that the first proposition was A's *reason* for the
second.

In terms of our amended account, this case has only fulfilled condition (ii): the *manifestation* condition. (A criticism which can
also be made of Watling's case.) To fulfil condition (i) we would
need to add that this causal relationship of beliefs is a manifestation
of a *disposition* of A's. A must be disposed to link together beliefs
according to a general principle, of which this particular linking is
a manifestation, and this general principle must be expressible in
an *unrestricted* universally quantified proposition. The case we considered included no supposition that such a general principle was
operating.

We might try to formulate such a principle and build it into
the case. For instance, the principle according to which A's mind is
disposed to operate might be 'whenever the third least distant planet
of a solar system contains a very able snub-nosed philosopher, then
the fourth least distant planet of that system has water on its surface'. If, then, Socrates is identified by A as 'a very able snub-nosed
philosopher living on the third least distant planet of a solar system'

and Mars as 'the fourth least distant planet of that system' then the case can be brought under the amended definition.

But, as soon as we have built this (absurd) general principle into A's mind, it also seems quite plausible to say that 'Socrates is snub-nosed' is now A's *reason* for believing that there is water on Mars. So there is still no counter-example here.

Finally, Objection 5. What if all causal connection between Baq and Bap is lacking, whether or not according to general patterns, yet A still *believes* that 'q' supports 'p'? Is this not possible? But, if it is possible, would not 'q' be A's *reason* for believing that p? The suggested causal relations between belief-states would *not* then be necessary conditions for 'q' being (one of) A's reason(s) for believing that p.

In answer to this difficulty, it will now be argued that, provided we accept a certain (independently plausible) account of what it is to have a general belief, the case put in the fifth objection is no proper case.

V   General Beliefs

It has been argued that, in order for there to be reasons which operate in a mind, there must be general principles which operate in that mind, so that, if certain beliefs are acquired, they are then disposed to create and/or causally sustain further beliefs according to a certain pattern. The operation of such general principles may be identified with dispositions in the persons in whom the principles operate. But now, following F. P. Ramsey, it is suggested that these dispositions are identical with the subject's *general beliefs*.

To believe a general proposition, according to this view, is to be so disposed that, if we have one belief, it is the efficient cause of another belief which is then causally sustained by the first belief (or, where the second belief is already held, for the first belief to give additional causal sustenance to the second belief in the believer's mind), the whole process proceeding according to certain patterns of antecedent and consequent. I come to believe that X's head has been cut off. Within my mind this belief generates and causally sustains the belief that X is dead. Furthermore, this process conforms to a general pattern such that I am disposed for it to occur whatever value is substituted for X. This *constitutes* my belief that the decapitated are dead.

It should be noticed that, as we have defined the terms 'manifestation' and 'expression' (Chapter Three, Section One), this manifestation of a general belief is not an *expression* of that belief. For the acquiring of a belief is not an *action* and we confined the term 'expression' to manifestations which are actions. General beliefs can, of course, have their expressions, for instance their being put into words. But the general belief can be held although the believer cannot put it into words.

It will be seen that this account of general beliefs is a *recursive* one, in that it uses the notion of a *belief* about a particular matter of fact. The account of general beliefs is given in terms of possible causal relations between beliefs about particular, spatio-temporally limited, matters of fact ('His head is cut off'). In some cases, the recursions will have more than one step. This becomes clear when we consider that a belief in the truth of a general proposition such as 'the decapitated are dead' may itself be (although it need not be) supported by reasons in the believer's mind. In such a case, the general principle in terms of which the reasoning proceeds will have the proposition that the decapitated are dead as an exemplification of its consequent. Sooner or later, however, the account will get down to beliefs about particular matters of fact. (But notice that our actual formula was framed only for the case where the immediate exemplifications are beliefs about particular matters of fact.)

I proceed to discuss certain objections to this account of general beliefs.

First, it may be objected that it is possible to believe a general proposition, simultaneously believe that some particular state of affairs obtains which falls under the antecedent of the general position but fail to draw the indicated conclusion. One sort of case is that where the general proposition is a very complex one, so that it is quite easy to fail to draw the conclusion. But even where there is no such intellectual difficulty, the conclusion may still not be drawn. A may believe that (x)(if Fx, then Gx), believe that b is F and it may be the case that *if he considered the matter for a moment* he would see that he ought also to believe that b is G. But he may nevertheless fail to bring together, fail to make the connection between, the general and the particular belief.

In replying to this objection, let us consider the second sort of case first. I think it is fair to say that, while we admit the case is a possible one, nevertheless it makes a peculiar impression upon us. If A really holds those two beliefs, must he not believe that b is G? If he does not, is it not some indication that he really does not believe one of the premisses?

The problem is solved by recalling a feature of dispositions which has already been referred to. The brittle glass breaks when struck, *but only under suitable circumstances.* And suitable circumstances will, in general, be *normal* circumstances. Similarly for general beliefs. There can be a case where the disposition is present, the initiating cause of the manifestation is present (belief that b is F), but the manifestation does not occur because circumstances are not suitable. But, in general, this will not be the normal case.

Now what of the case where the general proposition believed is so complex that the believer is unable to make the inference to b's being G, even although he explicitly considers what conclusion, if any, can be drawn from the general proposition together with b's being F, which he also believes? I suggest that here we can distinguish between actually grasping a proposition and merely grasping the symbolic vehicle by means of which it is expressed. It is commonplace to grasp a formula, believe that this formula expresses a truth, but to lack a clear grasp of the proposition expressed. As Berkeley pointed out (*Principles*, Introduction, Section 19), in much of our thinking we use symbols as in algebra, without bearing in mind the precise meaning of the symbols. May it not be this which occurs when we believe some complex general proposition, believe a particular proposition falling under the antecedent of the general proposition, bring the two beliefs together, but fail to embrace the proposition falling under the consequent? If we had really grasped the content of the general proposition, we would have been able to draw the conclusion.

Second, this account of general beliefs raises a problem about necessary propositions that are very obvious, for instance, '(x)(if Fx & Gx, then Gx & Fx)'. It may be said that this proposition is something we know, and so believe, to be true. But suppose we also believe 'Fb & Gb'. To believe this latter, it would seem, *is* to believe 'Gb & Fb'. But, if so, there are not *two* belief-states (Fb & Gb) and (Gb & Fb). Hence it is impossible that the belief-state 'Fb & Gb' should create and/or sustain the belief-state 'Gb & Fb'. So what account can we give of the corresponding general belief?

I think we should be resolute, and deny that this 'general belief' can be anything more than a belief about what symbolic manipulations are conventionally permitted without changing what is asserted. (Like translating a Russellian formula into Polish notation.) Only where the possible exemplifications of antecedent and consequent are genuinely distinct states do we have genuine general beliefs.

But where do we draw the line? Perhaps all would agree that the state of affairs Ba(Fb & Gb) is the very same state of affairs as Ba(Gb & Fb). But what of, say, Ba(if p, then q) and Ba(if ~q, then ~p)? Have we two beliefs here, or only one?

Tentatively, I suggest that the answers may be different for different believers. For one man, familiar with this logical equivalence, we may have the one belief-state expressed in two different ways. For another, we have two belief-states which nevertheless are disposed to sustain each other causally. The latter man might be said to have a general belief, which might on occasion fail to operate, by which he moves from one to the other.

Perhaps this casts light on the problem raised in Chapter Four, Section One, about the identity-conditions for the propositions which are the objects of belief. Given a belief-state, Bap, we can say that it is also the belief-state Baq if, and only if, 'p' and 'q' are simply different notational expressions of the same organization of Ideas in the one belief-state.

I do not think that such a criterion has a great deal of value in coming to a decision about particular cases. Introspection is not a very powerful instrument for revealing whether or not we have two distinct states which are causally related (and might become unrelated). Presumably, we would have to look to the future theoretical identification or correlations of neurophysiology to settle such questions with any show of decisiveness.

A *third* problem which may be raised is that of beliefs that have the form '(x)Fx'. Does such a general proposition provide for a movement from particular belief to particular belief?

I think that such a movement is provided for. Suppose A comes to believe a proposition of the form 'x exists'. He will then be disposed for this belief to create and/or sustain a belief of the form 'Fx'. Suppose, for instance, that A believes that everything there is is spatial. If, holding this belief, he comes to believe that there are disembodied spirits, he will be disposed to believe further that these spirits are spatial beings.

Finally, we must consider Objection 5, the objection raised at the end of Section Three. There we considered the case of an A who believed that q and believed that p, but who was *not* disposed to connect belief-states causally according to appropriate patterns. Might not such an A nevertheless believe that 'q' was a sufficient ground for accepting 'p'?

In posing this objection, I said that this belief seems to be distinct from the belief-states Baq and Bap. And I asked rhetorically what this third belief could have to do with a mere causal connection between beliefs. But now the situation should appear different. An account has now been given of what it is for A to take a proposition 'q' to be a sufficient ground for a further proposition 'p'. According to this account, A is manifesting a certain disposition, a disposition to connect causally in a certain fashion beliefs which fall under the antecedent and consequent of some general principle. This general principle according to which A reasons, was then identified with a general belief of A's (regardless of whether or not A can *state* the proposition in question). Both these theses, I hope, are independently plausible. But if we accept them, we see that A's belief that 'q' is a sufficient ground for 'p' does, after all, have everything to do with a causal connection between the belief-states Baq and Bap. A believes that 'q' is a sufficient ground for 'p' if, and only if, Baq and Bap are causally connected in the appropriate way.

I think we are therefore justified in rejecting Objection 5. We already noted, when originally posing the objection, that it would be peculiar if, in such a case, A's belief that p was not even potentially affected by possible fluctuations in his belief that q. A's mind would at least be working in an irrational fashion. Let us now be emboldened to declare that in the absence of the appropriate causal connections, it would not even be the case that A took 'q' to be a sufficient ground for 'p'. Our theory seems sufficiently plausible, and the case put in Objection 5 sufficiently shaky, to back the theory against the case.

So much for Objection 5. It may be noted, finally, that nothing in this account of general beliefs suggests that the general *propositions* believed are not true or false, or are true or false in some different sense from propositions concerning particular matters of fact.

VI   Inferring

Something must now be said about the psychological process of inferring. The situation we are concerned with is that where A believes that q, it is not the case that he believes that p, but he then comes to believe that p as a result of inferring it from 'q' (whether validly or invalidly, rightly or wrongly, is of no present concern). This may not be the only psychological situation to which the word 'inferring' is applied, but it is the most important one.

When we infer we are normally said to infer that something is the case from something else that we take to be the case. One proposition is inferred from another. But, just as in the case of reasons for believing, this linguistic fact seems no bar to giving an analysis of the situation in terms of causal relations between belief-states.

What are these causal relations? First, it is necessary that Baq be the efficient cause of Bap. The first belief-state must bring the second belief-state into existence. But this seems insufficient. (In *A Materialist Theory of the Mind*, Chapter Nine, Section III, I followed a suggestion of Max Deutscher's and argued that this simple causal relationship was sufficient as well as necessary. This now seems to me to be a greatly oversimplified account.) For if A infers 'p' from 'q' must not 'q' function as A's *reason* for believing that p? It seems, therefore, that Baq must not only create Bap, but must further act, for some period of time at least, as a sustaining cause of Bap. (It cannot be demanded that Baq go on sustaining Bap as long as the latter endures. For it is possible to retain, that is, believe, conclusions of our inferences after the evidence that caused us to draw them has been forgotten.)

A physical model for the causal relations involved in inferring is that of a crane hauling a weight to a certain point *and then holding it there*. The crane first brings it to be that W is at place P, and then sustains the situation. Imagine, further, that props are then put under W so that, although the crane's hook is removed, W remains at place P. This would model the situation where the inferred belief is retained, sustained either by other beliefs or by states of affairs which are not beliefs, although the premiss of the inference is no longer believed.

But, of course, if 'q' is to function as a *reason* for 'p', then this complex of causal relationships will be merely a manifestation of a *disposition* which A has: a disposition for causal relations to hold among belief-states according to a certain general pattern, where that disposition is identified with a general belief. (See the previous two Sections.) Then, and only then, do we have necessary and sufficient conditions for inferring.

Is our account of inferring too elaborate? Suppose that Baq gives rise to Bap, and that this causal process is a manifestation of some general pattern according to which A's mind is disposed to move, but that, after Bap comes to be, Baq stands in no particular causal relation to Bap. Baq might even cease to be at the instant, or before, Bap comes to be. Might one not describe this as inferring? After all, A's mental processes can be subjected to rational appraisal, just as in the case of the more elaborate process. We can consider whether the transition from 'q' to 'p' is a *truth-preserving* process. So why not speak of inferring?

I think that this may be a matter for linguistic decision. The sort of processes just described do seem to occur, for instance in the complex mental operations (largely unconscious) involved in perception. And they can be rationally appraised. But there is a vital difference from the cases where Baq still sustains Bap. In the latter case, not only can the process be appraised, but A himself remains open to rational persuasion. Convince A that 'q' is not true and he ceases to believe that p, or at any rate 'p' has one less support in his mind. But where Baq does nothing to sustain Bap, although it generated Bap, criticism of 'q' cannot, by hypothesis, affect A's belief that p. And so there is an important motive for refusing to talk of 'inferring' here.

VII   Reasons and Rationalization

A causal account of what it is for a man to have a reason for believing something enables a persuasive account to be given of the distinction between such reasons and mere *rationalizations*. (The same point is made by A. M. MacIver, MacIver 1958, p. 17.)

The term 'rationalization' is most generally used in connection with reasons for *actions*, but it can also be applied in connection with reasons for beliefs. (*Cf.* F. H. Bradley's definition of philosophy as finding bad reasons for what we believe on instinct.) The following seem to be sufficient conditions for saying that A is rationalizing:

(i) A believes that q and A believes that p.

(ii) It is not the case that Baq causally sustains Bap in any way.

(iii) A *believes* that 'q' is for him (a) reason for believing that p.

(iv) A desires that p should be true, and this desire is the sustaining cause of the state of affairs (iii).

We can see the plausibility of describing A as a rationalizer, by considering what happens if A ceases to believe that q despite the sustaining effect of his desire that p be true. By hypothesis, his belief that p remains unaffected. Under the influence of his desires, he has deceived himself about his reasoning processes, and so is properly regarded as a rationalizer.

The necessity for condition (iv) was pointed out to me by Bernard Williams. If we only demanded that conditions (i) to (iii) obtain, then the following case would have to be accounted rationalization. A man perceives that a certain object is of the sort X. In fact, though he does not know it, he does this by using cues of the sort Y. *He* thinks that he does it by using cues of the sort Z, which are in fact worthless. Psychologists investigating perception uncover this sort of situation quite frequently, and we certainly do not want to describe such perceivers as rationalizers. The missing factor seems to be that their false belief about the cues which they are using is not causally dependent upon any *desire* that their conclusion ('It is an X') be true.

It must be remembered that causal connection, or lack of causal connection, is often hard to establish. The task can be particularly difficult in the mental sphere, whether it is our own mind or that of another which is in question. But this should not make us suspicious of a partially causal criterion for distinguishing between genuine reasoning and mere rationalization. Indeed, it is some evidence in favour of such a criterion. For honesty compels us to admit that it is often perilously difficult to discern whether we are really reasoning or simply rationalizing.

VIII   Good Reasons

In all this discussion of what it is for a proposition actually to function in a man's mind as a reason for a belief, nothing has been said about the *goodness* of such reasons. This is because the goodness or badness of a reason has nothing essential to do with its actually operating for somebody as a reason. It is true that when we think particularly badly of some proffered reason we may say 'One couldn't call that a reason.' But I think that this remark is made in the spirit of one who says 'One couldn't call that a horse', not because it is a cow, but because it is a very poor specimen of a horse. A poor specimen of a horse is still a horse, and however bad a man's reason may be, if it actually operates in his mind it is *his reason*.

But what makes a reason (for believing) good? It is simplest to begin by considering the highest grade of goodness in this field: the notion of a conclusive reason.

I think that an account of conclusive reasons can be given very easily. 'q' is a conclusive reason for believing that p if, and only if, it is the case that 'if q, then p'. Conclusiveness of reasons is simply a matter of *the truth of a proposition*. ('q' may in fact be a conclusive reason for believing that p even if nobody knows, or even suspects, that 'if q, then p' is true.)

The proposition 'if q, then p' need not be true of logical necessity. It may be, but it need not be. It is a conclusive reason for believing that X is dead that his head has been cut off, but decapitation does not logically ensure death. All that cannot be allowed is reading 'if q, then p' simply as the logician's 'q ⊃ p'. And a logical link does not make 'q' a more conclusive reason than in the case of a non-logical link.

This last point, which is important, may be put thus. To be conclusive, an argument from 'q' to 'p' must be completely *truth-preserving*. But it does not have to be *valid*, in the logician's use of the term 'valid'. Valid arguments are simply one species of conclusive argument. (And they are not 'more conclusive' than other conclusive arguments.)

Having defined 'conclusive reason', we can define 'good reason' as follows. 'q' is a good reason for 'p' if, and only if, it is the case that 'if q, then p is (more or less) probable'.

This proposition, 'if q, then p is (more or less) probable', may be logically warranted, but it need not be. The hypothetical 'if 90% of A's are B's and this is an A, then this is a B' is logically warranted and the corresponding argument is less than conclusive. The hypothetical 'if this is a live man, then he is less than a hundred years old' is not logically warranted, nor is the corresponding argument conclusive. (Although it has a greater degree of conclusiveness than the previous argument.) Yet in both bases the antecedents constitute quite good reasons for believing the consequent to be true.

This exceedingly brisk treatment of the topic of 'good reasons' may perhaps seem more acceptable when it is pointed out that to say that a man's reason for believing some proposition is a *good* reason, is by no means to endorse his *reasoning*. Suppose that 'q' operates in A's mind as a reason for believing that p. And suppose it is the case that 'if q, then p'. Even if we altogether waive the question whether 'q' is true, and whether A knows it to be true, A might still be open to two epistemological criticisms.

In the first place, it must be remembered that it is possible to reason in accordance with a false principle and yet, if one is lucky, obtain the same results which one would have obtained by reasoning in accordance with a true one. Consider, for instance, self-cancelling errors in reasoning. It is therefore possible that, although 'if q, then p' is true, the principle of inference (general belief) which causes A to link together 'q' and 'p' in his mind, is false.

But even if A has linked together 'q' and 'p' in accordance with a true principle, can we not ask whether A's possession of this principle amounts to *knowledge*, or is merely true belief? We have given an account in this chapter of what it is for A to *believe* a general proposition: as a disposition to proceed from one belief to another, or to link beliefs together, in accordance with some general pattern. But, as in every case of belief, we want to distinguish between merely believing such propositions and knowing them to be true. Nothing said in this chapter is intended to cast any light on what it is to *know* that a general proposition is true. The topic must await discussion in Part III of this book.

7

Existential Beliefs

In this essay, beliefs about particular, spatio-temporally limited, states of affairs have been compared to maps (in many cases, inaccurate ones) which, taken together, form one great map of the world, with the believer as central reference point. General beliefs, however, are not part of the map. They are dispositions to *extend* the map according to certain principles, or, where there is no extension possible because the belief in question is already held, dispositions to create sustaining relations between one portion of the map and another.

It remains only to consider beliefs in the truth of unrestricted existentially quantified propositions ('existential beliefs'). Genuinely unrestricted existential beliefs about contingent matters of fact are not common. For instance, one who is said to believe 'that flying saucers exist' will normally believe that they exist *in the vicinity of the earth*. His belief is therefore not an 'existential belief'. But it is clearly *possible* that somebody should believe that something exists without relating the thing in question in any way to himself or to his spatio-temporal framework. In any case, such propositions are entailments of propositions that he does believe. Over and above existential beliefs of this sort, there are beliefs in the existence of mathematical entities, for instance, the true belief that there is a prime number between seven and thirteen, or that the number of the natural numbers is infinite.

This brief chapter will therefore consider the class of existential beliefs, beginning with those which are contingently true or false.

Let us go back to the analogy of a map of the world. Suppose we have a map, or connected series of maps, of the world. There might be certain islands which we believed to exist, and to have certain features, but which we were completely unable to place in the great map. Maps of these islands could be presented in an appendix with a heading 'for insertion somewhere in the main map'. Such added maps serve as a model for unrestricted existential beliefs concerning contingent matters of fact.

99

But to move beyond mere analogy. Such beliefs are mind-maps which *completely lack any referential component*. There is nothing in the belief-map that represents any sort of linking relationship (spatio-temporal, causal, *etc.*) between the object believed to exist and the believer. The problem which then arises is how to distinguish such beliefs from the corresponding mere thought. In Chapter Five, Section Four, an appeal was made to the often-remarked link between belief and action, a link which is lacking in the case of the corresponding mere thought. But that solution seems unavailable for the very special class of beliefs which we are now considering. If I believe that there is a post-box in the next street, then, if I want to post a letter, my belief may cause me to walk to the next street. But if I believe that somewhere in space and time, or beyond it, there are angelic beings, what possible effect will this belief have on my actions? I might think that they were watching what I did, to approve or disapprove, and provided I were concerned about their supposed attitude, this might affect my conduct. But to suppose this is to change the case. For if I believe that the angelic beings have such a relation to me, there is, after all, a referential component in my belief.

Once we see clearly how completely such beliefs must be cut off from the rest of our life to be genuine 'existential beliefs', the size and importance of our present problem is diminished. It can be seriously doubted, for instance, whether anybody actually ever holds beliefs of this sort. Nevertheless, it is clear that such beliefs are possible, and so the problem remains to be solved.

I suggest the following solution. As we have seen, if a referential component were added to an unrestricted existential belief, then the belief would have the usual potentiality for guiding action. The belief is not even potentially action-guiding, but it has the potential to be potentially action-guiding if it is referentially supplemented. This would not be the case with the corresponding mere thought. This difference, then, constitutes the difference between the belief and the mere thought.

It may be noted, however, that here we have a class of beliefs that cannot be given *expression* except linguistically. And in the absence of other expressions there will be the characteristic difficulty (even for ourselves) of determining whether what we say expresses a genuine *belief*, or is simply a mere thought.

I think that this is all which needs to be said about such beliefs.

A moment's consideration may be given to beliefs in the existence of an infinite collection of contingent beings: the belief, for instance, that there is an infinity of angels or other such subordinate heavenly powers. This can be broken down into a conjunction of two beliefs. First, there is the existential belief that at least one angel exists. The account just given suffices for this belief. Second, there is a *general* belief of the following form: for all values of n, if a set of angels exists having n members, then a set of angels exists having n + 1 members. The two believed propositions suffice between them to 'generate' an infinite set of angels. An account of the general belief can be given just as for any other general belief.

We can now consider beliefs in the existence of logical and mathematical entities. But before doing so, it may be advisable to say something about belief in logical and mathematical propositions generally, a topic we have so far avoided.

The belief that '2 + 3 = 5' or, for that matter, the belief that '2 + 3 = 6', appears to be a general belief, the proposition believed being unrestricted and universally quantified. If this is so, such beliefs can be treated in the same way as other general beliefs, the distinction between necessary and contingent propositions being irrelevant here.

I suggest the following analysis for '2 + 3 = 5'. It can be rewritten as two general propositions. (1) For all x and all y, *if* x is a set having two and only two members, and y is a wholly distinct set having three and only three members, *then* the union of x and y has five and only five members. (2) For all z, *if* z is a set having five and only five members, *then* there exist wholly distinct sub-sets of z, v and w, such that v has two members and w has three members. So belief that '2 + 3 = 5' is a belief in the conjunction of these two general propositions.

The advantage of this analysis is that it now becomes clear what sort of propositions are the particular beliefs which are dispositionally connected by the belief that 2 + 3 = 5. An instance of an appropriate antecedent belief might be the conjunctive belief that there are two and only two apples in this bowl *and* that there are three and only three apples in that other bowl. This belief might then create and sustain the belief that there are five and only five apples in the two bowls taken together. Of course, not all substitutions for the variables in the antecedents and consequents of propositions (1) and (2) will yield propositions about particular, spatio-temporally limited, matters of fact. Some may be further mathematical propositions. But if these propositions are believed, they can be treated as further cases of general beliefs, and analysed accordingly.

If A is disposed to reason according to the pattern given by (1) and (2), illustrated for (1) by the particular example of the apples in the bowl, then, and only then, he believes that $2 + 3 = 5$.

But our task in this chapter is to consider 'existential beliefs'. Beliefs that logical and mathematical entities exist are *prima facie* cases of such beliefs. Let us therefore consider the status of the belief that there exists at least one prime number between 7 and 13. I will propose an analysis of the proposition believed. What emerges from the analysis, I think, is that the proposition is as much an unrestricted universally quantified proposition as '$2 + 3 = 5$'.

As a preliminary we may offer: '*If* there is a set of things eight in number, and a set of things nine in number, ... and a set of things twelve in number, *then* at least one of these sets of things is prime in number.' This is the sort of thing wanted, but the formulation is not good enough because the antecedent simply *enumerates* the sets in question. The following may be more satisfactory. '*If* there is a set of sub-sets, such that, for each number of members between 7 and 13 members, there is at least one of these sub-sets that has this number of members, *then* at least one of these sub-sets is prime in number.'

This translation makes no attempt to analyse the notion of number, any more than the earlier translation of '$2 + 3 = 5$'. But it does treat numbers, and further notions such as primeness of number, as *properties of sets*. (In Part II I will be arguing for the onto-logical reality of properties.) To this extent, I am 'quantifying over numbers'. But I am rejecting the view that there are individual objects such as the number seven. There are sets which have the seven-ness property, or the primeness-in-number property, but there is no such thing as the Seven or the Prime. The sets themselves are sets of anything whatsoever: cabbages, marbles or whatever else can be counted. The corresponding *belief* is then treated like other general beliefs, as discussed in the last chapter. In this way, a belief that appears to be an existential belief turns out in fact to be a *general* belief.

If this excursion into the philosophy of mathematics is correct, and the same trick can be worked with all other 'existential' claims in logic and mathematics, then it seems that beliefs of this sort will *all* turn out to be general beliefs. (A proposition like 'There exists an infinite number of natural numbers' simply involves more of the same complications.)

These analyses of 'There is at least one prime number between 7 and 13', and equally of '$2 + 3 = 5$', are intrusions into the philosophy of mathematics. The justification of such analyses is that they allow us to give a naturalistic account of what it is to believe (and, as we shall see, to know) such propositions to be true. This is a subordination of general ontology to the demands of epistemological theory. But since the gain is so great, and the analyses of the mathematical propositions look reasonably plausible in their own right, I hope that the procedure is justified.

8

Further Considerations about Belief

1 Contradictory Beliefs

Before leaving the topic of belief something must be said about three topics, beginning with that of contradictory beliefs.

It will be argued in this section that it is possible to believe contradictory propositions simultaneously. The conjunction of Bap and Ba~p is a possible state of affairs. By contrast, the conjunction of Bap and ~Bap is not a possible state of affairs, although perhaps there are borderline situations where saying 'he believes it and it is not the case that he believes it' has a point, just as saying 'it is raining and it is not raining' has a point when a scotch mist is in question.

There are various different cases where contradictory beliefs are held simultaneously. The first and least controversial case is that where A believes that p and believes that q, 'q' is in fact logically equivalent to '~p', but A is not aware of this equivalence, perhaps because it is not easy to see. Whether or not one should speak of 'q' and '~p' as 'the same proposition', 'q' and 'p' are certainly contradictories.

But it is perfectly possible to hold simultaneously beliefs that are quite obviously contradictory. As the American philosopher Brian Skyrms has remarked 'the human mind is often a disorderly thing' (Skyrms 1967, fn. 4). It is a large place and an untidy place, and we may believe 'p' and '~p' simultaneously but fail to bring the two beliefs together, perhaps for emotional reasons. (*Cf.* Orwell on 'double-think'.)

Such a holding of obviously contradictory beliefs simultaneously is something of a puzzle for Behaviourist or Behaviourist-oriented theories of belief. For such theories, an account of the situation will have to be given primarily in terms of a set of manifestations, or potential manifestations, which are appropriate *both* to believing that p and believing that ~p. And so such cases will naturally be treated as being 'conflict-cases' or as involving 'conflicts of criteria'. They will be like borderline cases of which it is hard to say either that they are cases of raining or that they are cases of not raining. In other words, Behaviourist theories of belief will find it difficult to distinguish between the conjunction Bap & Ba~p, on the one hand, and the conjunction Bap & ~Bap, on the other.

But if we identify beliefs with categorical, structured, states of the believer, we can give a straightforward account of a situation of the sort Bap & Ba~p. There are simply two numerically different states, the one encoded for the proposition 'p', the other for '~p'. Manifestations, if they occur, are divided without difficulty into two classes by their *causes*: the two different states. The manifestations of the belief that p are brought about (in conjunction with other factors) by the belief-state which is the belief that p, while the manifestations of the belief that ~p are caused by the belief that ~p. Only if, for instance, one and the same state give rise to both sets of manifestations would any talk of 'conflict-cases' be necessary. But there seems no reason to think that such a confusing situation is more than logically possible.

In the above sorts of case, the believer has two beliefs which are very obviously logically incompatible, but, because he does not bring them together, is not aware of holding incompatible beliefs. But finally, it seems possible to become aware that we hold incompatible beliefs. Very often one of these beliefs will not originally be a belief which we were aware of holding. Bringing it to consciousness, and then contrasting it with its consciously-held contradictory or contrary, will often result in some modification of the situation. For instance, the previously unconsciously-held belief may be given up when dragged into the light of day. But awareness that we hold contradictory beliefs *need* not have this result.

Hume provides us with an example. In the Appendix to the *Treatise* he says that '... there are two principles which I cannot render consistent, nor is it in my power to renounce either of them'. It is not easy to see why Hume thinks that the particular two propositions he then states are incompatible, but it seems clear that the situation in himself which he purports to describe could have obtained with propositions that are more obviously logically incompatible. Unless it is possible to believe propositions of the form 'p& ~p', the possibility of which will not be investigated here, a man who recognizes the simultaneous existence of logically incompatible beliefs in his own mind must also recognize that his cognitive state is irrational. But recognition of one's own irrationality does not necessarily abolish it. And if distinct beliefs are distinct structured states, then it is easy to see how the belief that p, the belief that ∼ p, and the knowledge both that the two beliefs are held and that they are incompatible, could co-exist in the one mind.

The analogy between beliefs and *maps* is, of course, unaffected by the existence of contradictory beliefs simultaneously held. A map might contain contradictions. Suppose that ⚭ symbolizes the presence of a church, while ⚭ symbolizes that there is no church within five miles. Then suppose that the two symbols are put together on the map at a distance which represents less than five miles in the situation mapped.

Granted that one mind can contain contradictory beliefs simultaneously, can it contain two beliefs with exactly the same content? Should we say that Bap & Bap is a possible state of affairs?

We must certainly admit the possibility of two belief-states with exactly the same content. Indeed, the phenomenon actually seems to occur. It is a plausible psychological hypothesis that there is more than one belief-system in the human mind, systems which exist in relative isolation from each other. In particular, there seems to be a pre-verbal belief-system associated with perception and another system which has the closer links with our linguistic competence. It is commonplace for cross-system contradictions to exist. Must there not also be cross-system agreements?

But should we speak of this as a case where A holds two beliefs simultaneously that have the same content? A verbal decision seems necessary here. A factor influencing my decision is what has already been said about concepts in Chapter Five, Section One. It was said there that we could only have one concept with a particular content at a particular time, just as we can only have one skill of a certain sort. Yet if concepts and skills are identified with states, it seems clear that somebody may be in more than one state which nevertheless is encoded for the same concept or the same skill. However, it seems to me more natural still to speak of only one concept or skill here, and so I will adopt the same practice in the case of beliefs. So 'Bap & Bap' will say no more than 'Bap'.

II   Conjunctive Beliefs

It was argued in the previous section that it is possible to hold simultaneously, and without any awareness of irrationality, beliefs

which are clearly contradictory. This occurs when we fail to 'bring
the two beliefs together'. This situation is a particular exemplification of a general principle of some importance. Given that, at a certain time, A believes that p and A believes that q, it is not entailed
that A believes the conjunction of p and q:

$$\sim \{(Bap \, \& \, Baq) \rightarrow Ba(p \, \& \, q)\}.$$

The reverse entailment seems to hold. If A believes the conjunction
of p and q, then, it seems, he believes that p and he believes that q:

$$Ba(p \, \& \, q) \rightarrow (Bap \, \& \, Baq).$$

(This latter entailment, by the way, indicates that the rule of inference (p & q) → p does not represent any genuine 'movement of
thought'.)

Where the beliefs are clear contradictories, it may be argued that
the *only* way of believing the two propositions is by not bringing
them together. That is to say, Ba(p & ∼p) may not be a possible
situation. But I can reach no certainty on this difficult point.

Given the theory of belief developed in this book, how are we to
distinguish between merely holding two beliefs, on the one hand,
and believing their conjunction, on the other? The first situation
involves two belief-states, the second only one. But the principle by
which we count 'one' or 'two' states here is hardly perspicuous.

I think the answer must lie in the different causal powers of the
state(s). Suppose, for instance, that A comes to believe that r, as
the result of inferring it from p & q jointly. Bap & Baq brought
about Bar, but neither Bap nor Baq would have been sufficient
separately. We can surely say then that Bar comes to be as a result
of Ba(p & q). Or suppose A *acts* in a certain way because he believes
that p and believes that q, but neither belief on its own would have
initiated that action. Ba(p & q) caused, or was a causal factor in
bringing about, the action. It should not be demanded that it must
be the case that inferences occur, or action be initiated, for a case
of conjunctive belief to exist. But for Ba(p & q) to obtain, A's state
must be such that Bap & Baq have the *power* to produce a joint
effect, either in the realm of belief or of action.

One conclusion which follows is this. Where a set of believed
propositions actually functions for somebody as a reason for
believing something further, or for acting in some way, then these

propositions form the content of a single conjunctive belief. So in every actual piece of reasoning to a single conclusion there is a sense in which the reasoner reasons from one single premiss.

III Degrees of Belief

It seems clear that there are degrees of belief. There is a highest degree: perfect certainty that a proposition is true. There is a lowest degree: perfect certainty that the proposition is false. In between there are various degrees of belief. The scale has a middle, where judgement is equally poised between the proposition and its contradictory. Of course, the 'belief-scale' is not a scale like the temperature-scale, for it cannot be given a very exact quantification. It is more like the degree of disorder at a party or the degree of freedom which obtains in a society. But some parties are more disorderly than others, some societies freer than others, and equally we are more certain of some propositions than others. Where the degree of certainty is not high we sometimes talk of 'an inclination to believe' instead of a belief.

To accord a degree of belief to 'p', from the 1 of perfect certainty to the 0 of perfect disbelief, is automatically to assign some degree of belief to ' ∼p'. And so, except for the case of perfect certainty (a case that actually occurs, indeed is common), there is a sense in which one's mind is split between 'p' and ' ∼p'. But the situation is different from that where the believer believes contradictory things simultaneously. For the degrees of belief fluctuate in inverse proportion to each other, or, as we may put it, their sum remains 1. So there need be no element of irrationality in the situation. A degree of belief in 'p' which is less than 1 *is* also a positive degree of belief that ' ∼p', so that what we have here is simply a *single* state of mind.

The having of a degree of belief that p which is less than 1 must, of course, be distinguished from the belief that p has some *probability* which is less than 1, where there is some objective measure of p's probability. For one can be perfectly certain or, alternatively, less than perfectly certain that p has a certain objective probability. (Probability is relative to evidence, degree of belief need not be, even if it should be.)

What is the difference between believing unhesitatingly that p and merely having some degree of belief that p? As opposed to mere thought, belief is linked to action. (See Chapter Four, Section Four.) It seems reasonable, therefore, to place the difference between different degrees of belief in different causal relations to action. Full belief is a map by which we steer, a mere thought is a map by which we do not steer, partial belief should therefore be a map by which we steer . . . in some possible circumstances but not in others. (Are our circumstances such that we can afford to be wrong?) The problem is to set this out in causal terms.

I will content myself here with brief general remarks. (I think that Ramsey indicated the proper line of solution in Section 3 of his paper 'Truth and Probability' in Ramsey 1931.) Consider the difference between being absolutely certain that p and being almost, but not quite, certain of this. What difference will this make to conduct? For most values of 'p', and for most situations which A finds himself in, where 'situation' includes but is not exhausted by A's purposes, desires and other beliefs, the difference to A's conduct will be nil. It is only in a relatively few situations, for instance where A believes 'p' is more likely to be true than not, but also judges that the cost of acting as if 'p' were true would be unacceptably great if 'p' were false, that any difference would show up. The situation is like the difference between having a very powerful motor, and an exceedingly powerful motor, in a car. This might make no difference to the car's performance except in a small number of quite special situations (especially good road, especially good driver, *etc.*).

The 'rational betting situation', therefore, which Ramsey envisages, in which a man puts his money where his mouth is, and does it completely rationally, may therefore be considered as simply being an, or the, ideal situation in which degree of belief would show up most clearly, unaffected by the inconstancy of other factors which continually obtain in ordinary life. (There may also be an element of conceptual revision. The situation may enable a precision to be given to 'degree of belief' which is not present in ordinary thought.) The belief is a central state, and degree of certainty of this belief is a degree of causal efficacy of this state in relation to conduct. Conduct is a hypothetical 'rational betting situation' is a mere effect of this degree of causal efficacy. At the same time, there is no mere contingent connection between the degree of certainty and the conduct. Degree of certainty *is*, among other things, the thing which is measured by such situations as the rational betting situation. In the same way, temperature *is* that property of substances measured by (properly constructed) thermometers.

So much seems clear. The detail of the matter is not so clear, but, I hope, the detail is not very important for the argument of this book.

Part II

Truth

9

Truth

I   Correspondence

If A believes that p, he believes that p *is true*. What is it for p to be true? In this chapter, a version of the *correspondence* theory of truth will be developed. There is a good deal of overlap between what I say in this chapter, and a paper 'Materialism, Properties and Predicates' (Armstrong 1972).

The traditional correspondence theory holds that p is true if, and only if, it corresponds to reality. *Propositions* correspond, or fail to correspond, to *facts* or to *states of affairs*. But a relation of correspondence demands that the correspondents be distinct from each other, and for true propositions this demand is not met. Suppose that the proposition in question is 'that the earth is round'. The fact or state of affairs to which this proposition corresponds is the fact that the earth is round or the state of affairs of the earth's being round. But the proposition does not correspond with this fact or state of affairs, rather it coalesces with it.

However, it is a mistake to make propositions correspond or fail to correspond to anything. A proposition may or may not have a 'bearer'. That is to say, it may or it may not be believed, entertained or asserted. It is the (possible) 'bearer', the (possible) belief-state, thought-episode or act of asserting which corresponds, or fails to correspond, to reality.

The analogy of a map is as helpful as usual. Consider a completely accurate map. A certain arrangement of features on the map may be thought of as making a number of true assertions about reality. The arrangement is the 'bearer' of certain true propositions. It is this arrangement, and not the propositions that it bears, which corresponds with certain features of reality, in virtue of the mapping-conventions.

The problem now is to spell out this correspondence-relation in a more concrete way. Two points can be made immediately.

First, belief-states, thought-episodes and assertings will not correspond *qua* individual objects, *qua* tokens. For each proposition, there can in principle be many 'bearers', and each bearer must correspond in the requisite way. So the 'bearers' correspond *qua* types, *qua* instances of a certain sort of thing (instances of that map-type).

What constitutes sameness or difference of type here? In the case of belief-states and thought-episodes, it will be a matter of that particular structure of Ideas (in our technical sense of the term) which makes the belief-state or thought-episode the belief or thought that p. In the case of assertings it will be that sort of linguistic structure which, in accordance with a set of semantic and syntactic rules, suitably represents that particular structure of Ideas.

Second, given such a 'bearer' of a proposition, and given that the bearer has a 'correspondent' in the world (that is, that the proposition is true), the correspondent will only be a correspondent because it is of a certain type. In the case of a map, it is not simply a matter of a certain map-arrangement corresponding to a particular portion of reality. Correspondence will occur only because that portion of reality is of a certain sort (is a church, say).

It seems, then, that the correspondence-relation holds or does not hold in virtue of the nature of the things related. But this raises a very difficult problem. When we speak of a thing being of a certain type, sort, kind or nature, are we really speaking of some objective feature of reality which can stand over against our beliefs, thoughts and assertions? Nominalists and conceptualists would deny that we are. Yet, unless we are dealing with objective features, have we got the distinctness of terms which we demand for a correspondence relation?

I think that there are good reasons for holding Nominalism and Conceptualism to be false. What is more, the examination and refutation of these doctrines, and their replacement by a satisfactory form of Realism, will go a long way to clarify the nature of the correspondence-relation between 'bearers' of propositions and the world.

II Nominalism

The 'Problem of Universals', I take it, is to give an account of what it is for a thing (in the widest sense of 'thing') to be of some type, kind, sort, nature or to have some property. There may be somewhat different notions associated with these different words, but, from the standpoint of the general problem of universals, I think the differences are irrelevant. In what follows I shall restrict myself, for the most part, to talking about *properties*. The word 'property' will be used in its widest sense, the sense, for instance, which allows a distinction between relational and non-relational properties of things.

There is a crude form of Nominalism according to which general words, such as 'red' and 'zebra', should be assimilated to proper names, such as 'Peter'. It is an accidental feature of the name 'Peter' that it is used to name many individuals. But according to this form of Nominalism, 'red' and 'zebra' are fundamentally no different from 'Peter': they, too, are names that just happen to be the names of many individuals. The redness of an object is constituted by the fact that 'red' is (one) name of the object. I will not waste time with this implausible version of Nominalism.

A sophisticated Nominalism will instead try to give an account of a thing's having a certain property in terms of a *predicate* being applicable to that thing. Such a Nominalism may be said to offer the following definition:

Fa = .Def. 'F' is applicable to a

Parallel to this Nominalist doctrine there will be a form of Conceptualism which gives an account of a thing's having a certain property in terms of a particular concept (some sort of mental entity) being applicable to that thing:

Fa = .Def. Concept 'F' is applicable to a

But, since the important strengths and weaknesses of this form of Conceptualism are identical with the form of Nominalism just presented, in this discussion I will omit any further consideration of Conceptualism.

The definition of Nominalism might have been written:

Fa = .Def. 'F' is *true of* a

but, although no great harm would be done, it seems best to avoid using the phrase 'true of'. In the past, philosophers often meant by the term 'predicate' a constituent of propositions, and, if this older usage is adopted, a predicate in a true subject-predicate proposition could be said to be 'true of' the subject. But 'predicates' in our formulation of Nominalism are *linguistic* entities (they are expressions), and in saying that such entities could be 'true of' individuals such as a, we would be departing from the ordinary usage of the word 'true' (see Chapter Four, Section Four). So I will say that, where F is true of a, 'F' is *applicable to* a.

For the form of Nominalism we are considering, an account is given of 'same property' in terms of the applicability of the same (linguistic) predicate. To give the doctrine any content, therefore, Nominalists will have to explain what identity-conditions for predicates are being assumed. Purely phonemic or inscriptional identity-conditions would clearly be inadequate: we would be committed to the view that all banks, whether the retaining walls of rivers or financial institutions, had something in common which made them all banks. We would also be committed to the view that there are two distinct, although co-intensive, properties corresponding to the two distinct predicates 'oculist' and 'eye-doctor'. These conclusions seem absurd.

For the statement of Nominalism, the identity-conditions which it is natural to adopt are *semantic* ones: predicates are identical if, and only if, they have the same meaning. On this criterion 'oculist' and 'eye-doctor' are the same predicate, while 'bank' meaning the retaining wall of a river and 'bank' meaning a financial institution are not.

Certain difficulties may be raised against the adoption of identity-conditions for predicates in terms of meaning. *First*, it is impossible to combine this adoption with the denial that synonymy, or sameness of meaning, is a coherent concept. Somebody who does deny the coherency of the concept of synonymy will have to reformulate his Nominalism in a different way. But I do not know of a plausible reformulation.

Second, the notion of meaning, even if itself coherent, is wrapped in philosophical obscurity, and there are difficult borderline cases where it is unclear whether predicates have the same meaning or not (for instance, 'eighty one' and 'square of nine'). However, I do not think that this should be a great worry. The notion of meaning certainly involves philosophical difficulties, but the difficulties seem no worse than those involved in many other concepts which are cheerfully accepted as primitives in the course of particular philosophical investigations. Nor do the difficult borderline cases seem to create any more (though no less) trouble than the disputed borderline cases which can be cited in the case of other important concepts.

Third, it may be objected that a correct account of the concept of meaning might turn out to involve the notion of property, thus rendering the Nominalist analysis covertly circular. *Fourth*, it may be objected that the concept of meaning involves postulating entities which will function as 'meanings', a postulation which, because of the reductionist and anti-metaphysical temper of Nominalism, will be just as unsatisfactory as the Realists' properties. For the sake of examining the Nominalist position, I will assume that these objections can be met.

The Nominalist has been presented as giving an account of a thing's having a property in terms of a predicate being applicable to that thing. But, it may be objected, the Nominalist does not give an account of properties, rather, he denies their existence. And it is certainly true that the Nominalist gives a deflationary account of properties. For the Nominalist, the *objective* properties postulated by the Realist are a mere reflection cast upon the world by predicates. Nevertheless, the Nominalist does not deny that there are true propositions having the form 'Fa'. He does not deny that the rose is red, or larger than the buttercup. In this minimal sense, then, he accepts the existence of properties.

We come now to ask whether the Nominalist analysis is correct. Is it a sufficient account of a's being F to say that it is nothing but the predicate 'F' being applicable to a? Presumably 'applicable to' ('true of' as others would say) must be conceived of as a relation holding between the predicate 'F' and the object a. Now it is clear that it is not an arbitrary matter what predicate is applicable to what object. If 'F' is applicable to a, this in general depends upon (i) the nature of 'F', apart from whether 'F' has the 'applicable to' relation to a; (ii) the nature of a, apart from whether it stands to 'F' as an object stands to the predicate that is applicable to it. The relation is completely determined by the nature of the terms.

But if this is so, the Nominalist has not given a full account of what it is for a to be F. To make this clear, suppose that 'F' is applicable to a, but 'G' is not, and suppose also that 'G' is applicable to b, but 'F' is not. It cannot be the case that the *only* difference between a and b is that 'F' has the 'applicable to' relation to a, but lacks it to b, while 'G' has the 'applicable to' relation to b, but lacks it to a. There must be some further difference between a and

b. The predicate's applicability or lack of it is in some way founded on the nature of the objects. It follows that the Nominalist has not given us a full account of what it is for a to be F and b to be G. (For a careful examination of this form of Nominalism see Hochberg 1967.)

III   Semi-Nominalism

The weakness of a pure Nominalism has long been recognized. The Nominalist's opponent, the Realist, explains the situation by saying that 'F' is applicable to a because a has, possesses or instantiates some property or properties which exist independently of the predicate, actual or possible. I think that this is the correct answer, but before examining it let us examine two positions that are intermediate between pure Nominalism and Realism.

(1) The classical attempt to overcome the weakness of a pure Nominalism is to appeal to the notion of Resemblance. As Locke puts it, although our 'Abstract Ideas' (concepts rather than predicates, but the difference is immaterial here) are 'the workmanship of the understanding' yet they are based upon 'the similitudes in things (*Essay*, Book III, Chapter III, Section 13). Objective resemblance ('similitude') is thus admitted in order to avoid admitting objective properties.

This traditional manoeuvre faces traditional difficulties.

First, to say that two or more things resemble each other is to say something incomplete. We need to add in what *respect* it is that the things resemble each other. And what are 'respects' but 'properties' under another name? It is true that sometimes we can observe that, for example, two faces have a resemblance without being able to detect in what the resemblance consists. But, as modern philosophy has made clear, it does not follow from the fact that we do not know what the respect of the resemblance is that it is resemblance in no respect. And experimental psychology, after research, may inform us what in fact the respect is.

The following argument shows that resemblance is always resemblance in some respect. Whenever A resembles B it is conceivable, at any rate with respect to contingent things, that A should have existed while B did not. But in this projected circumstance, A would retain all its properties except those which are logically dependent upon the relations of A to B. And so for every thing which A resembles. But, if this is so, these properties of A cannot depend upon its relations of resemblance to other things. Rather, the relations of resemblance depend upon the properties of A.

Second, as Russell pointed out (Russell 1912, Chapter Nine), even if this analysis of resemblance be not conceded, in admitting the relation of resemblance as an objective, predicate-independent, repeatable feature of the world, the Resemblance analysis is admitting one objective property: the relational property things have of resembling other things. The denial of other objective properties then appears arbitrary.

(2) Another possible attempt to overcome the weakness of pure Nominalism is an appeal to *class-membership*. The predicate 'F' is applicable to a in virtue of a's membership of a certain class of things. However, this view faces much the same difficulties as those which face the Resemblance view.

First, either the relevant class of which a is a member is a unit-class, a being the only member, or there are other members. Suppose that there are other members. It is surely obvious that a's being F has nothing to do (save *per accidens*) with these other members. Imagine them away. a is still F. 'Fa' is still true. It is clear that it is the nature of a which determines a's membership of the class rather than the other way round. Suppose, alternatively, that the relevant class which a is a member of, is a unit-class. What philosophical gain is there in explaining a's possession of F in terms of a's membership of this unit-class?

Second, a's membership of the relevant class must be admitted to be an objective relational property of a. The denial of other objective properties to a then seems arbitrary.

But if pure Nominalism is unsatisfactory, and if a's being F is neither a matter of a resembling certain other objects, nor a's membership of a certain class of objects, what can it be? What is it in general which makes 'F' applicable to a? The only further answer which seems plausible is the Realist answer that a has some predicate-independent property or properties in virtue of which the predicate 'F' is applicable to a.

IV   Realisms

But perhaps it is a mistake to speak of 'the Realist answer'. There are, after all, various forms of Realism about properties, and it is important to distinguish them and make clear what form of Realism is defensible.

First, it is vital to distinguish between an immoderate or Platonistic view of properties and the moderate view which I think is the true conclusion to be drawn from the failure of Nominalism and its variants. The Platonist believes in the existence of objective, predicate-independent, properties which exist *apart from particular things*. He believes in a *realm* of universals. It seems to me that anybody who believes in the existence of such a realm lacks what Russell called 'a robust sense of reality'. But, in any case, the arguments brought against Nominalism give us no justification for postulating such a realm. What the weakness of Nominalist and semi-Nominalist doctrines indicate is that particulars – individual objects – have objective properties. The natural view to maintain is that properties, although predicate-independent, must be instantiated. The critique of Nominalism leads naturally to a position closer to that of Aristotle than that usually attributed to Plato.

Indeed, Nominalist accounts of properties have got much aid and comfort from the assimilation of a doctrine of objective properties to a Platonistic account of properties. Nominalists have menaced us with the Platonist alternative. But the moderate man need not choose either.

I pass on to consider somewhat more subtle distortions of a Realist account of properties.

First, a Realistic view of properties does not entail that a particular thing is nothing but the sum of its properties. The latter view entails the doctrine of the Identity of Indiscernibles: that it is impossible for numerically distinct things to have exactly the same properties, relational and non-relational. Now it does seem clear that sameness in every property is a logically necessary condition for numerical identity:

$$(1) \quad (x)(y) \, [(x = y) \supset (F)(Fx \equiv Fy)]$$

But it seems that it is not a logical necessity that sameness in every property, relational and non-relational, ensures numerical identity:

$$(2) \quad (x)(y)[(F)(Fx \equiv Fy) \supset (x = y)]$$

(2) may be true in fact, but it is not necessarily true. I can only be dogmatic here, but it is fairly easy to see, by describing possible worlds of a symmetrical sort, that there could be two things which had every property in common, but yet are still two. (See, for in-

stance, Max Black 1952.) The particularity of a particular is not to be reduced to its peculiar properties.

(Indeed, I should like to turn the contingency of (2) into a proposal for distinguishing between genuine particulars (individuals) and anything else which we may have occasion to refer to. It seems plausible to say that if properties or numbers or relations have all their properties in common, then *they* logically must be the very same property, number or relation. The Identity of Indiscernibles is necessarily true of such entities. But if a thing is a genuine particular, it is at least logically possible that another particular should exist which differs from the first particular in number alone.)

But, *second*, the rejection of the Identity of Indiscernibles as applied to particulars should not lead us to embrace either of two further doctrines: the Lockean doctrine of substratum or a Stoutian doctrine of universals.

One reaction to the insight that a particular thing is not just the sum of its properties is to postulate an unknowable substratum which 'supports' the properties. Locke gave at least formal allegiance to the doctrine of substratum, perhaps for this reason. But the weakness of the Lockean doctrine is well-known. Either this substratum has a nature, even if an unknowable nature, or it has not. If it has a nature, then it has properties, which contradicts the hypothesis. But if it lacks a nature how can it 'support' or 'underlie' properties? It seems that the doctrine of the substratum is just a desperately misleading way of paying tribute to the impossibility of analysing away numerical difference in terms of difference of properties.

Nor should we accept G. F. Stout's account of properties (Stout 1923). According to this view, when two objects are, for example, red, then not only do we have two numerically different objects but we have two numerically different rednesses. C. B. Martin has spoken in this connection of *property-instances*. The point here is not that the two objects might be two different shades of red. Even if the two objects are exactly the same shade of red, according to this view we have two different *rednesses*.

The difficulty for this analysis seems to be much the same as that facing the Resemblance and Class-membership views. Consider two objects which are of exactly the same shade of red. In respect of colour, they are exactly similar. This relation of exact similarity must clearly be founded on the nature of the related things. And what can this be except their common nature: the quality which they *both* have? If this quality dissolves into different rednesses, the problem of what is common recurs. If, alternatively, they really do have a common quality, then we can drop talk of numerical difference for all except the *things* which are red. (Stout's doctrine treats a universal as a great thing, chopped into numerically different and separated bits. But then a common quality is again needed to explain the unity of the great thing – but the quality gets again chopped up.)

This quick gallop through alternative forms of Realism about properties is hardly a substitute for a thorough examination of these alternatives, but I do not want this part of my argument, which may seem to have strayed so far from the topic of *truth*, to attain an unwieldy bulk. The position I am led to as a result of rejecting Nominalism and semi-Nominalist doctrines is that of Aristotle who holds that the least thing capable of *independent* existence is a 'this-such': a particular having certain properties. Particulars must be propertied, and properties must be the properties of particulars.

Notice that Aristotelian Realism about properties is independent of Aristotelian Essentialism. The latter is the doctrine that some property or properties of a thing stand in a specially intimate relationship to, constitute the essence of, that thing. I incline to the democratic, or Lockean view, that all properties of a thing are on an ontological level and that 'essence' is always relative to the particular *predicates* or *concepts* that we happen to have applied to the object.

But having argued for an Aristotelian form of Realism about properties, we come now to a relatively novel but absolutely vital point. We have seen that for Nominalism, where properties are defined in terms of predicates, to each distinct predicate its own peculiar property must correspond. It is easy to carry this assumption over into the Realist alternative. It is easy to assume that for each distinct predicate which is applicable to a thing, a Realist must provide its own peculiar property. But, when we then recall that, for instance, negative and disjunctive predicates are applied to the thing, we are led into an absurd inflation of our ontology. The result is taken to be a reason for rejecting Realism about properties. Realist over-inflation leads to Nominalist revulsion.

In the next section, then, an account of some of the relations between predicates and properties will be sketched which does not assume that to each predicate its own peculiar property corresponds. This in turn will call into question the parallel assumption, so often and so fatally made by upholders of a correspondence theory of truth, that to each distinct truth-bearer there corresponds its own peculiar correspondent. The way is then open for a purged correspondence theory.

V   Predicates and Properties

Given *one* predicate, then there may be nothing to which it is applicable. In that case, there is *no* property which corresponds to the predicate. Given, however, that there are things which the predicate is applicable to, then this may be in virtue of just one property of these things or else in virtue of more than one property of the things. These three possibilities will now be spelled out.

One predicate, but nothing which this predicate is applicable to. An example of such a predicate may be 'travels faster than light *in vacuo*'. This example depends upon the assumption that in fact nothing ever has travelled, or does or will travel, faster than light *in vacuo*. (If tachyons exist – particles which *always* travel faster than light (Feinberg 1970) – then the example would have to be changed.) If the assumption is true, then nothing has the property of travelling faster than light. But, given a moderate Realism about properties, if nothing has the property then there is no such property. So, although it is clear that the expression 'travels faster than light *in vacuo*' is a perfectly good *predicate*, there is no property to correspond to this predicate.

It cannot be retorted that, although nothing *has* the property of travelling faster than light *in vacuo*, the property still exists. What does this mean? It would have meaning for a Platonic Realist with his hypostatized properties. But if moderate Realism is true, all properties are instantiated properties. What is true is that travelling faster than light *in vacuo* is a *logically possible* property. It is an intelligible conception that something should travel faster than light *in vacuo*. But a logically possible property is not a property any more than a logically possible horse is a horse (else beggars would ride).

Of course, those who accept an ontology of possible worlds could say that there are possible worlds in which something travels faster than light *in vacuo*, and so argue that the property *is* instantiated in such possible worlds. But I do not believe that this is an ontology to be taken seriously. There is only the actual world.

One predicate, which is applicable in virtue of a single property. The predicate 'spherical' may be offered as an example. It is very plausible to say that this predicate is applicable to spherical things in virtue of a single, somewhat complex, property which all these things have in common. The grounds for saying this will best be given after a discussion of the third class of predicates.

One predicate, which is applicable in virtue of more than one property. As soon as we look for such predicates with an instructed eye, examples abound.

Consider, first, disjunctive predicates such as 'either a raven or a writing-desk'. This predicate is applicable to each member of the class formed by the union of the class of ravens with the class of writing-desks. But it would be absurd to imagine that ravens and writing-desks must therefore share a common property. The members of the class of ravens may well have a common property which makes them all ravens, the members of the class of writing-desks may perhaps have a common property which makes them all writing-desks. But to the one predicate at least two properties correspond.

Consider, second, negative predicates such as 'not a raven'. This predicate is applicable to most of the objects in the universe. But what common property do these objects have which makes this predicate applicable? It cannot be said that the common property is some relation which each member has to the class of ravens. For what then is to be made of the predicate 'not a unicorn'? There are no unicorns to be related to. Yet it is clear that a parallel account must be given of the predicates 'not a raven' and 'not a unicorn'. It seems reasonable to say instead that the nature of a thing is exhausted by its *positive* properties. That is to say, positive properties are a thing's only properties. It is they, in all their multitude and diversity, which make negative predicates applicable to objects.

The following argument might be brought against the view that the only properties are positive properties. Suppose that we are able to enumerate the complete set of positive properties of an object. Certain negative predicates will be applicable to the object, but that they are applicable will not be entailed by the fact that the object possesses the set of positive properties that it does possess. We require in addition the premiss that that set of positive properties is the complete set of the thing's positive properties. So the object will require at least one negative property *viz*. that it lacks any other property besides those enumerated in the list of positive properties.

I think that this argument is unsound. Consider some predicate that predicates a positive property of a thing, but which is in fact not applicable to the thing. It is the actual positive properties of the thing, and these alone, which make the predicate inapplicable. But the inapplicability of this predicate is the same thing as the applicability of the corresponding negative predicate. So it is the conjunction of the thing's positive properties which exhausts the thing's properties.

What of conjunctive predicates? They raise a number of important points which enable us to develop further a theory of properties. Conjunctive predicates should not be treated in the same way as disjunctive and negative ones. There seems to be no reason to deny that there is a property of being both red and spherical, possessed by those objects to which the predicate 'red and spherical' is applicable. Such a property may well be said to be an 'ontologically insignificant' property, on the ground that there is no nomic connection of any sort between redness and sphericity. But an insignificant property is a property nevertheless.

There is, however, no call to postulate three *distinct* properties: redness, sphericity and (redness and sphericity). Once an object has the first two properties then it automatically has the 'third' property. The position concerning properties seems to be the same as that with particulars. Two particulars may be completely distinct from each other, but one may contain the other (an arm in a body) or they may overlap. In the same way, two properties may be completely distinct from each other, but it is also possible that one 'contains' the other or that they 'overlap'. Consider, for instance, the proposition 'red is a colour'. Given that this is a necessary truth, and that redness and colour are genuine *properties* (assumptions which might be disputed) then it would seem that this particular necessity is best explained by saying that the property of redness is a complex property which contains the property of colour. (See also the discussion of this proposition in Chapter Five, Section Two. It is, of course, quite incorrect to say that redness is 'contained' in colour on the grounds that colour is the determinable of which redness is a determinate. All that is true is that the class of red things is contained in the class of coloured things. Intension and extension vary inversely.)

More generally, there seems to be nothing in a Realism about properties which forces us to conclude that properties must necessarily be analysable into ultimate 'atomic' properties which are wholly distinct from each other. Just as spatio-temporal particulars may be continuous, so 'property-space' may be continuous. And, phenomenologically, this is the situation which we seem to be presented with, for instance in the case of the colours.

So much for reflections inspired by contemplating conjunctive predicates. What of other predicates which are not defined by means of the disjunctive or negative operator? Must they be applicable to the objects which they are applicable to in view of some one property of the object? Not necessarily. A *possible* example here is the predicate 'game'. One intelligible way to understand Wittgenstein's assertions about the word 'game' (Wittgenstein 1953, Section 66) is that this predicate is not applied to the activities it is applicable to in virtue of a *single* objective property which they all have in common. (I do not claim it is the only interpretation, and I do not claim that Wittgenstein would have any sympathy with this interpretation.) Whether such a claim is true or not, I do not venture to say. But I suggest that it is an intelligible one.

But how are such claims adjudged? On what basis can it be decided that the predicate 'spherical' is applicable to the things it is applicable to in virtue of some objective property which they all have in common, while the predicate 'game', perhaps, is applicable in virtue of some rather complex disjunctive pattern of properties?

The position seems to be like this. We start with mastery of a certain stock of predicates which do not appear to be disjunctive or negative predicates. We automatically take it that each of these predicates applies in virtue of some common property. For such predicates exist in order to take account of what things have in common. But as inquiry and science proceed, we find that certain predicates, although they apply to certain objects, do not fit in properly with the rest of our predicate-stock. In order to protect the assumption that, by-and-large, the stock apply in virtue of common properties, it becomes necessary to convict selected predicates of not doing their work properly and of applying to the things which they do apply to in virtue of an irreducible diversity of properties possessed by those things. Such predicates, we judge, and the methods by which we judge are as complex as the whole process of inquiry and science itself, fail, in Plato's image (Phaedrus 265e) to carve the beast of

reality along the joints. (We can think of the 'ontologically significant' properties as the *major* joints.) It follows, I think, that they
are predicates whose proper place is in practice, not theory. They
are not wanted in science, save *faute de mieux*.

The position is similar to that involving our beliefs. We must
take it that our beliefs are true. But this very necessity we are
under eventually forces us to recognize that selected beliefs clash
with the mass and must be struck out as false.

Let us now suppose that we have a single property (pleonastically:
instantiated property). Corresponding to this property, there may
exist no predicate, one predicate or many predicates.

One property, for which there exists no predicate. This case pre-
sents no difficulty. It is simply a case of a property of objects which,
for one reason or another, through human incapacity or inattention
or lack of interest, is taken no notice of by any of our schemes of
classification. In the nature of the case, no example can be given.

One property, for which there exists only one predicate. The
second sort of case, a property for which there exists only one predicate, is not as easy to find a clear case of as one might imagine.
The property of sphericity, for instance, may not be an example.
For besides the predicate 'spherical' there will be complex logical
equivalents that geometers will know and apply. And it may be
that such complex logical equivalents should be accounted *different*
predicates. The best examples to take are things about which we
have very little theoretical knowledge. It is plausible to say that all
itches have something in common in virtue of which the predicate
'itchy' is applied, and that this is the only actual predicate which
corresponds to this common property.

One property, for which there exists more than one predicate.
Considerations of symmetry lead us to expect that this slot will also
be filled. The really interesting question here is whether there can
be two or more predicates which are *not* logically equivalent, but
which apply to an object in virtue of just *one* property of that
object.

To bring up the question is, in effect, to bring up the vexed
question of the 'contingent identification' of properties. So I will
begin by putting forward what seems to me to be a knock-down
case for showing at least the possibility of different predicates applying to the same thing in virtue of just one property of that thing.

Consider an old philosophical friend: the chicken-sexer. He is able to look at newly-born chicks and to tell just from looking what their sex is. But although he knows that it is some property of the chick's surface, apprehended by vision, that gives him the clue, that is about as far as his knowledge goes. It seems that there is for him an unanalysable, but recognizable, male *gestalt* and an unanalysable, but recognizable, female *gestalt*. These *gestalten* are, of course, only contingently connected with being a male chick and being a female chick. It is perfectly possible that the world should change, so that the *gestalt* which had once been the mark of a male was now the mark of a female, and *vice versa*. What the chicken-sexer once used to put in the box for males he would now have to learn to put in the box for females, and the other way around. We can imagine, finally, that the sexer introduces two predicates 'M' and 'F' for the two *gestalten*. These are distinct predicates from the predicates 'male' and 'female' and, indeed, the distinct predicates 'M' and 'male' (equally 'F' and 'female') apply to the chicks they apply to in virtue of distinct properties of the chicks.

Suppose, now, that the chicken-sexer's abilities are made the subject of scientific investigation, for instance by psychologists, and that visual features which correlate with the two *gestalten* are mapped out in the M-formula and the F-formula. It is clear that the M-formula and the F-formula are logically distinct predicates from the two predicates 'M' and 'F'. Yet, in all likelihood, *property* M is the property picked out by the M-formula, and property F is the property picked out by the F-formula. If so, then two predicates apply to the chick in virtue of just one property of the chick's rear surface, apprehended in a totalistic or *gestalt* way by chicken-sexers and painfully articulated by scientists. (All this links up with the point made in Chapter Five, Section Two, that simple Ideas are Ideas of features that need only be *epistemologically* simple.)

It might be objected that it is perfectly possible that a chick should lack the properties described by the M-formula, and yet the predicate 'M' should be applicable to it. Hence, it may be inferred, we are dealing with two distinct properties of the chick. In reply to this, it must be agreed that this is a possible situation. But this only shows that the predicate 'M' and the M-formula *might* pick out two ontologically distinct, but co-extensive, properties of male chicks. But *may it not also be* that the *gestalt*-property is nothing but the property described by the M-formula?

But how is it decided whether we have two (co-extensive) properties here or only one? I think that this can only be decided on grounds of theoretical economy. There cannot be apodeictic proof that the two predicates apply in virtue of only one property of the object. But it can be, it would seem to be in this case, the simplest supposition.

Here, then, it seems that two logically distinct predicates are applicable to the very same class of objects, and applicable in virtue of the very same property of these objects. The relation of the two predicates to this one property is different. One might say that the predicate 'M' 'indicates' or 'names' this property, while the M-formula 'analyses' that property. These terms 'indicate', 'name' and 'analyse' must be treated with the greatest care. We must be clear that they are analogical terms for semantic relationships that have hardly been recognized in philosophy. (The quotation marks are not meant to symbolize a shift from use to mention, but rather a shift from one use to a different but analogical meaning.)

We are familiar with the idea that predicates may be applicable to, or true of, objects. It is an advance to recognize that the predicates are applicable to the objects they are applicable to in virtue of some (predicate-independent) property or properties of the object. This is one of the insights encapsulated in an Aristotelian Realism about properties. I have argued further in this chapter that it is wrong to assume that, for each distinct predicate applicable to an object, there corresponds in the object a property peculiar to that predicate. And now we should recognize that where two distinct predicates apply to an object in virtue of the very same property, even then the two predicates may stand in somewhat different semantic relations to that property. The chicken-sexer situation is a case in point.

It is not relevant to the concerns of this essay, but I think that the chicken-sexer situation will serve as a model for physicalist reductions of the secondary qualities. Thus, the predicates 'hot' and 'higher than average mean kinetic energy of molecules' are logically distinct predicates if any predicates are. But, perhaps, when we feel that something is hot, what we feel, in our uncomprehending, *gestaltist*, way is *nothing* but higher than average mean kinetic energy of the molecules of the substance felt.

There are other sorts of case where two predicates are applicable to one and the same object, or class of objects, in virtue of just one property of this object or objects. Consider 'Brittleness is a certain sort of molecular bonding'. Let us assume that the promissory phrase 'a certain sort of' is spelt out in some formula. The predicate 'brittle' then applies to the very same class of things to which the predicate 'having a certain sort of molecular bonding' applies. The latter predicate seems fairly straightforward. It 'analyses' the property in virtue of which it applies to the class it applies to. It is like the M-formula in the chicken-sexer case. But what of the predicate 'brittle'? We might say: 'brittle' applies to things in virtue of their *brittleness*, and brittleness is just a certain sort of molecular bonding. But this is not very helpful! I suggest that the special semantic relationship between the predicate 'brittle' and the property in virtue of which the predicate applies could be called that of 'definite description', though once again this phrase stands for a previously hardly recognized semantic relation. For brittleness, after all, is that state (property) of objects that renders them liable to shatter when struck (Chapter Two, Section Two). So the predicate 'brittle' is applicable to objects in virtue of a property. But it is a property which the predicate neither 'indicates' *nor* 'analyses' but instead *identifies* as that property, whatever it may be, that is responsible for the outcome of certain actual or possible causal sequences.

I will not follow up these points any further here. I hope enough has been said to open up a vista of deep and fascinating questions about the relations of predicates to properties. Much further work is indicated. But here I did not want to pursue the topic for its own sake. I wanted rather to cast light on the notion of truth. In getting away from the oversimple notion that to each distinct predicate there corresponds its own peculiar property, we put ourselves in a position to see that the correspondence or lack of correspondence between belief-states, thought-episodes and assertions, on the one hand, and the world on the other, need not be a simple invariable relation either. This will be the business of a brief final section of this chapter.

VI The Correspondence relation

Suppose that A believes of an individual, b, that it has the *property* F. There will be just one correspondent for this belief-state: b's instantiating F. If this state of affairs obtains, the proposition is true, if it does not, it is false. Notice that the 'correspondent' is not the *thing* b, but a state of affairs or situation: b's instantiation of F.

It will be seen how important it was to argue for a Realistic account of properties.

But this simple picture does not hold in all cases. Consider, for instance, the true proposition that at least one black swan exists (where 'exists' is simply the existential quantifier, ranging over all space and time). If we insist on having only *one* correspondent for bearers of this proposition the correspondent will have to be the existential state of affairs that at least one black swan exists. But it seems much better to say that such bearers have many, perhaps infinitely many, correspondents *viz.* each instantiation of the complex property of being a black swan. (Assuming, for the sake of argument, that to the predicates 'black' and 'swan' correspond genuine properties.) If the proposition is changed to 'At least two black swans exist' then the correspondents for bearers of this proposition will be every class of two instantiations of the same complex property.

Suppose, now, that our proposition is 'Either at least one black swan exists or at least one unicorn exists'. Since there are black swans, but there are no unicorns, the correspondents for the bearers of this true proposition will be exactly the same as the correspondents for 'At least one black swan exists'. And with this insight vanishes any necessity to postulate 'disjunctive facts' or 'disjunctive states of affairs'. If unicorns had not been fabulous creatures, then each instantiation of the complex property which makes a thing a unicorn would have served as additional correspondent.

But true unrestricted universally quantified propositions of the form (x)(if Fx, then Gx), where F and G are both properties, are like true propositions of the form 'Fa'. The single correspondent will be the state of affairs: each instance of F being an instance of G. (Since F is a *property*, there must be instances of F.)

Negative propositions have been a traditional teaser. If it is true that there are no zebras in the room, do we require a negative fact or state of affairs as correspondent? We have already rejected negative properties. Let us make the simplifying assumption that a zebra can be as small as we please and still count as a zebra. The correspondent for bearers of this proposition would then seem to be *the room and its entire contents, with their properties.* We shall, however, require only the non-relational properties of the room and its contents, together with no more relational properties than are required to make it 'the room'. Anything less than this and the correspondent would presumably permit the presence of a zebra or it would not be 'the room'. This correspondent, of course, will serve as correspondent for the bearers of indefinitely many other true negative propositions, for instance, that there are no crocodiles in the room. In the case of unrestricted negative existential truths, such as 'There are no unicorns' and 'There are no centaurs' the entire universe with all its properties is required for correspondent. This becomes more obvious if, instead of saying 'There are no centaurs', we say 'Nothing is a centaur'. That is to say, from our point of view here, '$(x) \sim$ centaur x' is more perspicuous than '$\sim (\exists x)$ centaur x'. But by abandoning the notion that the correspondence relation requires a unique correspondent for each bearer of a distinct proposition, we abolish the need to postulate negative facts or negative states of affairs.

Turning now to cases where logically distinct predicates apply to objects in virtue of one and the same property of that object, we have a further case where the one state of affairs serves as correspondent for the bearers of quite distinct propositions. The chicken has a certain property, M, perceived by chicken-sexers. The instantiation of the properties of the chicken which make it 'this chicken' together with this *gestalt* property, are correspondent for bearers of the proposition that this chicken has the male *gestalt*. The identical correspondent also serves for bearers of the proposition that this chicken has the property described by the M-formula.

What will be the correspondent for a bearer of the proposition that this indicated object is brittle? Unlike the case of the chick, the state of affairs of the object instantiating a certain sort of molecular bonding does not seem sufficient. It must further be the case that, if an object having this sort of molecular bonding is struck, then, in ordinary circumstances, it shatters. So we also require a correspondent for bearers of this proposition. However, this is an unrestricted universally quantified proposition, and we have already indicated the sort of correspondent required.

This is as far as I have been able to get in working out a version of the correspondence theory of truth which does not demand that the correspondence be of a simple sort. In ordinary maps, if they are accurate, the mapping-features and the features mapped generally do stand in a one-one correspondence. But my suggestion is that our mind-maps (and language-maps) stand to reality in other, looser, sorts of correspondence-relation.

Among the problems that I leave hanging in the air, the most urgent appears to be that of necessary truth. What could the correspondent be for bearers of such true propositions? The truth of a necessary truth is independent of the existence of any contingent being. If we postulate necessarily existing universals as correspondents instead, then we are back with the hypostatized properties of Plato which we have already rejected. The alternatives appear to be (i) to find the correspondents for these truths in words-with-their-meanings or in mental furniture such as concepts; or (ii) to argue that in the case of necessary truths *no correspondent is required*. The first manoeuvre, though it strikes me as the most hopeful, faces the familiar difficulty that it threatens to turn necessary truths into contingent truths about meanings or concepts. The second sets such a wide gulf between contingent and necessary truths that it becomes unclear what the word 'truth' could mean in the case of necessary truth.

Finally, of course, there is the possibility of denying the whole distinction between necessary and contingent truth. Truths of logic and mathematics would then be assimilated to other unrestricted universally quantified propositions.

But despite the difficulties raised by the truths of logic and mathematics, there is something intuitively appealing in the idea that truth involves correspondence. The suggestion that this correspondence is not the same sort of relation in each case, together with a (moderate) Realism about properties, may enable us to give that intuition some definite content.

Part III

□□□□□□□□□□□□□

Knowledge

10

Knowledge Entails True Belief

I The Classical account of knowledge

Having attempted to give an account of what it is for A to believe that p, and having said something about what it is for a belief to be true, we ask now what it is for A to *know* that p.

There is an analysis of the concept of knowledge which has been put forward again and again in the history of philosophy. Its first recorded occurrence is in Plato's *Meno* (87–8). According to this analysis A knows that p if, and only if, three conditions are satisfied. Two of these conditions differ somewhat (and not merely verbally) in different formulations. But there is a common form which all the formulations satisfy.

A knows that p if, and only if:

  (i) *The Truth-condition is satisfied*: p is true
  (ii) *The Belief-condition is satisfied*: A believes that p *or* A is certain that p, *etc.*
  (iii) *The Evidence-condition is satisfied*: A has adequate evidence for p *or* A has good reasons for believing that p, *etc.*

Knowledge, on this view, is true belief properly evidenced, or some similar formula.

This classical analysis of knowledge seems a good place to begin our own investigations, so we will proceed by examining the three suggested conditions. The present chapter deals only with the first two: The Truth-condition and the Belief-condition.

II The Truth-condition

We can begin with something uncontroversial. I do not think that there has ever been any serious doubt that it is a necessary condition for knowledge that what is known be *true*. As the catchphrase has it: 'If you know, you can't be wrong.' Knowledge is here contrasted with belief, which can be false as well as true.

What is controversial is how we are to understand this necessary condition.

According to an older tradition of thought upon the subject, knowledge is a special state or act of the mind which, unlike mere belief or opinion, logically cannot but hit upon the truth. The mind has a special faculty, with special powers, which, to the extent that it can be exercised, is infallible. (This is the view put forward by Plato in the *Republic*, 509–14.)

The modern view is much more deflationary. It sees the guarantee of truth which knowledge gives us as no more than the reflection of a relatively trivial linguistic necessity. 'If you know, you can't be wrong' does no more than pay tribute, in a misleadingly portentous way, to the meaning of the word 'know'. You can only call a fox a 'vixen' if it is a *female* fox. If it is not a female, then it is a semantic rule of English that it should not be called a 'vixen'. In the same way, you can only speak of 'knowledge' if the thing said to be known is in fact the case. If it is not the case, then it is a semantic rule of English that the cognitive attitude involved is not to be called 'knowledge'. The word has a demand for truth built into its meaning, just as 'vixen' has a demand for female nature built into its meaning. Any more recondite explanation of the truth-condition is a metaphysical illusion: a misleading shadow cast by language on the world.

So there is an inflationary and a deflationary way of taking the truth-condition. At a later stage it will be argued that the truth about the truth-condition lies midway between these inflationary and deflationary views. It will also be argued that, in a correct analysis of the concept of knowledge, the truth-condition, although it is indeed a necessary condition, is a *redundant* one.

III   Different Views concerning the Belief-condition

It is uncontroversial that 'A knows that p' entails 'p', even if different philosophers have understood the inner meaning of the entailment differently. By contrast, there has been much controversy over the Belief-condition.

Some have asserted that knowledge entails belief: $Kap \rightarrow Bap$, others have denied this: $\sim(Kap \rightarrow Bap)$. Among those who have accepted the Belief-condition we can distinguish between those who have held that knowledge entails certainty: $Kap \rightarrow Cap$, and those who have denied this: $\sim(Kap \rightarrow Cap)$. By 'certainty' is simply meant being quite sure or perfectly confident that something is true, where certainty does not entail truth. (Despite the existence of the obscure idiom 'It is certain that . . .' it is dubious whether there is any other non-technical concept of certainty than this concept, sometimes pejoratively called 'subjective certainty' by philosophers.) Now certainty is a stronger notion than mere belief. 'A is certain that p' entails that 'A believes that p' $(Cap \rightarrow Bap)$, for it is a contradiction to say that A is certain that the earth is flat but does not believe it to be flat. At the same time, that A believes p to be true does not entail that A is certain that p is true: $\sim(Bap \rightarrow Cap)$. We may therefore distinguish between a Strong and a Weak assertion of the Belief-condition, according to whether it is asserted or denied that knowledge entails ('subjective') certainty.

Among those who have denied the necessity for any Belief-condition we can similarly distinguish between a Weak and a Strong denial. According to the Weak denial, although it is possible to know something but not believe it, knowledge does not entail the absence of belief: $\sim(Kap \rightarrow \sim Bap)$. But according to the Strong denial, knowing that p actually excludes believing it: $Kap \rightarrow \sim Bap$.

We thus have four important positions (as will be indicated, each view has had its supporters) with respect to the Belief-condition for knowledge:

Assertion of the Belief-condition: $(Kap \rightarrow Bap)$
- in a strong form: $(Kap \rightarrow Cap)$
- in a weak form: $\sim(Kap \rightarrow Cap)$

Denial of the Belief-condition: $\sim(Kap \rightarrow Bap)$
- in a weak form: $\sim(Kap \rightarrow \sim Bap)$
- in a strong form: $(Kap \rightarrow \sim Bap)$

The view which will be upheld here is a Weak Assertion of the Belief-condition. The defence of this view will proceed by a criticism of the other three alternatives, beginning with the Strong Denial of the Belief-condition. Much of this chapter was given a preliminary statement in a paper 'Does Knowledge entail Belief?' (Armstrong 1969).

IV   Rejection of the Strong Denial of the Belief-condition

The view that knowledge excludes the corresponding belief was first put forward by Plato in the *Republic* 476–9 (in startling contrast to what appears to be his view elsewhere that knowledge entails belief). His argument, which will not be examined here, started from the premiss that knowledge is infallible, belief fallible. In recent decades the Strong Denial has frequently been supported by linguistic arguments. For example, it has been pointed out that when a speaker knows that p, and desires to be candid in his speech, it would be inappropriate for him to say that he believes that p is the case. If somebody tells you that he believes the last train has gone, you will naturally conclude that he does not know this for a fact. Linguistic points of this kind were taken to show that knowledge excludes belief.

The invalidity of these arguments from what it is natural to say in certain situations has been widely recognized in recent years. (See, in particular, Jonathan Harrison, 1957.) I will not therefore give them any attention except to remark that they seem to confuse what is *misleading* for a candid man to say in a certain situation with saying what he believes to be false. Misleading speech is speech which tends to create in its hearers' minds false beliefs about what the speaker believes. It does not follow that the content of what is actually said is something the speaker does not believe. But instead of following this point up, I will offer a simple argument which seems to *prove* that it is false that knowledge excludes the corresponding belief.

We have already noted in Section III that certainty entails belief: (Cap → Bap). It is also clear that, although certainty does not entail knowledge or even truth, it is possible for A to be both certain that p is true and know it to be true: $\diamondsuit$ (Cap & Kap). The readers of this book are perfectly certain that the earth is round, indeed they know it for a fact. But if knowledge logically excludes the corresponding belief, one of these two obvious assumptions must be given up. For consider an A who is both certain that, and knows that, p: Cap & Kap. If knowledge excludes belief, then it is not the case that he believes that p: Cap & Kap & ~ Bap. So A is certain that p is true but does not believe that p! The only alternative is to deny that knowledge and certainty are compatible.

The argument can be presented in another way. Consider the situation of somebody, B, who knows that A is certain that p, but who does not know whether or not A knows that p. If knowledge excludes belief, B will not be entitled to say that A believes that p. For, for all B knows, A knows that p and so does not believe it. But it is clear that in fact B *is* entitled to say that A believes that p.

It should be noticed that this argument would be relatively in-effective against the position developed by Plato in the *Republic*. For my argument assumes, what Plato there contests, that the one state of affairs, for instance the roundness of the earth, can be the object of the distinct cognitive attitudes: knowledge, certainty and belief. But the justification for my assumption has been taught us by G. E. Moore. It is one of those obvious facts which we should appeal to in the course of testing philosophical theses and arguments, rather than allow philosophical theses and arguments to cast doubt upon. For the 'assumption' is something we are far more certain of than almost any philosophical thesis or argument.

V   Rejection of the Strong Assertion of the Belief-condition

Many modern philosophers have asserted that if A knows that p it is entailed that A is certain or sure that p. An example is A. J. Ayer in *The Problem of Knowledge* (Chapter One, Section (v)). But there exists a strong argument against the existence of an entail-ment between knowledge and certainty, first put forward in print, to my knowledge, by A. D. Woozley in a paper 'Knowing and not Knowing' (Woozley 1952). He calls attention to a not uncommon type of case where we attribute knowledge in the absence of cer-tainty. His example may be called 'The Case of the Unconfident Examinee'.

Suppose that an examinee gives fumbling, unconfident, but always correct answers to a series of questions. He is not sure that his answers are the true ones. But might we not credit him with *know-ing* that the answers are correct? We might say to such an examinee: 'You see, you *knew* the answers all the time.' And such encourage-ment need not be mere encouragement.

I think that this case is conclusive. It seems that the Strong Assertion of the Belief-condition is as easily refuted as its Strong Denial.

Nevertheless, it is important to notice, as Woozley and others have, that there is some conceptual link between knowledge and certainty. Suppose that A *asserts* that he knows that p. On pain of uttering something paradoxical, he cannot go on to deny that he is certain that p is true:

I know that p is true, but it is not the case that I am certain that p is true.

is a paradoxical sentence.

If Woozley's interpretation of the case of the Unconfident Examinee is correct, A has not contradicted himself. But it is paradoxical to say what he says. This may be contrasted with the sentence obtained by substituting 'believe' for 'know':

I believe that p is true, but it is not the case that I am certain p is true.

There is nothing paradoxical about this sentence.

The paradoxical sentence can be turned round, and still produce a strange sentence:

I am certain that p is true, but it is not the case that I know that p is true.

Since it is quite clear that A could be certain that p is true, but not know p to be true, A has certainly not contradicated himself. (To substitute 'believe' for 'know' here does produce a contradiction.) But there may be a difference from the original paradoxical sentence. P. F. Strawson has pointed out to me that the second sentence might possibly be used by A as a report on his mental state. A might observe that, in part of his mind at least, he was certain that p. At the same time he might judge this certainty unwarranted. And so he might utter the sentence: 'I am certain that p is true, but it is not the case that I know that p is true.' Even here, however, the sentence is in a degree paradoxical. For A is judging his own certainty to be unwarranted, and hence admitting that he is in an irrational state.

What conclusion should be drawn from the paradoxical nature of these first-person sentences linking knowledge and certainty? I think they indicate that the Strong Assertion of the Belief-condition, although incorrect, is groping for some truth about the nature of knowledge. The concepts of knowledge and certainty stand in some connection, direct or indirect. After our account has been given of the nature of knowledge, an hypothesis about the exact nature of the connection will be suggested (see Chapter Fifteen, Section Three).

VI Rejection of the Weak Denial of the Belief-condition

We are left with a choice between the Weak Denial and the Weak Assertion of the Belief-condition. The Weak Denial, which is now to be discussed, has only been proposed, so far as I know, in recent years. This position asserts that, although knowledge does not exclude belief, cases of knowledge without belief (Kap & ~ Bap) are *possible*.

Consider a case of a sort that is sometimes cited. A woman appears to know that her explorer-husband has perished. She has been given the proofs, and she verbally acknowledges their force. Yet, at the same time, much of her conduct appears to belie her acknowledgements. She does and says all sorts of things which would be naturally interpreted as expressions of a belief that he is still alive. She may say of herself that, although she knows he is dead, she cannot bring herself to believe it. Is this a possible case of knowledge in the absence of the corresponding belief?

Let us admit, for the sake of argument at least, that what we have here is a case of somebody who knows something but does not believe it. Is it therefore a case of Kap and ~ Bap? Not necessarily. Here we must remember the ambiguity of the phrase 'She doesn't believe it'. It might mean 'It is not the case that she believes it' or it might mean 'She believes it is not the case'. The phrase, in ordinary usage, is ambiguous between ~ Bap and Ba ~ p. Only if the phrase can be interpreted in the first way does the case establish the Weak Denial of the Belief-condition.

It might be thought that the ambiguity is of no importance. Suppose that the phrase is taken to mean 'She believes it is not the case'. Can we not argue from this to the conclusion 'It is not the case that she believes it'? Can we not argue from Ba ~ p to ~ Bap? (It is obvious that we cannot argue the other way.)

Given the Ba ~ p, it will in general be the case that ~ Bap. If you believe that it is not the case that Jack will be coming, then, in general, it will not be the case that you believe that Jack will be coming. But there is no entailment here. For it is possible that you have a split mind on the question, that you hold contradictory beliefs on the matter, believing both that it is not the case that Jack will be coming and that it is the case that Jack will be coming. Ba ~ p & Bap is a possible state of affairs. The matter was discussed in Chapter Eight, Section One, where it was argued that it is always possible for one person to hold contradictory beliefs simultaneously, even where he is aware that he holds such beliefs.

So now it emerges that there are at least two ways of interpreting the case of the woman and her explorer husband. Someone who wished to argue for the Weak Denial of the Belief-condition might interpret it as a case of Kap & ~ Bap. But somebody who thought that knowledge entailed belief might suggest that it was a case of Kap, *and therefore a case of Bap*, but *also*, in addition, a case of Ba ~ p. The woman knows, and so believes, that her husband is dead, but at the same time she is unable to excise from her mind the belief that it is not the case that her husband is dead. She holds contradictory beliefs, *one* of the beliefs satisfying the further conditions for knowledge.

How do we decide between these two interpretations? We might, of course, decide that it is not a case of *knowledge* at all, and so that both interpretations are incorrect. But then the case would not serve the interests of the Weak Denial. And since, in any case, I think the case *could* be a case of knowledge, at any rate if the account of knowledge still to be developed in this essay is correct, I will assume that our task is to choose between the two interpretations.

One way we can accomplish this is to set the case in a context of further cases. Wittgenstein has warned us against the dangers of a *one-sided* diet of cases in philosophy. To surround a case with other cases can sometimes cause us to reconsider what we want to say about the first case. (An intuition can be corrected by intuitions.) I believe that this is the situation here.

Suppose, therefore, that we change the case in just one respect. We alter the proofs that the woman is given, and which she acknowledges, to 'proofs'. Although the evidence she is given seems to her to be satisfactory, it is in fact not satisfactory. Her husband is not dead, or perhaps he is dead but still the evidence she is given for his death is not really satisfactory. Now we cannot say that she knows her husband is dead. We will have to say that she believes he is dead (Bap). But what of her other conduct that belies her acknowledgements? We cannot now interpret this other conduct as indicating that it is not the case that she believes her husband is dead (~ Bap), for Bap & ~ Bap is not a possible state of affairs. So we ought to interpret the other conduct as indicating that she believes it is not the case that her husband is dead (Ba ~ p). *But if this is the way we interpret the altered case, we must interpret the original case in the same way.* For there is no relevant difference in the cases. So the original case is a case of Kap & Ba ~ p, and there is nothing in it to indicate that it is a case of ~ Bap. The Weak Denial of the Belief-condition is not established by the original case.

It may be objected (it has been objected by P. F. Strawson) that my argument here shows a rather superstitious faith in the Law of Non-Contradiction. Might we not say of the woman both that she believed, and it was not the case that she believed, her husband was dead, in the same spirit that we might say in certain meteorological conditions both that it was and was not raining?

But suppose this interpretation to be conceded, although I concede it purely for the sake of argument. The original case must then be interpreted as one of Kap and Bap & ~ Bap. Despite the fact that the belief that p is a borderline case, it is a case of *belief that p.* So the case will be of no use as a counter-instance to the thesis that knowledge entails belief. Incidentally, it might plausibly be maintained that if it is a borderline case of belief, it is a borderline case of knowledge also, and so that the borderlines of the two concepts coincide.

What I have been considering here is simply one case that purports to be one of knowledge without the corresponding belief. But I believe (although I do not know how to prove) that a parallel line of argument can be developed against any other such purported case. All I will do by way of supporting my view is to apply the same line of thought deployed in the case of the woman to an ingenious case recently put forward by Mr Colin Radford (Radford 1966).

Radford's case is essentially an attempt to extend the case of the Unconfident Examinee. He takes the case of a French-Canadian who believes himself to be ignorant of English history but who, in the course of a game, makes what appear to him to be sheer guesses in answer to questions about this subject. Surprisingly, he gets a number of questions right, including the death of Queen Elizabeth in 1603. He subsequently recollects, what he had previously forgotten, that he did once learn certain dates in English history. It is concluded that his 'guess', although it appeared to himself at the time to be a sheer guess, was in fact something he remembered, and so that he really *knew* the answer to the question. In this case, then, Radford claims, somebody knew that Queen Elizabeth died in 1603, but it is false that they believed that Queen Elizabeth died in 1603.

The question arises, as it already did in the case of the woman, whether this is a genuine case of knowledge. In my view, it is such a case. I do not think that the description Radford gives of the case *entails* that it is a case of knowledge. But it is a *prima facie* case. (See the analysis of knowledge which is to come.) The chief difficulty many will find in calling it a case of knowledge is that the French-Canadian neither knows nor believes that he knows that Elizabeth died in 1603 ($\sim$KaKap & $\sim$BaKap). This contradicts the common assumption that if A knows that p then it is entailed that he knows that he knows that p (Kap $\rightarrow$ KaKap). But in Chapter Two, Section Five (iv) I briefly indicated, what I have elsewhere argued, that it is logically possible to be mistaken about, or unaware of the existence of, any of our own current mental states just as much as any other state of affairs in the world. So I think we should accept Radford's case as a possible case of knowledge.

Further, it seems clear that the Canadian believes it is not the case that Elizabeth died in 1603 (Ba$\sim$p). For, consciously, he regards his saying of '1603' as the merest guess, and therefore as very much more likely to be wrong than right. He would bet heavily against his 'guess' being correct. Admittedly, he believes that it is just possible that Elizabeth died in 1603. But if somebody believes that p is just possible, but no more than just possible, then he believes, although he is not certain, that $\sim$p is true.

But, as we can now appreciate after the discussion of the previous case of the woman, this is not sufficient to clinch Radford's case. He needs to show that $\sim$Bap obtains: that it is not the case that the Canadian believes that Elizabeth died in 1603. But somebody who holds, against Radford, that knowledge entails belief will maintain that the case is one where the Canadian knows *and so believes* that Elizabeth died in 1603 yet also believes (without certainty) that it is not the case that Elizabeth died in 1603 (Kap & Bap & Ba$\sim$p). How do we decide between Radford and his opponent?

Once again, additional cases can be constructed. Strictly, only one is necessary, but I will construct two. For ease of following the argument, I will in addition first repeat Radford's case, giving us three cases in all.

Case 1. A person who is currently quite ignorant of English history is asked to give the date of the death of Queen Elizabeth. As it seems to him, he 'simply guesses' 1603. But in fact he was once taught this date, as he later recollects. The memory-trace which was produced by this teaching continued to exist right up to the time of the guess (although leading a subterranean life in the subject's mind) and was responsible for his picking this date rather than any other. This is Radford's case, with the causal mechanism which must surely be involved made explicit.

Case 2. The subject is asked the question, and, as it seems to him, 'simply guesses' 1630. In fact, as he later recollects, he had in the past been taught that date (wrongly as we know), thus acquiring the false belief that Queen Elizabeth died in 1630. The memory-trace which was produced by this teaching continued to exist right up to the time of the guess (although leading a subterranean life in the subject's mind) and was responsible for his picking this date rather than any other.

It seems to me plausible to say that this guess was in fact, or at any rate could be, a manifestation of a *false belief*. (Perhaps other 'unconscious manifestations' would be required to clinch the case as a case of unconscious false belief. These can easily be added, without affecting the argument in any way.) Radford, at least, ought to admit the plausibility of this. Many philosophers, of course, would deny that it was a case of false belief. But they are the same philosophers who would deny that Radford's case (Case 1) was a case of knowledge. They accept neither unconscious knowledge nor unconscious belief.

To spell out the argument for saying that Case 2 is a case of false belief. Case 2 stands to *ordinary* false belief (for instance, the false belief which the subject held just after the incorrect teaching) exactly as Case 1 stands to *ordinary* knowledge (for instance, the knowledge which the subject had just after being taught the correct date). Case 2 and Case 1 are simply the two ordinary cases trimmed down in *identical* fashion. In each case, the subject fails to take the words which he utters as being manifestations of belief or knowledge, but instead thinks that what he says is a mere guess. So whoever wants to say that Case 1 is a case of knowledge ought to find it plausible to say that Case 2 (or at least an enriched Case 2) is a case of false belief.

The argument is not apodeictic. There seems no way to *prove* that the two cases are parallel. There may even be some way to demonstrate, or make plausible, that there is some difference between knowledge and belief such that, while Case 1 is, or can be, a case of unconscious knowledge, Case 2 cannot be a case of unconscious belief. But I know of no plausible grounds of differentiation.

Case 3. The subject is asked the question and, as it seems to him, 'simply guesses' 1603. In fact he had in the past been taught wrongly that the date was 1630. Shortly afterwards he became muddled in his recollection of the (incorrect) teaching and came to believe that the date was 1603. The muddled memory-trace continued to exist right up to the time of the guess (although leading a subterranean life in the subject's mind) and was responsible for his picking '1603' rather than any other date.

Clearly this cannot be a case of knowledge. But if Case 2 is a case of unconscious false belief, as argued above, then this must be a case of unconscious (mere) true belief.

What has been done now is to show that, alongside Radford's putative case of knowledge, equally plausible cases of the same sort can be constructed, but ones involving false and (mere) true belief. Alongside *ordinary* cases of knowledge, it is easy to construct parallel ordinary cases of false belief and (mere) true belief. Now, I hope, the same has been done for Radford's case. It was also done in the case of the woman and her husband, though there it could be done without difficulty. And now, just as in the case of the woman, a second step of the argument follows.

Consider, in particular, Case 3. It is a case (we have now agreed) of unconscious (mere) true belief. It therefore involves the Canadian in believing that Elizabeth died in 1603 (Bap). At the same time, he disowns his 'guess' at the conscious level. So, just as in Radford's original case, and for exactly the same reasons, it is the case that, at the *conscious* level, A believes (without being certain) that it is not the case that Elizabeth died in 1603 (Ba $\sim$ p). Now, *in this case*, we cannot interpret the conscious disavowal of the 'guess' as showing that it is false that the Canadian believes that Elizabeth died in 1603 ($\sim$ Bap). For this would introduce a contradiction into the description of the case. So we must interpret the *identical* conscious disavowal of the guess in Radford's original case (Case 1) as nothing more than a belief that Elizabeth did not die in 1603 (Ba $\sim$ p), and not in addition, as Radford would have it, $\sim$ Bap.

So, in default of other evidence, I conclude that the Weak Denial of the Belief-condition should be rejected. And so, by elimination of all other possibilities, we are entitled to assert the Belief-condition in its weak form. Although knowing that something is true does not entail being certain that that thing is true:

$$\cdot \quad \sim(\text{Kap} \rightarrow \text{Cap})$$

nevertheless knowing that something is true does entail believing that that thing is true:

$$\text{Kap} \rightarrow \text{Bap}.$$

11

The Infinite Regress of Reasons

I The Evidence-condition

If the argument of the previous chapter was correct, then 'A knows that p' entails 'A truly believes that p'. But true belief does not entail knowledge. The latter point is made by Plato in the *Theaetetus* 200D–201C). It may be illustrated, for instance, by *The Case of the Optimistic Punter*. Because he is optimistic, he regularly *believes* that the horses he bets on will win. But he never has any reliable information about these horses. As a result, he normally loses. From time to time, however, his horses win. On such occasions his beliefs are true. But we do not think that he *knows* that these horses will win.

This is the occasion for introducing the Evidence-condition. The trouble about the punter, it is plausibly suggested, is that he lacks *good reasons* or *sufficient evidence* for his true belief. If only he had that, he would know.

However, when the Evidence-condition is scrutinized more closely, all sorts of problems emerge. In this section no less than five sub-conditions will be outlined which the Evidence-condition must satisfy, if it is accepted at all. All these sub-conditions raise important problems.

Condition 1. Suppose that p is true, A believes that p and A has evidence for 'p', namely 'q'. It cannot be the case that A *knows* that p unless, as a matter of objective fact, 'q' constitutes *sufficient evidence* to establish the truth of 'p'. It will be argued at a later point (Chapter Fourteen, Section One) that, for knowledge, such 'sufficient evidence' must be *conclusive* evidence. We have already discussed what it is for one proposition, 'q', to be a conclusive reason for the truth of another proposition, 'p', in Chapter Six, Section Seven. It is simply a matter of the hypothetical proposition 'if q, then p' being true. (The relation between 'q' and 'p' need not be entailment, though it cannot simply be 'q ⊃ p'.)

Condition 2. Suppose that 'p' is true, A believes that p, A has evidence 'q' for 'p', and 'q' is in fact sufficient evidence for the truth of 'p'. It may still be the case that A does not realize, or has not noticed, the relevance of his evidence 'q' to 'p'. He may, for instance, have failed to 'put two and two together'.

What is needed is that A's evidence should be actually operative in A's mind, supporting his belief that p. We must therefore have an account of what it is for somebody actually to *take* one proposition as a (conclusive) reason for accepting another. An answer to this question has also been given, in Chapter Six. It is a matter of certain quite complex causal relationships between belief-states.

Condition 3. But even if 'p' is true, A believes that p, A has evidence 'q' for the truth of 'p', 'q' is in fact sufficient evidence for 'p', and the evidence actually operates in A's mind to support his belief that p, it still does not follow that A *knows* that p. For although 'q' in fact supports 'p' conclusively, might not A be reasoning from 'q' to 'p' according to some *false* principle which in this particular case moves from a truth to a truth? For instance, A's reasoning from 'q' to 'p' might involve a compensating error peculiar to the case in hand. It seems that we need to say that the principle of reasoning according to which A operates, when his belief that q operates in his mind to support his belief that p, is a *true* principle. This stipulation, by the way, makes Condition 1 redundant.

Condition 4. We now stipulate that 'p' is true, A believes that p, A has evidence 'q' for 'p', the evidence actually operates in A's mind to support his belief that p, and the principle of reasoning according to which A operates is a true principle. It still does not follow that A *knows* that p. For although the principle of A's reasoning is true, may it not be that A accepts this principle on thoroughly bad grounds? And could we then say that he knew that p? It seems that we ought to amend Condition 3 by saying that the principle of A's reasoning is not simply true, but is *known* by A to be true. But this raises the difficulty that our analysis of A knows that p now involves *knowledge* by A of at least one general principle. What account shall we give of *this* knowledge?

Condition 5. Let us waive this difficulty (for the present). Suppose 'p' is true, A believes that p, A has evidence 'q' for 'p', the evidence actually operates in A's mind to support his belief that p, and the principle of reasoning according to which A operates is known by A to be true. Even now it is not entailed that A knows p. For consider A's evidence 'q'. Do we not require the further stipulation that A *know* that q is true? Suppose it not to be the case that A knows that q ($\sim$Kaq). Is not 'p' insufficiently supported?

But if this is correct, then knowledge that p can be defined only in terms of *knowledge* that q. 'q' will then demand support in A's mind from evidence 'r', and an infinite regress threatens.

Although the apparent necessity for Condition 4 also introduces the threat of an infinite regress, historically it is the regress which results from the demand that the evidence be itself something which A knows which has especially troubled supporters of the classical 'good reasons' analysis of knowledge. Let us begin, therefore, by discussing the problem raised by the apparent necessity for Condition 5. Only much later will we return to the problems posed by Conditions 2, 3 and 4.

II   The Infinite Regress of Reasons

Knowledge entails true belief, but true belief does not entail knowledge. It is therefore suggested that knowledge is a true belief for which the believer has sufficient evidence, or some such formula. But the evidence will have to be some proposition, 'q', which is *known* to A. I think that this becomes evident if the 'method of subtraction' is applied, and we contemplate the situation where this condition *fails* to obtain. Let us suppose that it is not the case that A knows that q is true ($\sim$Kaq). Surely this weakness in the foundations ensures that the belief founded upon it is not known either? If I claim to know that p solely on the basis of evidence 'q', but go on to admit that it is not the case that I know that q is true, you will laugh at my claim to know.

This simple consideration seems to make redundant the ingenious argument of Edmund L. Gettier's brief but influential article 'Is Justified True Belief Knowledge?' (Gettier 1963). Gettier produces counter-examples to the thesis that justified true belief is knowledge by producing true beliefs based on justifiably believed grounds, in the 'ordinary language' sense of 'justifiably believed', but where these grounds are in fact *false*. But because possession of such grounds could not constitute possession of *knowledge*, I should have thought it obvious that they are too weak to serve as suitable grounds. It is not surprising, therefore, that Gettier is able to construct examples where a true belief is justified in an ordinary sense of 'justified', but the true belief is clearly not a case of knowledge.

Gettier's paper has been commented upon, with a view to excluding his counter-example by judiciously chosen extra conditions, in a truly alarming and ever-increasing series of papers. For instance, it has been suggested that in order to count as proper grounds, the justifying beliefs must be not only 'justifiably believed' but also true. But whatever amendments have been proposed, counter-examples have still been constructed. It seems to me clear that it must always be possible to construct counter-examples until a condition is introduced that the justifying beliefs are *known* to be true.

Of course, it is easy to see why those who try to introduce extra conditions to exclude Gettier's counter-examples do not introduce *knowledge* of the justifying beliefs into their analyses. For then the very notion of knowledge which an analysis is being sought for crops up again in the analysis. Knowledge that p will be analysed in terms of knowledge that q, knowledge that q in terms of knowledge that r, and so, it would seem, *ad infinitum*.

Nevertheless, if we are going to have an Evidence-condition at all, then, as has been argued, it *must* involve *knowledge* of the evidence. And the threatened infinite regress – first noticed in the literature by Plato at the end of the *Theaetetus* (209E–210B) – does not leave the supporter of an Evidence-condition completely without resource. Knowledge that q is used in defining knowledge that p. This is not flat circularity. The term 'knowledge' crops up both in *definiendum* and *definiens*. But one piece of knowledge is defined in terms of *another* piece of knowledge. This gives a little space for manoeuvre and there have been all sorts of attempts to exploit this space.

Indeed, Gregory O'Hair has attempted, in unpublished work, to classify all the various philosophers' analyses or accounts of knowledge as *different reactions to the threatened regress*. The sketch which follows is greatly indebted to this idea of his, although I have not stuck to all his particular sub-divisions. I am not proposing to discuss exhaustively the alternatives to my own view, but will content myself simply with a brief indication of objections. My object is only to place the type of solution to the problem which I defend in a perspective of other attempted solutions. Gettier-type analyses must, of course, be excluded, because they do not allow the regress even to begin. But we have argued that they operate with too weak a form of the Evidence-condition.

III Different Reactions to the Regress

1. *The 'Sceptical' Reaction.* We may begin by distinguishing between 'sceptical' and 'non-sceptical' reactions to the regress. An extreme form of the sceptical reaction would be to say that the infinite regress showed that the concept of knowledge involves a contradiction. A moderate view would be that the word 'know', although it attributes true belief, attributes nothing further of an objective nature to the belief – no relation to the facts – except truth.

One straightforwardly sceptical account of knowledge is the view suggested in much of Karl Popper's work that the word 'know' is not theoretically useful, and that all our beliefs should be treated as 'hypotheses'. (To avoid possible misunderstanding, let me say now that it is not being claimed that all the views mentioned are actually formed under the stimulus of the threatened infinite regress. The claim is only that these views can usefully be classified *as if* they were reactions to the regress.)

In J. L. Austin's well-known article 'Other Minds' (Austin 1961) it is suggested that the special linguistic function of the phrase 'I know . . .' is to pledge the speaker's word, or give his authority, that the statement which follows is true. This suggests, although it may not actually entail, a 'sceptical' view of knowledge. (For what seems definitive criticism of this so-called 'performative' view of 'I know . . .' see Jonathan Harrison 1962, and W. H. F. Barnes 1963.)

The only comment which seems required about 'sceptical' views of knowledge is this. A non-sceptical solution to the problem posed by the infinite regress is to be preferred if it can be found. After all, there does appear to be a clear, objective, distinction between knowledge and mere true belief (*vide* the optimistic punter).

2. *The regress is infinite but virtuous.* The first non-sceptical solution which may be canvassed is that the regress exists, but is virtuous. Suppose that event A has a prior cause B, B has a prior cause C, and so, perhaps, *ad infinitum*. Few modern philosophers would consider this latter progression to infinity a vicious one. So perhaps A's knowledge that p rests upon knowledge that q which rests upon knowledge that r, and so on without stop. Such a view

was held by C. S. Peirce. (See 'Some Consequences of Four Incapacities', Peirce 1940.)

This solution depends upon maintaining that, in order to know anything, we must know an infinite number of things. And so it might seem to be sufficiently refuted by pointing out that the mind of man is finite. However, this does not completely dispose of the suggestion. For instance, if we know a rule for generating an open set of formulae then, it can be argued, we have potential access to an infinite number of formulae, despite the fact that our minds are finite. In some similar way to this, it may be suggested, we could know the infinite number of things which serve as the infinite chain of good reasons standing behind everything we know.

It can hardly be pretended, however, that this reaction to the regress has much plausibility. Like the 'sceptical' solution, it is a *desperate* solution, to be considered only if all others are clearly seen to be unsatisfactory.

3. *The regress is finite, but has no end.* Suppose, then, that the regress is not virtuous. Then either the regress has no end, or it has an end. If it has no end, then at some point the reasons must come back upon their own tail, so that 'p' is supported by 'q', which is supported by 'r', which is supported by 's', . . . which is supported by . . ., which is supported by 'p'. This may seem to involve *vicious* circularity. But perhaps it need not. If we have a circle of true beliefs which mutually support each other in this way, then it might be suggested that, once the circle is sufficiently comprehensive and the mutual support sufficiently strong, we would not have mere true beliefs but pieces of knowledge. This may be called the *Coherence* analysis of the concept of knowledge. I do not know anywhere that it has been worked out in detail, but it is close in spirit to the Coherence theory of truth.

There are complications here, depending upon the theory of truth accepted. If one took the Coherence view of truth also, then the notions of knowledge and truth might come into close logical connection. But if one accepted the sort of view of truth already argued for in Part II, truth and knowledge would be quite independent. One would have an objective view of truth, but combine it with the idea that coherence of such true beliefs turned the cohering beliefs into knowledge. The traditional analysis of knowledge implicitly assumes that the Truth-condition and the Belief-condition are logically independent.

Clearly, there are many difficulties for this 'Coherence theory of knowledge'. For instance, what criterion can be given to show that a circle of true beliefs is 'sufficiently comprehensive'? It is not easy to say. And might there not be a sufficiently comprehensive circle of true beliefs which was arrived at so irregularly and luckily that we would not want to call it knowledge?

4. *The regress ends in self-evident truths.* If the Coherence analysis is rejected, then at some point in the regress of reasons (perhaps right at the beginning) we will reach knowledge which is *not* based on reasons. I will call such knowledge 'non-inferential' knowledge. I oppose it to 'inferential' knowledge, which *is* based on reasons. Once it is granted that there is an objective notion of knowledge; that the infinite regress of reasons is in some way vicious; and that the regress cannot be stopped by judicious circularity; then it must be granted that, when A knows that p, then *either* this knowledge is non-inferential, or it is based on a finite set of reasons terminating in non-inferential knowledge.

The problem then comes to be that of giving an account of non-inferential knowledge. Suppose that A believes that p, but that A's belief does not rest upon any reason for believing that p. We have already (Chapter Six, Section One) called such a case 'non-inferential belief'. It is clear that non-inferential knowledge entails true non-inferential belief, but that the reverse entailment does not hold. So the question becomes: what further restriction must be placed on true non-inferential beliefs to yield non-inferential *knowledge*?

The classical answer is: non-inferential beliefs which are self-evident, indubitable or incorrigible. They will serve to stop the regress and act as the foundations of knowledge. This has been the *standard* solution from the time of Descartes until quite recently.

However, I reject the whole notion of beliefs that it is logically impossible to be wrong about. I think the logical possibility of error is always present in any belief about any subject matter whatsoever. In any case, it has been demonstrated again and again that, even if there is such self-evident knowledge, it is completely insufficient in *extent* to serve as a foundation for all the things we ordinarily claim to know, even when we have circumscribed that claim by careful reflection. In the past, defenders of this Cartesian solution have regularly had to cut down the scope of our supposed knowledge in a completely unacceptable manner. (For instance, it becomes difficult to claim that there is any empirical knowledge, non-inferential or inferential, beyond that of our own current states of mind.)

5. '*Initial credibility*'. The alternative is to attempt an account of non-inferential knowledge without appealing to such self-evident truths. O'Hair has distinguished two sorts of view here, which he calls 'Initial credibility' and 'Externalist' views.

First a word about 'Initial credibility' theories. It might be maintained that certain classes of our non-inferential beliefs have an intrinsic claim to credibility, even although error about them is a logical and even an empirical possibility. Instances might be beliefs based directly upon sense-perception, upon memory, upon intuition of the simpler logical necessities, or perhaps only upon suitable sub-classes of these classes. Now suppose that a belief is non-inferential, is 'initially credible' and is also *true*. Might it not then be accounted a case of non-inferential *knowledge*?

This approach strikes me as more hopeful than the possible reactions to the infinite regress which have already been mentioned. But it involves certain difficulties. It is easy, for instance, to construct non-inferential memory beliefs which are true, but which we certainly would not call knowledge. Thus, a probe in my brain might produce the belief in me that I had an itch in my little finger three days ago. By sheer coincidence, the belief might be true. Or a veridical memory-trace might degenerate but, in the course of a multi-stage degeneration, the original encoding might be reinstated by a sheer fluke. Some way of excluding such cases would have to be found. I myself am convinced, although I will not try to demonstrate the point here, that the only way to achieve such exclusions satisfactorily is to pass over into an 'Externalist' theory.

6. '*Externalist*' *theories*. According to 'Externalist' accounts of non-inferential knowledge, what makes a true non-inferential belief a case of *knowledge* is some natural relation which holds between the belief-state, Bap, and the situation which makes the belief true. It is a matter of a certain relation holding between the believer and the world. It is important to notice that, unlike 'Cartesian' and 'Initial Credibility' theories, Externalist theories are regularly developed as theories of the nature of knowledge *generally* and not simply as theories of non-inferential knowledge. But they still have a peculiar importance in the case of non-inferential knowledge because they serve to solve the problem of the infinite regress.

Externalist theories may be further sub-divided into 'Causal' and 'Reliability' theories.

6 (i) *Causal theories.* The central notion in causal theories may be illustrated by the simplest case. The suggestion is that Bap is a case of Kap if 'p' is true and, furthermore, the situation that makes 'p' true is causally responsible for the existence of the belief-state Bap. I not only believe, but *know*, that the room is rather hot. Now it is certainly *the excessive heat of the room* which has caused me to have this belief. This causal relation, it may then be suggested, is what makes my belief a case of knowledge.

Ramsey's brief note on 'Knowledge', to be found among his 'Last Papers' in *The Foundations of Mathematics*, puts forward a causal view. A sophisticated recent version of a causal theory is to be found in 'A Causal Theory of Knowing' by Alvin I. Goldman (Goldman 1967).

Causal theories face two main types of difficulty. In the first place, even if we restrict ourselves to knowledge of particular matters of fact, not every case of knowledge is a case where the situation known is causally responsible for the existence of the belief. For instance, we appear to have some knowledge of the future. And even if all such knowledge is in practice inferential, non-inferential knowledge of the future (for example, that I will be ill tomorrow) seems to be an intelligible possibility. Yet it could hardly be held that my illness tomorrow causes my belief today that I will be ill tomorrow. Such cases can perhaps be dealt with by sophisticating the Causal analysis. In such a case, one could say, both the illness tomorrow and today's belief that I will be ill tomorrow have a *common* cause, for instance some condition of my body today which not only leads to illness but casts its shadow before by giving rise to the belief. (An 'early-warning' system.)

In the second place, and much more seriously, cases can be envisaged where the situation that makes 'p' true gives rise to Bap, but we would not want to say that A *knew* that p. Suppose, for instance, that A is in a hypersensitive and deranged state, so that almost any considerable sensory stimulus causes him to believe that there is a sound of a certain sort in his immediate environment. Now suppose that, on a particular occasion, the considerable sensory stimulus which produces that belief is, in fact, *a sound of just that sort in his immediate environment.* Here the p-situation produces Bap, but we would not want to say that it was a case of knowledge.

I believe that such cases can be excluded only by filling out the Causal Analysis with a Reliability condition. But once this is done, I think it turns out that the Causal part of the analysis becomes redundant, and that the Reliability condition is sufficient by itself for giving an account of non-inferential (and inferential) knowledge.

6 (ii) *Reliability theories.* The second 'Externalist' approach is in terms of the *empirical reliability* of the belief involved. Knowledge is empirically reliable belief. Since the next chapter will be devoted to a defence of a form of the Reliability view, it will be only courteous to indicate the major precursors of this sort of view which I am acquainted with.

Once again, Ramsey is the pioneer. The paper 'Knowledge', already mentioned, combines elements of the Causal and the Reliability view. There followed John Watling's 'Inference from the Known to the Unknown' (Watling 1954), which first converted me to a Reliability view. Since then there has been Brian Skyrms' very difficult paper 'The Explication of "X knows that p" ' (Skyrms 1967), and Peter Unger's 'An Analysis of Factual Knowledge' (Unger 1968), both of which appear to defend versions of the Reliability view. There is also my own first version in Chapter Nine of *A Materialist Theory of the Mind.* A still more recent paper, which I think can be said to put forward a Reliability view, and which in any case anticipates a number of the results I arrive at in this Part, is Fred Dretske's 'Conclusive Reasons' (Dretske 1971).

It is interesting to notice that a Reliability analysis is considered for a moment by Plato in the *Meno,* only to be dropped immediately. At 97b Socrates asserts that '. . . true opinion is as good a guide as knowledge for the purpose of acting rightly', and goes on to ask whether we should not draw the conclusion that 'right opinion is something no less useful than knowledge'. Meno however objects:

Except that the man with knowledge will always be successful, and the man with right opinion only sometimes.

Unfortunately, however, Socrates brushes aside this tentative development of a Reliability view, saying:

What? Will he not always be successful so long as he has the right opinion?

Meno immediately concedes the point.

This concludes our brief survey. In philosophy, when one finds

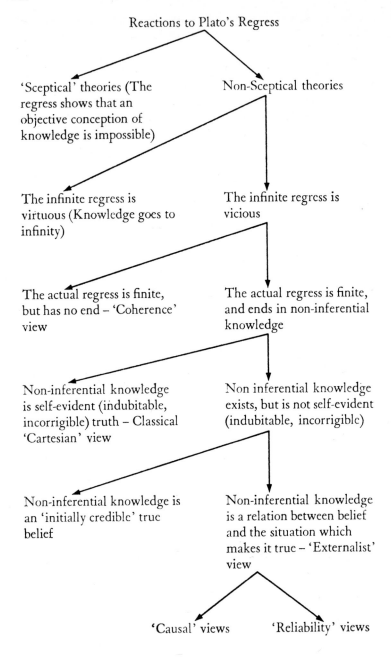

Reactions to Plato's Regress

'Sceptical' theories (The regress shows that an objective conception of knowledge is impossible)

Non-Sceptical theories

The infinite regress is virtuous (Knowledge goes to infinity)

The infinite regress is vicious

The actual regress is finite, but has no end – 'Coherence' view

The actual regress is finite, and ends in non-inferential knowledge

Non-inferential knowledge is self-evident (indubitable, incorrigible) truth – Classical 'Cartesian' view

Non inferential knowledge exists, but is not self-evident (indubitable, incorrigible)

Non-inferential knowledge is an 'initially credible' true belief

Non-inferential knowledge is a relation between belief and the situation which makes it true – 'Externalist' view

'Causal' views   'Reliability' views

oneself in a difficult intellectual situation, it is often vitally important to be aware of the full range of response which is open to one. And in philosophy, if one practises it honestly, one invariably is in a more or less difficult intellectual situation. The survey just made was intended to create an awareness of the many different responses open to us in the difficult situation created by the threatened infinite regress involved in the classical analysis of knowledge. Against this background, I proceed to put forward a suggested solution of the problem.

12

Non-Inferential Knowledge (1)

In this chapter a theory of non-inferential knowledge will be developed. The restriction to *non-inferential* knowledge is not essential, and in a subsequent chapter the analysis developed here will be extended to inferential knowledge. But the case of non-inferential knowledge is peculiarly important. Thinking about the threatened infinite regress in the classical analysis of knowledge seems to lead to the conclusion that there must be non-inferential knowledge. Furthermore, we seem *forced* in the case of this sort of knowledge to look for some non-classical solution to the problem. (The classical or 'Cartesian' postulation of self-evident truths can rather easily be shown to be an insufficient account of the basis of all that we think we know.) If we can find a non-classical solution to the problem of non-inferential knowledge, where such a solution is clearly required, we may then try to extend the solution to cover all cases of knowledge.

I   What are the paradigms of non-inferential knowledge?

It would be extremely convenient if, in the course of discussion of non-inferential knowledge, one could point to uncontroversial examples of such knowledge. The examples could then be used in testing whether particular philosophical accounts of non-inferential knowledge are correct or not.

In the case of knowledge *simpliciter*, such uncontroversial cases are available. I *know* that the earth is round. I *know* that there is a piece of paper in front of me now. If a philosophical theory of the nature of knowledge yields the consequence that I do *not* know these things, then this is a conclusive (I do not say logically conclusive) reason for rejecting the theory.

Unfortunately, however, in the case of the more technical notion of *non-inferential* knowledge, no such uncontroversial examples are available. It has taken an abstract argument even to show that there must be such knowledge, and it is hard to give cases that are clearly beyond controversy. At the same time, it is unsatisfactory if no examples are used, or at least borne in mind. I shall therefore put forward a view of where non-inferential knowledge is to be found. At the same time, however, the actual *analysis* of non-inferential knowledge, which will be our subsequent business, will not depend upon the identification of cases of non-inferential knowledge to be suggested in this section.

I suggest that at least one place where non-inferential knowledge is to be found is in *the simpler judgements of perception*. I do not say that this is the only place where non-inferential knowledge is found. (The simpler judgements of introspection would be one further *locus* of such knowledge.) Nor is it the case that all our simpler judgements of perception are instances of non-inferential knowledge. First, such judgements can be false. Second, even where they are true, it is possible for them to fall short of being knowledge. Third, even where they are knowledge, it is possible for them to be inferential knowledge. All that is asserted is that instances of non-inferential knowledge are common among the simpler judgements of perception.

What is meant by 'the simpler judgements of perception'? I have in mind such judgements as 'There is a noise within earshot', 'It is getting hotter', 'There is something red and round over there', 'There is something pressing on my body' and so on. Very often, I suggest, such judgements are instances of non-inferential knowledge.

It may help to illuminate this suggestion if I contrast it with two other views of where non-inferential knowledge is to be found which have some currency in modern philosophy. The two views are, respectively, more pessimistic and more optimistic than the moderate view advocated here.

According to the 'pessimistic' view of non-inferential knowledge, it is not possible, as our moderate view assumes, to have non-inferential knowledge of states of affairs in the physical world. Non-inferential knowledge of sensory matters, the pessimists hold, is confined to knowledge of the perceiver's own sensory states. All that we can possibly know non-inferentially about sensory matters is such things as 'It sounds to me as if there is a noise within earshot', 'It feels to me as if it is getting hotter', 'It looks to me as if there is something red and round over there', 'It feels to me as if there is something pressing on my body', where thèse statements are taken simply to express judgements about the perceiver's current sensory state.

Historically, this 'pessimistic' view is linked with the idea that non-inferential knowledge must be logically indubitable. It is, however, logically independent of this idea. The 'pessimistic' view is even more closely bound up with the Representative theory of perception, according to which all our knowledge of the physical environment is an inference, however unselfconscious, from the *data* of the perceiver's own sensory states. It is because I see no reason to accept the Representative theory (for reasons which do not concern us here) that I see no reason to accept the 'pessimistic' view that non-inferential knowledge is confined to the subject's own sensory states.

Notice, however, that the 'moderate' view need in no way reject the positive contentions of the 'pessimistic' view. A moderate can perfectly well admit that there can be, and regularly is, non-inferential knowledge of our own sensory states, and mental states generally.

The 'optimist' about non-inferential knowledge will again be perfectly prepared to accept the positive contentions of the 'pessimist' and the 'moderate'. But he thinks that the sphere of non-inferential knowledge is wider still. He thinks that we know non-inferentially things of a much more complex sort than those admitted by the 'pessimist' and the 'moderate'. Suppose that I am looking at a dog just in front of me, that the light is good, and that I am in my right mind. Unless other conditions are quite extraordinary, I will *know* that there is a dog in front of me. But the 'optimist' about non-inferential knowledge will claim further that this is *non-inferential* knowledge.

The strength of the 'optimistic' view lies in our ordinary speech and thought. It seems extraordinary, when there is a dog slap in front of our eyes, to say we *infer* that there is a dog there. Surely we *contrast* cases like that of the dog with cases where it is a matter of inferring?

On the other hand, if we consider the actual process by which we come to know that there is a dog before our eyes, it becomes more plausible to say that the knowledge involves inference. We come to know that there is a dog there as a result of light-waves reaching our eyes, and the information which can be conveyed by the light-waves is limited. A material thing having a similar physical constitution to the portion of the surface of the dog which is in our field of view, but which did not resemble a dog in any other way (a 'surface-simulacrum'), would have the same effect on the eyes and mind as the dog. It is tempting, and I think correct, to conclude that the presence of a *whole* dog is inferred from more elementary information.

One thing which gives trouble here is the temptation to make inferring a far more explicit, hesitating and self-conscious affair than it always is. When we start thinking about the psychological process of inferring, it is natural to concentrate upon such cases. For, by hypothesis, these are the cases where we take special notice of the inferring. But it is wrong to restrict inferring to such cases. In Chapter Six, Section Six, we gave an account of inferring in terms of one belief being the efficient, and then, for some finite duration, the sustaining, cause of another belief, provided that this causal process exemplifies some general *pattern* of connection of beliefs which the believer is disposed to exhibit. Such a process could be automatic, instantaneous and unselfconscious – indeed, it could be below the surface of consciousness. Now, once we take such a view of inferring, it becomes far easier to accept the conclusion that even seeing that there is a dog before one's eyes involves inference. One is not conscious of inferring, but that is little reason for denying that inferring occurs if there are other reasons for postulating its occurrence.

Notice that this dispute between 'pessimistic, 'moderate' and 'optimistic' views of where non-inferential knowledge is to be found is an *empirical* dispute. There is certainly no *a priori* objection to the idea that we could have non-inferential knowledge that there is a dog before us. It is simply that, from what we know of perception, it seems (to me, at any rate) an unlikely hypothesis. The question in what areas non-inferential knowledge is found seems to be a *psychological* question, a question about the cognitive structure and powers of the human mind. In espousing the 'moderate' view I am opting for a psychological theory which seems to me to be plausible.

In Chapter Five, Section Two, it was argued that the question what concepts and Ideas are *simple* is also a psychological question, not to be settled *a priori* or by off-hand introspection. The parallel is obvious.

II The 'Thermometer' view of non-inferential knowledge

Suppose that 'p' is true, and A believes that p, but his belief is not supported by any reasons. 'p' might be the proposition that there is a sound in A's evironment. (The previous section indicates why this example is chosen.) What makes such a belief a case of knowledge? My suggestion is that there must be a *law-like connection* between the state of affairs Bap and the state of affairs that makes 'p' true such that, given Bap, it must be the case that p.

The quickest way to grasp the suggestion is to use a model. Let us compare non-inferential beliefs to the temperature-readings given by a thermometer. In some cases, the thermometer-reading will fail to correspond to the temperature of the environment. Such a reading may be compared to non-inferential false belief. In other cases, the reading will correspond to the actual temperature. Such a reading is like non-inferential true belief. The second case, where reading and actual environmental temperature coincide, is then sub-divided into two sorts of case. First, suppose that the thermometer is a bad one, but that, on a certain occasion, the thermometer-reading coincides with the actual temperature. (*Cf.* the stopped clock that shows the right time twice a day.) Such a reading is to be compared with non-inferential true belief which falls short of knowledge. Suppose finally that the thermometer is a good one, so that a reading of 'T°' on the thermometer ensures that the environmental temperature is T°. Such a reading is to be compared with non-inferential *knowledge*. When a true belief unsupported by reasons stands to the situation truly believed to exist as a thermometer-reading in a good thermometer stands to the actual temperature, then we have non-inferential knowledge.

I think the picture given by the thermometer-model is intuitively clear. The problem is to give a formal account of the situation.

Here is one immediate difficulty. Laws of nature are connections between things (in the widest sense of 'things') of certain *sorts*. But the suggested connection between belief-state and situation which makes the belief true is a connection between particular states of affairs: between singulars.

The reply to this is that the belief-state is an *instance* of a certain sort of thing: a person believing a certain sort of proposition. Equally, the situation is an instance of a certain sort of thing: say, a certain sort of sound within earshot of the believer. So we can say that a law-like connection holds between the two singulars in virtue of the fact that the two are of certain sorts, and things of these sorts are connected by a law.

Here, however, we must be careful. What is the law that is involved? Take the example of knowing non-inferentially that there is a sound in one's environment. A believes that there is a sound in his environment now, and indeed there is. Do we want to say that A *knows* there is a sound in his environment only if the whole situation is covered by the following law-like generalization: 'If anybody believes that there is a sound in his environment, then there is indeed a sound in his environment'? Of course not. The proposed generalization is clearly false, because people have sometimes believed that there was a sound in their environment when there was none. Yet we are not led by this to say that nobody ever *knows* that such sounds are occurring.

The model of the thermometer gives us further assistance here. For a thermometer to be reliable on a certain occasion in registering a certain temperature as T° we do not demand that there be a true law-like generalization: 'If any thermometer registers "T°", then the temperature is T°.' In the first place, we recognize that there can be good and bad thermometers. In the second place, we do not even demand that a good thermometer provide a reliable reading under every condition. We recognize that there may be special environmental conditions under which even a 'good' thermometer is unreliable.

What do we demand? Let us investigate a far less stringent condition. Suppose, on a certain occasion, a thermometer is reliably registering 'T°'. There must be some property of the instrument and/or its circumstances such that, if anything has this property, and registers 'T°', it must be the case, as a matter of natural law, that the temperature *is* T°. We might find it extremely hard to specify this property (set of properties). The specification might have to be given in the form of a blank cheque to be filled in only after extensive investigation. But it may be relatively easy to recognize that a certain thermometer is operating reliably, and so that such specification is possible. (In general, the recognition of the existence of general connections in nature precedes their specification. Some light will be thrown on this fact later on. See Chapter Thirteen, Section Three.)

Let us now try applying this to the case of non-inferential knowledge. A's non-inferential belief that p is non-inferential *knowledge* if, and only if:

   (i) p is the case
   (ii) There is some specification of A such that, if any person is so specified, then, if they further believe that p, then p is the case.

Putting the suggestion in a more formal way (though it will soon be seen that the formula is ill-formed as it stands, and requires amendment):

A's non-inferential belief that p is a case of non-inferential *knowledge* if, and only if:

   (i) p
   (ii) ($\exists$H)[Ha & there is a law-like connection in nature (x) if Hx, then (if Bxp, then p)]

It is important to remember that in condition (ii) Bxp and p are here to be taken as states of affairs rather than propositions. We might have written ^{s}Bxp and ^{s}p. Notice also that H is being used as a 'predicate variable' in the predicate position. Many would object to this practice, but it is by far the most convenient way of saying what I want to say.

It may seem strange that there can be a law-like connection holding between a state of affairs of a certain sort, on the one hand, and a further law-like connection, on the other. But in fact this is a commonplace in nature, as the thermometer case shows. *If* the thermometer is properly constructed, *then*, as a result of this, *if* the thermometer registers 'T°', *then* the temperature is T°. The same thing may therefore hold in the case of beliefs.

What are law-like connections of nature? I should like to avoid committing myself on this issue beyond what is absolutely necessary. The essential points seem to be these.

First, they are the sort of connections which can in principle be investigated by scientific method: by observation and, in particular, by experiment. In the case of a thermometer the investigation would not be difficult, in the case of beliefs it could be very difficult indeed, but there is no difference in principle between the cases. Were the particular thermometer-reading and the actual temperature at that time connected in a law-like way? We experiment with the thermometer, or a sufficiently similar one, and so draw a conclusion about the original situation. It is far harder to experiment with the beliefs of human beings, and so there may be much more guess-work in the assertion that a similar connection exists. But I take this to be a mere practical difficulty. (It does have the consequence, which seems to be perfectly acceptable, that it will often be difficult to determine when we do, and when we do not, *know*.)

Second, the law-like generalizations which record the existence of such connections yield counterfactual or, more generally, subjunc-tive conditionals. If the temperature of the environment on that occasion had not been T°, then the reading on the thermometer would not have been 'T°'. If p had not been the case, then it would not have been the case that A believed that p.

Third, the connection between belief and state of affairs is a connection which holds independently of us who may record its existence. It is an ontological connection. It is not, however, a *causal* connection. The state of affairs Bap does not bring the state of affairs that makes 'p' true into existence. (There is a difficulty here, which will be discussed in Section Six.) It is frequently the case that this state of affairs brings the state of affairs Bap into existence. But even that does not occur in all cases.

This, I hope, is as far as it is necessary to commit ourselves on the nature of the general connections involved. Some philosophers, in the spirit of Hume, maintain that a satisfactory account of law-like connection can be given without assuming the existence of any-thing except regularities of various sorts among otherwise uncon-nected phenomena. Other philosophers argue that some far stronger necessity in the nature of things is required. But this whole great dispute is an ontological problem which will receive no attention here. It may be hoped that, whatever answers are given to the problem, an account of non-inferential knowledge in terms of law-like connection will be unaffected. For in our account the notion of law-like connection is taken as a largely unanalysed primitive.

So much by way of explaining our formula. Unfortunately, it is not in its final form. A series of objections require discussion and some of these require that the formula be modified.

One modification is urgently required. As the formula has just been presented it is certainly ill-formed. p is a place-holder or dummy for a particular state of affairs. How then is it possible to bring p within the scope of a universal quantifier? How can we talk of states of affairs of the *sort* p?

But at this point we remember that the *proposition* p asserts a particular matter of fact ('It is hot here now'). All such propositions must involve (a) reference to some individual and (b) predicating some property of that individual. Putting it another way, such propositions must have the form Fa, or, as it will be more convenient to write because the letters 'F' and 'a' have already been given another use in this book, the form Jc. It is not just that there must exist a proposition with the form Jc that is logically equivalent to p. The structure of Ideas in the belief-state must actually have the form Jc. And once this point is appreciated, we can say that the second condition asserts a general connection between (a) beliefs that have the form Jc and (b) the actual obtaining of what is believed.

Our formula can now be rewritten. A's non-inferential belief that c is a J is a case of non-inferential *knowledge* if, and only if:

(i) Jc
(ii) (∃ H)[Ha & there is a law-like connection in nature (x)(y) {ifHx, then (if BxJy, then Jy)}].

x ranges over beings capable of cognition. Since this account of non-inferential knowledge is restricted to beliefs about 'particular matters of fact', in the sense given to that phrase in Chapter One, y can range over particulars which figure in such beliefs. Suppose that what is believed is the proposition that it is hot here now. 'J' might then be 'hot in the immediate environment of the believer'. A believes it is hot here now, that is, he believes it is hot in his immediate environment. Further, A's current condition and situation is such that if *any* person who is in that condition and situation believes that it is hot in his immediate environment then, indeed, that immediate environment is hot.

Notice that, because the beliefs involved are *true*, there is no problem about y ranging over individuals which do not exist. In Chapter Six, Sections Four and Five, an account was given of what it is to hold a general belief. In our formula there, we used a quantifier outside a belief-context that was supposed to range over individuals within that context: (x)(BaFx ⊃ BaGx). We noted that this was unsatisfactory, but said that the formula was used for simplicity's sake. A proper re-statement of the condition would render belief-states as mental structures of Ideas, and the quantifier involved would range over tokens of Ideas of particulars. The difficulties involved in our present formula are rather less. As just noted, there is no question in the present formula of the quantifier trying to range over non-existent individuals, a problem that did arise in the case of general beliefs. Nevertheless, ideally our formula should express a law-like connection between belief-states involving certain sorts of Ideas, on the one hand, and certain sorts of states of affairs, on the other. I cannot see that such a re-statement involves any difficulties of principle (although self-deception here is all too easy), but its complexity would be nightmarish in practice.

III   Deutscher's objection

We must now take notice of an objection, due to Max Deutscher (private communication), which will force us to place a restriction on H, that is, the specification of A's condition and circumstances within which a belief of that sort is reliable.

We noticed briefly that the situation of c's being J is, very often, the thing which brings BaJc into existence. For instance, the sound in my environment is the thing which brings it about that I come to believe that there is a sound in my environment. (Just as the environmental temperature $T°$ brings it about that the thermometer registers '$T°$'.) At the same time, however, not every case where the situation of c's being J brings about the situation BaJc is a case where KaJc. We have already seen this in our brief discussion of Causal analyses of non-inferential knowledge. To re-describe the case mentioned there. A is suffering from auditory hallucinations, which he takes to be genuine. Like an object which is liable to explode under the impact of almost any slight shock, he is in such a state that almost any sensory stimulus will make him believe (normally falsely) that there is a sound in his environment. From time to time, however, the stimulus that makes him believe that there is a sound in his environment *is in fact a sound*. He has a 'veridical hallucination'! Here c's being J was causally responsible for BaJc, but we should want to deny that the belief was a case of knowledge.

At first sight, this 'veridical hallucination' case may seem to pose no problems for our formula. What we speak of as a cause is seldom a *necessary* condition of its effect. In the case under discussion, the sound is certainly not a necessary condition for producing the belief that there is a sound in the environment. Only if c's being J were a *necessary* causal condition of BaJc, which would make BaJc sufficient for c's being J (although coming after that state of affairs in time), would it seem that the conditions laid down in our formula for knowledge were met.

But, and this is Deutscher's point, we have forgotten about conditions H. Our formula set no limits on H. Condition (ii) of our formula, it will be remembered, was:

$$(\exists H)[Ha \ \& \ \text{there is a law-like connection in nature } (x)(y)$$
$$\{\text{if Hx, then (if BxJy, then Jy)}\}].$$

H can be any general property, non-relational and/or relational, that the believer A has, however complex this property may be. Now suppose that in the 'veridical hallucination' situation we go on specifying certain of A's properties in indefinitely greater and greater detail. Will we not inevitably arrive at a complex property H that A has, such that, given a believer who had just that complex property *and* believed that there was a sound in his environment, then there *must* (nomically must) have been a sound there? In a situation so closely specified, the *only* thing which could cause the belief that there is a sound in the environment *is* such a sound. For the detailed description of A and his environment, if it is *sufficiently* detailed, will be such as to rule out any other cause. (Whatever operates, leaves signs of its operations about. Absence of these signs means that thing is not operating. These are not necessary truths. But we believe them to be true!) So even in the 'veridical hallucination' case, it seems, the law-like condition 'if Hx, then (if BxJy, then Jy)' will be satisfied, provided H is specified in sufficient detail. And there is no bar in the formula to specifying H in indefinite detail. Which yields us a result we cannot accept, that the 'veridical hallucination' case is a case of knowledge.

It seems that some restricting condition must be placed upon H in order to rule out such a counter-case.

In order to solve the problem, let us go back to our ever-useful model of the thermometer. Let us first construct the thermometer-equivalent of the 'veridical hallucination' case. It is possible to conceive of a thoroughly unsatisfactory thermometer which is acted upon by an environment at T°, and that this environmental temperature, by some strange fluke, happens on a particular occasion to make the thermometer register 'T°'. Yet if we were to specify the thermometer's constitution *and environment* on that occasion in sufficient detail, it would (almost certainly) be empirically impossible that the thermometer *as so specified* should have registered 'T°' except through the action of an environment at T°.

Now have we got a thermometer which is *reliable* (in respect of registering 'T°') in these highly specific conditions? We would resist this conclusion. Why? The answer, I think, is that thermometers are built to *use*, and a thermometer of that sort would be no use, even if we knew and could identify the conditions in which its reading of 'T°' had to be correct. For the conditions would be so highly idiosyncratic that in all probability they would never occur more than once. Rather, what is wanted is a thermometer which will register correctly *in a variety of conditions*. But in order to ensure this, the conditions in which it gives a correct reading must not be specified too closely. Indeed, the more unspecified these are, then, all other things being equal, the more useful the thermometer will be. These conditions are the thermometer-equivalent of condition H in our formula.

The same sort of considerations apply in the case of non-inferential knowledge. There is a sense in which knowledge is a pragmatic concept. Why are we interested in the distinction between knowledge and mere true belief? Because the man who has *mere* true belief is unreliable. He was right this time, but if the same sort of situation crops up again he is likely to get it wrong. (The point made by the luckless Meno, but brushed aside by Socrates.) But if it is empirically impossible or even very unlikely that the situation will crop up again, then the distinction loses almost all its *point*.

So I think it is fair to put the following restriction upon H. H must not be so specified that the situation becomes unique, or for all practical purposes unique. H must be such that the situation has some real probability or at least possibility of being repeated. And, all other things being equal, the less specific H is the greater the 'value' of A's knowledge, because this increases the probability of repetition.

It is clear that this restriction on H is not a very precise one. (Notice the ambiguity in the formulations of the previous paragraph.) It may therefore leave us with borderline cases which are awkward to adjudicate upon. But it does seem an intelligible and real restriction, it is not a relative one, and it is one which flows naturally out of the 'pragmatic' nature of the concept of knowledge. Furthermore, in the next section it will be shown that exactly the same line of solution is available and plausible in giving an analysis of what it is for an *action* of A's to be a manifestation of A's *ability* to do that action. That is, Deutscher's problem about non-inferential knowledge can also be applied to manifestations of ability or skill, and our solution to his problem will also apply in this new field.

But although the scope of H is thus restricted so that it cannot be too specific, it is important to notice that there is one restriction on H's scope which must not be demanded. H must not be restricted to the *non-relational* properties of the believer A. That this restriction is too severe is most simply seen in terms of the analogy of the thermometer. It is not a conclusive objection to a thermometer that it is only reliable in a certain sort of environment. In the same way, reliability of belief, but only within a certain sort of environment, would seem to be sufficient for the believer to earn the accolade of knowledge if that sort of environment is part of his boundary-conditions.

The fact that H's scope can extend to *relational* properties of A has an important consequence. It was argued in Part I of this book that *belief* was a state (and in the case of general beliefs a dispositional state) of the believer. States are (a sub-class of) non-relational properties of the object which is in that state. But it now seems that non-inferential knowledge, at least, is not, or at any rate need not be, a state. A belief-state which is not knowledge might be knowledge, if the circumstances had been more favourable, without necessitating any difference in the believer's mind. So, although any particular belief-state is or is not knowledge (or is a border-line case), there is *this* element of 'relativity' in the notion of knowledge.

Before concluding this section, I shall make one note on the model of the thermometer. This model has proved so useful in explicating my view, which might even be called the 'thermometer' account of non-inferential knowledge, that it is important to notice that one characteristic of a good thermometer plays no part in the account. Registration of temperature and actual temperature reflect each other. Given that a reliable thermometer is registering 'T°', then the environmental temperature is T°. It is this feature which has been important for us. But, equally, given that the environmental temperature is T°, then the good thermometer will register 'T°'. Now this second feature is not necessary for non-inferential knowledge. Given that a person knows that c is J non-inferentially, then his belief is a reliable one, in the way which we have spelt out. He is in some condition and/or circumstances H which must not be too narrowly specified, such that if a person is in H, and believes something of that sort, then, as a matter of law-like connection, that thing believed is the case. But it does not follow that if a person is in circumstances/condition H, and c is J, then that person believes that c is J. Such a person may have no opinion at all on the matter. He may fail to register 'Jc'. In this respect, then, the reliable thermometer is too strong a model for non-inferential knowledge.

In order to remove this defect from the thermometer-model it would be necessary to have a thermometer which, although reliable when it *was* operating, might give a non-reading from which nothing in general could be deduced about the temperature. A reliable watch exhibits this feature when it is not wound up, except that its hands do still register a time. (It is also worth noticing that in the case of a properly set, wound-up reliable watch the time of day is not the *cause* of the watch registering the time of day correctly. In this, it is unlike the reliable thermometer. Yet, like the reliable thermometer, a reliable watch is a useful model for non-inferential knowledge.)

IV   A parallel account of manifestations of skill

It may give extra support to our suggested account of non-inferential knowledge if we interpolate at this point a discussion of the nature of *practical* knowledge, that is to say, the mastery of a skill. I think it emerges that exactly parallel difficulties arise in distinguishing genuine manifestations of a skill from the thing being brought off by sheer chance, as arise in distinguishing genuine non-inferential knowledge from mere true belief. These parallel difficulties will be shown to have a parallel solution. This will help to remove the suspicion that the answer just given to Deutscher's difficulty is *ad hoc*. (At the same time, this section does nothing to *advance* the main line of the argument. It could therefore be omitted.)

Let us compare *trying* or *attempting* to do P (P might be anything from one's arm going up, to balancing on a tightrope) with believing that p is the case. In symbols, TaP is compared with Bap. Let us also compare the actual *occurrence* of P (whether as the result of the agent's attempts or not) with the *truth* of 'p'. Now let us ask what it is for P to occur as the manifestation of A's skill or ability to do things of the sort P.

Is it enough that (i) A try to do P (ii) occurs (TaP & P)? Clearly not. For consider the following case. I try to open a heavy gate. My *efforts* are in fact doomed to failure. But by coincidence, at exactly the moment that I try to open the gate, machinery operates and the gate swings open. This is clearly parallel to mere true belief (Bap & p).

It may now be suggested that what is needed is that (i) A try to do P and (ii) *as a direct result of this attempt*, P occurs (TaP brings about P). Surely this would be a manifestation of A's having the skill or ability to do P? But in fact it need not be. For although *in this particular situation* TaP made P occur, this might be wildest luck, which A could never hope to repeat. And how then could A be credited with the skill or ability to do P? (We might credit A with a *capacity* to do P, on the grounds that whatever a man does in a situation, he has the capacity to do in that situation. But it is rather an attenuated sense even of the word 'capacity'.) It seems that we need to add some general conditon about the results of trying to do P on other occasions.

It is clear that we cannot demand that *whenever* A or somebody like A attempts to do P, then, as a result, P occurs. This is far too strong. We are therefore led to the idea that there exists some set of conditions, H, which characterize A when he makes his attempt, and such that any person who is characterized by H, and further attempts to do P, brings P off. Is this the extra condition required?

But this suggested extra condition at once runs into Deutscher trouble. For we have set no limits upon what H may be. Let us go back to the case where A attempts to do P, and, as a result of this, P occurs, but only because of the wildest luck. If A's condition and situation can be specified as closely as we please, it must be the ease that a condition H exists, that A is in condition H, and that, given H, A is *assured* of bringing off P. The only trouble will be in the extreme unlikelihood that these conditions will ever recur. For instance, A might attempt to walk a tightrope, and, only because of some incredibly unlikely blowing of the local winds, succeed in so doing as a result of his attempt. If conditions H include just these atmospheric conditions, then this case fits our formula. But we would not want to say that A manifested an ability to walk a tight-rope. He lacks such an ability, but, because of the once-only winds, his effort to walk the tightrope was successful.

But as soon as we remember the pragmatic nature of the concept of a skill or ability – our interest in a man's *reliability* under certain conditions – the Deutscher type of objection can be answered. If a man is to be said to have the skill or ability to do something, then, although we do not demand that he be able to bring the thing off in *all* circumstances, the range of circumstances in which he succeeds must not be so circumscribed that it is improbable that such circumstances should ever occur again. The performance must be a *repeatable* one, in the sense that there must be a real, empirical, possibility of the circumstances recurring. Such a restriction of H is, of course, not all that precise. This means that there is no *sharp* distinction in every case between bringing a thing off because one has the ability to do so in the circumstances which obtain, and bringing a thing off by sheer luck. But this result does not appear counter-intuitive.

As Deutscher has pointed out to me, if the extraordinary weather conditions which allowed A to balance on his tightrope were not extraordinary, but usual, then we would turn round and allow that, in these conditions, A did have the *skill* or *ability* to walk a tightrope. There is the same element of relativity in skill as in knowledge.

The clear parallel with our account of non-inferential knowledge, should, I think, strengthen our confidence in the correctness both of the account of such knowledge and the account just given of what it is for an action to be a manifestation of a skill (ability).

The argument of this section may have another value. It has been fashionable for some years, largely as a result of Ryle's discussion of 'knowing how' and 'knowing that' (Ryle 1949, Chapter Two), to compare knowing that something is the case with having the ability to do something. This seems incorrect. Knowing that something is the case is more usefully compared with the successful *manifestation* on a particular occasion of an ability to do something; it is best compared with the successful manifestation on an occasion of skill or 'know how'. Abilities, skills and 'knowings how' are better compared with those *cognitive abilities* which issue if they have issue, in particular comings to know that. The word 'know' can indeed be used to refer to such cognitive abilities. Hamlet claimed to *know* a hawk from a handsaw. He was claiming to have an ability such that, if presented with such pairs of objects, he would, at any rate in suitable weather conditions, know *that* one was a hawk and know *that* the other was a handsaw. The claim to know a person involves, among other things, the claim to have a certain cognitive ability. The claim to know a person is, among other things, the claim that if this person is sensorily presented then, in suitable circumstances at least, one will know *that* this person is so-and-so (Mr Jones, the local plumber or whatever).

So, against Ryle, the suggestion arising out of our analysis of what it is to manifest an ability is that:

Having an ability, skill or 'know how'	*stands to*	Manifesting that ability, *etc.*
as Having ability for a certain sort of 'knowing that'	*stands to*	gaining knowledge that something of that sort is the case

V   Further objections

But our troubles are not over. The two objections now to be considered are naturally connected and may be considered together.

The first problem was pointed out by Christopher Murphy, then an undergraduate at Sydney University. The trouble lies in the latter portion of the second condition:

> (ii) . . .there is a law-like connection in nature $(x)(y)$
> {if Hx, then (if BxJy, then Jy)}.

By the logical operation of exportation, presumably valid in this context, this is equivalent to:

> . . . $(x)(y)${if(Hx & BxJy), then Jy}.

Now suppose that there is, as there might be, a law-like connection between situations of the sort H and situations of the sort J. Suppose in particular:

> (x)(if Hx, then $(\exists y)$Jy).

A simple example falling under this formula would be one where H is a physiological condition of a certain quickly fatal sort, J is death, and x is the very same person as y. If any person is in physiological condition H, then that person dies shortly. Suppose now that this person *irrationally* acquires a (true) belief that he will die shortly. On our formula, his belief would have to be accounted knowledge.

A similar difficulty has been pointed out by Ken Waller (private communication). To produce Waller's case, we set up a law-like connection between belief-states and situations of the sort J. Suppose, for instance, that there is a chemical which must be present in a man's brain if he is to have *any* belief. If he believes anything, then the belief-chemical must be present in his brain. But now suppose that he somehow acquires the belief that a certain chemical is present in his brain. It happens to be the belief-chemical. Given our formula, this belief *must* be knowledge. But it seems obvious that it might in fact be a case of mere true belief.

What seems to be required in order to exclude Murphy's and Waller's cases is that, in our formula, the conditions H and the particular nature of the belief held should all be *nomically* relevant to the situations of the sort J. In Murphy's case, if we consider simply the belief, there is no law-like connection between it and situations of the sort J. In Waller's case, if we consider simply the particular content of the belief, there is no law-like connection between beliefs with this sort of content and situations of the sort J. Where two particulars are connected in a law-like way, they are connected *qua* particulars *of a certain sort* and not in virtue of other characteristics they may happen to have. Murphy and Waller have simply constructed cases where the particulars involved are not connected *qua* believers (Murphy) or *qua* believers of a certain sort of proposition (Waller), although in fact the beliefs are true. So we meet Murphy's and Waller's objection simply by stipulating that nothing but *nomically relevant characterizations* appear in our formula.

The principle seems easy enough, but the formal statement of this new restriction is rather complex. It might be thought that we could exclude Murphy's case by modifying condition (ii), the relevant portion of which at present reads:

$$\ldots (x)(y)\{\text{if } Hx, \text{ then (if } BxJy, \text{ then } Jy)\}$$

simply by adding, within the scope of the quantifiers:

$$\sim(\text{if } Hx, \text{ then } Jy)$$

This, however, would be too strong. It can be the case that (if Hx, then Jy), and yet it still be possible to credit the believer with knowledge that c is J. If there is *a law-like connection between the belief and the condition H*, then, even if H by itself ensures J, we still have a case of knowledge. The belief will ensure Ha, which will ensure Jc, and so, by transitivity, the belief will ensure Jc. The addition should therefore instead take the form:

$$\text{if (if } Hx, \text{ then } Jy), \text{ then (if } BxJy, \text{ then } Hx)$$

In Waller's sort of case, H together with x's holding a belief ensures a situation of the sort J. This suggests adding to condition (ii), within the scope of the quantifiers, the following condition:

$$\sim (P)(\text{if } BxP, \text{ then } Jy)$$

where 'P' ranges over all propositions. Once again, however, this condition would be too restricting. It would make it impossible for somebody to *know* that he had the belief-chemical in his brain. What we should say, rather, is that *if* H together with any belief whatsoever ensures a situation of the sort J, then the actual belief held must ensure H. (The belief automatically ensures that *some* belief is held, so the latter condition need not be explicitly mentioned.) So the condition will become:

$$\text{if } (P)(\text{if } BxP, \text{ then } Jy), \text{ then } (\text{if } BxJy, \text{ then } Hx).$$

In this way, I think, we can exclude all but nomically relevant characteristics from our formula. But since, as we have just seen, formal statement is both complex and tricky, I will for the future simply allow the condition of nomic relevance to appear as an unformalized restriction on our formula.

VI   Self-fulfilling beliefs

But the last paragraph of the previous section brings up a point which will force a final modification in our formula.

A's believing that c is J is a certain sort of state: a state of A's mind. Like all states, it endows the object that is in that state with certain causal powers. Now suppose that A has a belief that c is J for which he has no reasons, but which, in the circumstances A is in, brings it about that c is J. The analogy in the case of the thermometer would be an instrument that, by registering 'T°', brought it about that the temperature of the environment *was* T°. Of course, we should not call it a thermometer.

Such cases are not merely conceivable, they are empirically possible and sometimes occur. Consider the case of a sick man who, for no reason at all, believes that he will recover. Is it not possible, in view of what we know about the effect of psychological states upon bodily conditions, that that belief should be the cause of his recovery? (Without it, he would have died.) Again, consider the case of a child who takes it into his head, for no reason at all, that he will receive a certain toy for Christmas. His kind-hearted parents, who had not intended to give him this toy, learn of his belief and proceed to make it true.

Now in both cases of self-fulfilling beliefs it seems that, in the situation the believer is in, the belief ensures its own truth. In A's situation, if BaJc, then Jc. Furthermore, the conditions, H, under which this sequence occurs, might well, on occasion, be sufficiently general to permit the real possibility of other believers with beliefs of the same sort to be in the situation H. So the suggested conditions for non-inferential knowledge might well obtain. But would we ever be prepared to speak of *knowledge* here?

The situation is a peculiar one, and my intuitions, and I would suppose other people's, are not completely clear on the matter. But it seems, on the whole, that we ought not to speak of knowledge here. The essential point of a 'faculty of knowledge', is that it should, in respect of what is known, be passive to the world. If the 'reflection' is achieved by our mind moulding the world, we are not knowing but creating. (Although there may be a model here for God's knowledge of his creation.)

How, then, should we amend our account of non-inferential knowledge to exclude such cases? It could be done by simply adding a third clause to our formula:

(iii) it is not the case that Bap is the cause of p.

If, however, we consider the second condition:

(ii) (∃ H)[Ha & there is a law-like connection in nature
(x)(y){if Hx, then (if BxJy, then Jy)}].

then we have already introduced one modification as a restriction upon the scope of H in this formula (there must be a real possibility of the repetition of conditions H), and another as a restriction to nomically relevant properties in the formula as a whole. We might therefore introduce this new restriction as a comment upon the relation between BxJy and Jy.

We must first introduce and define the notion of a (natural) *sign*. Black clouds, for instance, are a sign of rain. We may distinguish between sign as token and sign as type. The following definition of a sign-token is then attractive. It is a particular of a certain sort, such that if the particular comes under the cognizance of a suitably knowledgeable person as a particular of that sort, that person can make a more or less reliable (inductive) inference to the existence of some further particular state of affairs. (The inference might be that the very same particular was of some further sort.)

But this definition, although on the right track, is a trifle too wide. Suppose that a certain sort of wound ensures death. A suitably trained person might infer from the fact that A had that sort of wound that A would die. The wound answers to our definition of a sign. But we should be reluctant to say the wound was a sign of ensuing death. Compare this with a special pallor which the wounded man might exhibit from which death could also be inferred. We would be happy to say that the *pallor* was a sign that death approached.

What is the difference between the wound and the pallor? I think that we say that the wound is not a sign of death because it is, *qua* wound, the *cause* of death. An effect can be a sign of its cause. A corpse may be a sign of foul play. But a cause is not a sign of its effect. (Black clouds are a cause of rain, but not in virtue of their blackness.) But, I think, with this restriction, our original definition of 'sign' can stand.

Returning now to our definition of non-inferential knowledge, we need not now stipulate, as an independent condition, that it be not the case that BaJc bring it about that c is J. Instead we can stipulate that the relation in our second condition between BxJy and Jy, be that of sign to thing signified.

Our definition now becomes:

A's non-inferential belief that c is J is a case of non-inferential *knowledge* if, and only if:

    (i) Jc
    (ii) (∃ H)[Ha & there is a law-like connection in nature (x)(y) {if Hx, then (if BxJy, then Jy)}]

The following restrictions are placed on (ii)

    (*a*) H must be such that there is a real possibility of the situation covered by the law-like connection recurring.
    (*b*) The properties mentioned are nomically relevant to the law-like connection.
    (*c*) The relation of BxJy to Jy is that of *completely reliable sign* to thing signified.

It will be pointed out in the next chapter that, given that A believes that c is J, condition (i) – that c is in fact J – is redundant. But otherwise our definition of non-inferential knowledge in terms of non-inferential belief is now fully before us.

The formulation of restriction (c) to condition (ii) in terms of the notion of a reliable sign helps to bring out a very important point about our account of non-inferential knowledge. The knower himself will not have evidence for what he knows. That is the meaning of 'non-inferential'. But his own belief-state, together with the circumstances he is in, could function for somebody *else* (God perhaps) as completely reliable evidence, in particular as a completely reliable sign, of the truth of the thing he believes. The subject's belief is not based on reasons, but it might be said to be reasonable (justifiable), because it is a sign, a completely reliable sign, that the situation believed to exist does in fact exist.

13

Non-Inferential Knowledge (2)

I In support of our account of non-inferential knowledge

In the previous chapter an analysis of non-inferential knowledge was developed in terms of a law-like relation between beliefs and the thing believed. In response to various objections the analysis was complicated and modified. But no systematic defence of an analysis in terms of a law-like relation between beliefs and the world has yet been offered. This will be the business of this section.

The argument has two steps. *First*, it will be argued that a law-like connection between belief and thing believed is at least a *necessary* condition for non-inferential knowledge. *Second*, once this is granted, it will be argued that it is hard to find any further necessary condition, so that the condition is in fact necessary and sufficient.

The first step, that such a law-like connection is at least *necessary*, may be defended as usual by the 'method of subtraction'. Consider the case where the law-like connection *fails* to obtain. Suppose that A believes that c is J non-inferentially, and his belief is true. But suppose it is not the case that there exists any H, for which Ha is true, such that if anybody has property H then, if he further believes that c is J, it is indeed the case that c is J. (Or, if there is such an H, it is a property which is so specific that it excludes the real possibility of repetitions of situations of the sort H. I omit the full details of the analysis.) Apart, then, from the possibility of some ridiculously complex specification of A's nature and circumstances, it would have been *empirically* possible for BaJc to have obtained, and yet for c's being J not to be the case. But if there is an empirical, as opposed to a logical, possibility of error, surely we are not justified in attributing knowledge?

Consider, as usual, the parallel case of the thermometer. Suppose that a thermometer gives a certain reading, and the reading is correct. But suppose that there is a *physical* possibility that, on that occasion, the thermometer should have been giving that reading although the actual temperature did not correspond. That is to say, suppose that there exists no property H, characterizing the nature and/or circumstances of the thermometer, such that, given both that the theromometer registers 'T°' and has property H, the actual temperature must (as a matter of natural or nomic necessity) be T°. (Or if there is such an H it is so specific that it excludes the real possibility of repetitions of situations of the sort H.) I do not think it can then be said that this thermometer is an absolutely reliable instrument. But must not the *knower* be compared with an absolutely reliable instrument?

I think that consideration of the case provided by the 'method of subtraction' shows that empirical reliability of belief is necessary for non-inferential knowledge. If there is considerable empirical chance of the belief being wrong, it surely cannot be knowledge. But, it may be asked, is *absolute reliability* necessary? To demand absolute reliability, it may be thought, is screwing up our demands too tight. Would it not be sufficient to demand only that BaJc confer *high probability* on c's being J? (Of course, it must also be the case that c is J.)

In fact, however, I think this reasonable-seeming relaxation creates intolerable paradoxes, as I will now attempt to show. My argument here was originally derived from Herbert Heidelberger (Heidelberger 1963).

Modern philosophy is familiar with the so-called 'lottery paradox' (Kyburg 1965, p. 305). Suppose it is rational for A to believe that p (RBap), rational to believe that q (RBaq) and so on for a whole class of propositions. It is not entailed that it is rational for A to believe the conjunction of these propositions:

$$(RBap \ \& \ RBaq \ldots) \nrightarrow RBa(p \ \& \ q \ldots)$$

For example, if A knows that there are ten thousand ticket-holders in a fair lottery, then it is rational for him to believe concerning each ticket-holder that that person does not hold the one and only winning ticket. But it would not be rational for A to believe that nobody held the winning ticket.

For the purpose of our argument here, it should be noticed that the entailment still fails if the premiss is added that p & q . . . all be *true*. Consider, for instance, the case where a marble is drawn from a barrel of ten thousand marbles with the object of drawing a single specially marked marble. If the drawer is unsuccessful, his losing marble is replaced and stirred in with the others. Let us suppose that this process is repeated twenty thousand times, but that no winning draw is made. It would be rational for A at the beginning of this process to believe of any draw that it would fail to be a winning draw. And in fact no draw turns out to be a winning draw. But it was not rational for A to believe from the beginning that twenty thousand attempts would be unsuccessful, even although in fact they were.

But now consider another principle:

$$(Kap \ \& \ Kaq \ . \ . \ .) \to RBa \ (p \ \& \ q \ . \ . \ .)$$

Surely this is a true principle? Can it ever be irrational to believe a conjunction of propositions that we know individually to be true? I call this the principle of the *Conjunctivity of knowledge*. I suggest that it is a secure principle to base an argument upon. But, as I will now proceed to show, if we do not demand *absolute* empirical reliability for our non-inferential beliefs before accounting them cases of non-inferential knowledge, then the Conjunctivity principle must be given up.

Let us now suppose, once again, that there is a sound in A's environment and that this sound creates in A the belief that there is a sound in his environment. But now let us suppose, further, that although A's belief is a reliable one, it is not an absolutely reliable one. In the situation that A is in, there are no better, though no worse than, 99 chances out of a hundred that his belief is true (though it is true in this case). That is to say: there exists no H which characterizes A and his situation that, together with his belief-state, nomically ensures that the thing believed is true; but there does exist such an H that ensures 99 chances in 100 of the thing believed being true. (*Vide* a thermometer that is reliable, but not absolutely reliable.) Let us suppose that all other necessary conditions for non-inferential knowledge are satisfied. Let it also be assumed, for the sake of investigating the hypothesis, that *absolute* reliability of belief is not required for knowledge and that A knows that there is a sound in his environment.

Now suppose that the whole situation is repeated 200 times. Each time a sound causes A to believe that there is a sound in his environment. If he knew the first time, he knows on each subsequent occasion. Suppose that he were to sum his knowledge and as a result believe that there was this series of sounds in his environment. By the principle of the Conjunctivity of knowledge this conjunctive belief would be rational.

This result, however, is a *reductio ad absurdum* of the supposition. A would *truly* believe that there was a sound in his environment on each of the two hundred occasions. But he does not rationally believe this. For the *odds* were that on some of these occasions his belief was not caused by a sound in his environment. So it cannot have been the case that A ever knew on any occasion that there was a sound in his environment.

The trouble is quite general. Whenever it is not the case that A's belief is completely reliable, although true, it is possible that this belief should be conjoined with other similar true beliefs until a point is reached where the conjunction is a *mere* true belief. The moral I draw is that, for knowledge, the belief in question must strictly ensure truth.

The alternatives seem quite unacceptable. It must be allowed that knowledge entails truth. If this demand be dropped, there may be rational belief, but there cannot be knowledge. It is almost equally unacceptable to deny the Conjunctivity of knowledge. So knowledge requires a belief-state which *ensures* truth. (If, however, a philosopher is hardy enough to deny the Conjunctivity principle, then he need not require complete reliability of belief.)

This seems a good occasion to point out that the *first* condition in our suggested account of non-inferential knowledge in terms of non-inferential belief – *viz.* that c is J – is redundant. Referring back to the formula at the end of Chapter Twelve, then given BaJc and condition (ii), it is easily seen that 'Jc' is entailed. (The only operations required are Existential and Universal Instantiation, *Modus Ponens* and Simplification.) But if the law-like connection between BaJc and c's being J is weakened so that BaJc simply probabilifies c's being J, then the truth-condition would be no longer redundant. But then belief-state and truth would not be securely welded together, belief-state would not ensure truth, and, as we we have just seen, paradox would arise.

But does not this demand for *absolute* reliability of belief as a necessary condition for knowledge require that we tighten up ordinary language? Will it not have the consequence that some of the things we ordinarily say we know, we do not in fact know? And what then becomes of the method we earlier committed ourselves to, of testing our analysis of knowledge by reference to ordinary paradigms?

I think that in fact the paradigms remain unaffected. Our analysis would have no tendency to discredit the statement that I know that there is a piece of paper before me. Or if, as is likely, this knowledge involves an inferential component, then let the example be that I know that there is something white, oblong, more or less flat and with blue horizontal markings before me. For it seems completely reasonable to think that, situated as I am, in my right mind and with my sense-organs working normally, I could not in fact be mistaken about this. As a matter of contingent fact, the *only* thing which could create this belief in me would be an actual white, oblong, more or less flat object with blue horizontal markings, before my eyes. Error is logically possible, *but that is all.*

In the case of knowledge we are in the queer (but not unique) position that the paradigm or knock-down cases of knowledge are not the cases where we have much occasion to *speak* of knowledge. Because knowledge is generally considered a desirable commodity, and yet we are not much interested in the cases where it is *obvious* that there is knowledge, when we use the word 'know' we have a tendency to push our luck. We use the word in too liberal a way. But we are aware that we use the word over-optimistically, and we can be recalled to the standards for knowledge which we accept even while we flout them. 'You say you know. But do you really? Are you quite certain? Could you not, just possibly, be wrong?' This need not be the philosophical sceptic speaking, but the man in the street. The requirement that error be nomically impossible may condemn some usings of the word 'know' as over-optimistic. But so it should. Any 'scepticism' about knowledge that results will be moderate and mitigated, like the scepticism which Hume advocated at the end of his *Inquiry*. It will not touch the paradigms.

At this point, we are ready to see the deep truth enshrined in the old and now somewhat derided slogan 'If you know, you cannot be wrong', at any rate as applied to non-inferential knowledge. As contemporary philosophers have viewed the formula, the only truth it bears witness to is that 'Kap' entails 'p'. 'Of logical necessity, if Kap, then p.' But, they have said, it is a fallacy to move from this to 'if Kap, then necessarily p'.

Now certainly it is a fallacy, and a gross one, if this is interpreted to mean that 'p', to be known, must be a necessary truth. It is still a fallacy if the interpretation is that, when we know, we are in some state of mind which of its intrinsic nature, logically necessitates 'p'. This way we are led to the venerable, but I think utterly worthless, doctrine of logically indubitable or self-evident truths. But now we can see that there is a third way to read 'if Kap, then necessarily p'. We might read it as 'Knowledge is a state of mind which as a matter of law-like necessity ensures that p'. And then the formula is an epigrammatic statement of the account we have been arguing for of the nature of non-inferential knowledge.

In his book *Analytical Philosophy of Knowledge* (Danto 1968), Arthur C. Danto says that:

... whereas we will all acknowledge that, if *m* knows that *s*, then *m* cannot be in error, cannot be wrong, with respect to *s*, few of us would so readily countenance the direct contrapositive of this, *viz.* that if *m can* be in error, *can* be wrong with respect to *s*, then *m* does *not* know that *s* (p. 51).

It is interesting to observe that, if the 'can' is the 'can' of, roughly, empirical possibility in that situation, then, according to our account of non-inferential knowledge, the contrapositive is straightforwardly true.

Having said so much in favour of making it at least a necessary condition of non-inferential knowledge that the belief involved be (as a matter of contingent fact) absolutely reliable, two things can be said which mitigate this rigour a little.

First, when we claim to know that p is true, in quite a number of cases we would accept a reformulation of the claim as no more than knowing that it is true that p is very probable. Now, where BaJc is not sufficient for c's being J, it may nevertheless be sufficient for the *high probability* of c's being J. Knowledge of probabilities, whether non-inferential or inferential, will be discussed later (Chapter Fifteen, Section Two). But provided we can give an objective interpretation to 'the probability of c's being J' in that situation, there would seem to be no reason why Ba(c's being J is very probable) should not be an *absolutely* reliable belief.

Second, even where we do not have knowledge, we may still have *rational belief*. If BaJc is a reliable pointer to the high probability of c's being J, then the belief that c is J may be called rational (whether or not the believer knows it is rational). Such rational belief will not, of course, ensure that c is J. This requirement of truth could be added arbitrarily. But we have seen that the resultant set of conditions could not be called knowledge, at any rate if we accept the principle of the Conjunctivity of knowledge.

Excusably, the reader may have forgotten that the topic we were discussing was whether the demand for law-like connection between Bap and p was a *necessary* condition for turning non-inferential belief into non-inferential knowledge. I have been arguing that it is such a necessary condition, and that it must be taken perfectly strictly so that, given BaJc in that situation, it *must* be the case that c is J, as a matter of empirical necessity. The question now arises whether this condition is *sufficient* (as I think it is) to transform non-inferential belief into non-inferential knowledge.

The best way to proceed seems to be the method of challenge. What further conditions could be required? A suggestion of some plausibility, which recalls the 'Initial Credibility' approach to the analysis of knowledge, is that the belief must be acquired in a standard way, for instance by the stimulation of the senses, or that it be a certain *sort* of belief, for instance a memory-belief.

But it seems to be simply their superior truth-gaining capacity which recommends reliance upon the senses, or upon memory. Suppose, as seems possible, that our senses and memory were much less reliable than they are in fact. And suppose, as also seems possible, that we had non-inferential beliefs which were not acquired by the senses, were not memory-beliefs, and which were much more reliable than our senses and memory. Would we not think that this new class of beliefs were better candidates for knowledge than sensory or memory-beliefs? But the superior 'reliability' of this new class of beliefs would seem to be nothing more than that law-like link between belief and thing believed which we have suggested is required to turn non-inferential belief into non-inferential knowledge.

II An epistemological objection to our account of non-inferential knowledge

One objection which it is natural to make to this proposed account of non-inferential knowledge is that it would be completely useless as a way of *testing* whether the things we take ourselves to know non-inferentially are in fact known to us. Consider, by way of contrast, Descartes' criterion for knowledge: 'clear and distinct perception'. This is intended for *use*. I examine my beliefs, discover which of them I have a 'clear and distinct perception' of, and conclude that these are the things which I really know. We may be unsure what clarity and distinctness of perception comes to, and, even if we have settled that question, we may still be doubtful if Descartes' criterion is in fact any good. But, formally at least, it seems to provide us with a *means of identifying our knowledge*.

But how could the analysis we have proposed provide us with any such means of identification? A knows that p if his belief is such that, given the features of A's situation, his belief has to be true. But there would be no way of using this formula in the quest for knowledge unless we *already* knew that the thing believed was true, which would make the formula otiose. The uselessness of the formula, it may then be argued, shows that it must be false.

This objection, however, is the result of running together the two completely different questions: (i) 'What is (non-inferential) knowledge?', and 'What (non-inferential) knowledge do we have?'. These are distinct questions. The first is a question about the concept of knowledge and, because it is a conceptual question, is in some broad sense a logical question. The second is an empirical question. Now we have been trying to answer the first question, and it is no reproach to this answer that it gives us no particular assistance in answering the second question. Why should it? Since when has the arriving at definitions cast light upon questions of empirical fact? Yet it is somehow natural to be seduced into thinking that an answer to the first question can be tested by its usefulness in answering the second question. We cannot help thinking that a satisfactory account of the nature of knowledge should give us concrete assistance in determining its extent.

But let us hold fast to this: just as a definition of an albino is not a recipe for finding albinos, so a definition of knowledge is not a recipe for obtaining knowledge.

What I think is at bottom the same objection is that, although our definition of non-inferential knowledge leaves open the possibility of such knowledge, it does not allow us to say that we *know* that we have such knowledge. We have certain beliefs. Some correspond to the facts, and some do not. Among those which correspond to the facts, but are unsupported by reasons, some have that empirical correlation with the facts of the sort which has been described. All this may be granted, it will be said, but how can we who are, as it were, behind and locked up in our own beliefs, determine which of our beliefs are properly correlated? If such a correlation is knowledge, we may sometimes know, but we will never be in a position to know that a correlation obtains, that is, know that we know. But this is unacceptable scepticism.

The answer to this argument must be to give an analysis not only of what it is to know, but also what it is to know that we know (KaKap). There is no reason to think that this cannot be done, *and done along exactly the same lines as our account of (non-inferential) knowledge*. I know (non-inferentially) that I know that p if (i) I believe non-inferentially that I know that p; (ii) correlation of the sort already described holds between this belief-state of mine and that further state which is *my knowing that p*. And so for knowing that I know that I know that p, *ad indefinitum*. I will say nothing more here, but will return to the topic of knowledge of knowledge at a later point (Chapter Fifteen, Section One).

III   Restrictions on the scope of our account of non-inferential knowledge

There are, however, certain important limitations which must be placed on our results so far. We have said that there must be a law-like connection between Bap and p's being the case if we are to have non-inferential knowledge that p. But what sort of values could p take? Could p be a logically necessary truth like '2 + 3 = 5' or a true empirical generalization like 'arsenic is poisonous'? It does not seem so. We admitted this when we said that the believed proposition p will have the form 'Jc': that it be a claim about some particular matter of fact.

What could it mean to say 'If A believes that $2+3=5$, then $2+3$ *is* equal to 5'? Admittedly, we do say things of this sort. Let us substitute a somewhat more complex mathematical formula for '$2+3=5$'. We say things of the form 'If A (a professor of mathematics) believes that p, then p is certainly true', or 'If B (a pharmacological expert) believes that chemical X is poisonous, then chemical X certainly *is* poisonous'. But these statements do not seem to assert the sort of connection asserted in the proposed analysis of non-inferential knowledge. If A believes that there is a sound in his environment, then we can, in principle, test whether there is a law-like connection involving belief and sound *by experiment*. For instance, we can suppress the sound and note that, for that believer in that situation, it is impossible to generate the belief. The practical difficulties may be great, but the theoretical possibility of such testing exists. But we cannot set up a situation where 2 and 3 are not 5, or arsenic is not poisonous, and then see how this affects the believer!

The difficulty is that our formula is tailor-made to connect *particular states of affairs*. Whatever the content of a belief, the belief itself is always a particular state of affairs in the believer's mind. But it is not the case that the situation which makes a true belief true is always a particular state of affairs. True beliefs *about* particular states of affairs – about particular happenings at particular times and places – will, of course, fit the formula. But what we have called 'general beliefs', beliefs whose contents are universally quantified propositions which range over 'open' classes, will not so fit, whether they be necessary or contingent. (Nor will propositions which state probability-relations for 'open' classes.)

It cannot be denied that even in the case of 'open' universally quantified propositions we seem to be able to attach some sense to counterfactuals which tell us what we would, or would not, have believed if the state of affairs had not obtained. It seems intelligible, and even plausible, to say that if arsenic had not been poisonous we would not have believed it was poisonous, or even that if 2 and 3 had not been equal to 5 we would not have believed they were equal to 5. But it is not clear to me what such statements mean, still less how they are established. All that is clear is that the 'connection' between belief and fact which is involved is of a quite different nature from that involved in the connection between mental states and particular states of affairs.

It seems, then, that our account of non-inferential knowledge cannot be applied to non-inferential knowledge of law-like connection itself. But in view of the fact that in Part I we found it necessary to give a quite different account of general beliefs as opposed to beliefs concerning particular states of affairs, this should not surprise us. We might expect to have to give a different account of *knowledge* of general connection also.

It might be thought that our problem here could be by-passed. We are at present concerned with *non-inferential* knowledge. Now it is a traditional Empiricist doctrine, at least, that all knowledge *begins* with knowledge of particular matters of fact. Perhaps, then, if we are considering non-inferential knowledge, we need not go beyond knowledge of particular matters of fact.

Unfortunately, however, it seems impossible to maintain that non-inferential knowledge logically must be restricted to particular matters of fact. Consider the case of mathematical prodigies. Sometimes they give the correct answers to difficult mathematical problems, yet can give no account of how they reached the answers. It is difficult to deny that their beliefs on these matters are instances of knowledge. It is at least a possibility that their knowledge is not based on any reasons. If so, they have non-inferential knowledge of general propositions. And we can at least conceive of persons who had the same capacity with regard to some class of unrestricted *empirical* generalizations. An account of non-inferential knowledge of general propositions must therefore be sought. (A further argument to show that there must be some non-inferential knowledge of general propositions will be developed in the first section of Chapter Fourteen.)

IV   Enlargements of the scope of our account of non-inferential knowledge

However, there is one sort of non-inferential knowledge of law-like connection which *can* be brought within the scope of our formula. Very often, we are aware that a certain *particular* situation is governed by a law, but are quite unable to formulate the law. We know that the stone broke the window. On most views of causality, this entails the existence of a law-like connection in nature. If the happening were not governed by a law of some sort, it would not be a case of causation. Yet we might not be able to do more than make a vague gesture towards the specification of the law. Plausible examples of this sort can be found even in the sphere of non-inferential knowledge. If anything is a candidate for non-inferential knowledge, knowledge that pressure is being put upon our body would seem to be a strong candidate. Yet to know that something is pressing upon us is surely to know that something is acting causally. And it is plausible to say that such causal action, like all other causal action, entails that the phenomenon in question is an instance of some law-like connection, even if a law-like connection which we are unable to formulate.

Now, it might be argued, if causal connection entails law-like connection then knowledge of causal connection will entail know-

ledge of law-like connection, at any rate for those who appreciate
the existence of the entailment, even if the knowledge is not knowledge of the specific nature of the law-like connection. And then, it
may be further objected, the account of non-inferential knowledge so
far developed will not serve for knowledge of such law-like connections. It serves only for non-inferential knowledge of spatio-temporally restricted states of affairs. Hence, it might seem, our
account of non-inferential knowledge, as so far developed, is inadequate to deal with such simple matters as knowledge of pressure on
our own body, much less more sophisticated causal knowledge, or
other knowledge involving law-like connection, about particular
states of affairs.

It is important to see that in fact our formula can handle such non-
inferential knowledge. Suppose, for instance, that on a particular
occasion a stone breaks a window. It need not be necessary that an
object with just that nature coming into just that sort of collision
with a thing of the nature of that window should break the window.
For it may be that it breaks the window only because the set-up as a
whole – the standing conditions – is in some way appropriate. But
there must be a specification of the situation, involving the thing
operating, the thing operated upon, and the conditions under which
the operation takes place, which *ensures*, as a matter of natural law,
that the effect takes place. In the same way, if a reliable thermometer
registers 'T°', then this registration together with some specification
H of the thermometer and its circumstances, ensures that the temperature *is* T°. In these cases, then, we will have a particular state of
affairs which ensures the existence of a further state of affairs.

But now suppose that a person, A, non-inferentially believes that
some state of affairs, B, obtains where B, as it happens, ensures
some further state of affairs, C. B might be a physical object of a
certain nature, and moving at a certain speed, coming into contact
with the person's flesh. C might be that flesh yielding. Now there
might be the right sort of reliability in A's non-inferential belief
that B obtains, so that A *knows* this. Because B is a particular state
of affairs, this involves no difficulty. But now consider A's non-
inferential belief that B brought about C. Since B *ensured* C, *the
conditions for the reliability of this belief are exactly the same as the
conditions for the reliability of the belief that B obtained.* So our
formula can cover a belief of the form 'B ensures C', that is: a
belief that one particular state of affairs ensures another.

Hence, although knowledge of the specific *content* of general connections may lie outside the scope of our formula, non-inferential knowledge that, on a particular occasion, causal or other law-like connections hold between particulars – that is, non-inferential knowledge of the *existence* of general connections between particular states of affairs – does not. It may be remarked in passing that what has been said here will, at a later point, enable us to give a simple and convincing treatment of *knowledge of knowledge*.

We must now consider beliefs having as their content an unrestricted *existentially* quantified proposition: a proposition of the form (∃ x) Fx. In the case of necessary propositions which are apparently of this form, for instance 'existential claims' in logic and mathematics, it has already been argued that beliefs with this content can be treated as general beliefs (see Chapter Seven). For it emerges on investigation that the propositions involved are really unrestricted universally quantified ones. Corresponding *knowledge* will therefore be part of the problem of what it is to *know* such general propositions to be true, a problem to be tackled in the next chapter.

But what about knowledge of the following sort: that there exists at least one zebra? It is, of course, unlikely in the extreme that there should be *non-inferential* knowledge of such truths. In practice, no doubt, it would be deduced by existential generalization from knowledge of propositions of the form 'a is a zebra'. But non-inferential knowledge of such truths is an intelligible conception.

However, if there is such non-inferential knowledge, it can be covered by our formula. Why should it not be the case that A believes, without having any reasons for the belief, that there exists at least one zebra, and, furthermore, that A's nature and circumstances be of the sort H, where H is such that, if anybody's nature and circumstances be H, if they further believe that there exists at least one zebra, this belief-state is a completely reliable sign of the existence of at least one zebra? (The existence, of course, need not be *present* existence.)

From the general nature of law-like connection in the world we would expect, indeed demand, that the belief-state will stand in some *particular* natural relationship to at least one particular zebra. For instance, a zebra might have *caused* the belief-state, and, moreover, it might have been the case that nothing but an actual zebra could have caused the belief. This zebra's relationship to the belief-state would then be a factor such that, if it had been absent, the belief-state would not have existed. And so the law-like connection involved will still be between the particular belief-state and a particular zebra or finite collection of particular zebras. It would thus be a connection whose existence could be established, in principle at least, by the methods of natural science. But, unlike the case where A knows that there is a zebra *before him*, the proposition believed and known would not involve any 'mention' of the relationship which the zebra or zebras bore to the believer.

It seems, then, that our formula will serve to give an account of the knowledge-conditions for all non-inferential beliefs with the sole exception of 'general beliefs'.

Let us conclude these two chapters by a final formulation of the doctrine of non-inferential knowledge which we have arrived at.

A's non-inferential belief that c is J is a case of non-inferential *knowledge* if, and only if:

$$(\exists H)[\text{ Ha \& there is a law-like connection in nature}$$
$$(x)(y)\{\text{if Hx, then (if BxJy, then Jy)}\}].$$

(*a*) H must be such that there is a real possibility of the situation covered by the law-like connection recurring.

(*b*) x ranges over beings capable of cognition.

(*c*) y ranges over particulars.

(*d*) B is the belief-operator.

(*e*) The properties mentioned are nomically relevant to the law-like connection.

(*f*) The relationship is restricted to that of reliable sign to thing signified. (It is not the case that BxJy *causes* Jy).

With suitable modifications, for instance for 'existential beliefs', this formula can be adapted to cover all except 'general beliefs'.

14

Inferential and General Knowledge

I Difficulties about inferential knowledge

We must now try to extend our account to cover knowledge that *is* based upon reasons.

In Chapter Eleven, Section One, this problem was raised in a preliminary way. Suppose that A truly believes that p on the sole basis of evidence 'q'. What further stipulation must we make about 'q' in order to ensure that A *knows* that p is true?

We saw that A must know that q is true. This demand leads to an infinite regress if all knowledge is belief based upon further evidence. But we have now given an account of non-inferential knowledge, so that we can argue that the regress of reasons is finite. For simplicity, let us assume that the regress terminates at 'q', so that A knows that q *non-inferentially*.

But it is insufficient that 'p' be true, that A believes that p and that A know that q (non-inferentially). It is further necessary that 'q' be, as an objective matter of fact, a conclusive reason for believing that 'p'. 'q' need not be a *logically* conclusive reason for believing that p, but it must be a conclusive reason. (It will be remembered from the discussion in Chapter Six, Section Eight, that good reasons, of which conclusive reasons are the best sort, need not be reasons which actually operate in anybody's mind.)

For suppose it not to be the case that 'q' is a conclusive reason for 'p'. Then, although A knows that q, and so 'q' is true, it will be possible (and not merely logically possible) that 'p' is not true. A's knowledge that q will not ensure that it is the case that p. And so, by the same line of argument which was developed in Chapter Thirteen, Section One, in connection with non-inferential knowledge, it cannot be the case that A knows that p, even although A believes that p, and it is the case that p.

It was argued in Chapter Six, Section Eight, that to say that 'q' is a conclusive reason for 'p' is equivalent to asserting the truth of the hypothetical proposition 'if q, then p'. So we now add the stipulation that 'if q, then p'. Notice that this condition, together with the condition that A knows that q, makes the stipulation that p be the case a redundant one.

It is now demanded that A believe that p, know that q and that 'q' be in fact a conclusive reason for believing that p. But this is still insufficient for saying that A knows that p. For the belief that p and the knowledge that q may lie alongside each other in A's mind without A making any connection between them. In order to exclude this possibility it must further be stipulated that A's belief that q (entailed by A's knowledge that q) actually functions in A's mind so that A *takes* 'q' to be a conclusive reason for believing that p. (It is not necessary that A be *conscious* of this.)

But our conditions still do not entail that A knows that p. In Chapter Six we gave an account of what it is for somebody to take some proposition to be a conclusive reason for believing some further proposition. It is a matter of A's belief that q *causally sustaining* his belief that p. This sustaining, furthermore, must be an exemplification of some general principle such that, if A acquires, or has, a belief whose content exemplifies the *antecedent* of this general principle, then A is disposed to infer, or at least have causally sustained, beliefs which exemplify the *consequent* of this principle.

This disposition for A's mind to move from belief to belief according to some general principle was identified, following Ramsey, with a *general belief*: a belief that some unrestricted universally quantified proposition is true. But once we make this identification we see that the support of 'p' by 'q' in A's mind, though genuine support psychologically may spring from the operation of some false general principle which in this particular instance moves from truth (q) to truth (p). (We have already stipulated that 'if q, then p' be true. But *A* could be using some quite incorrect principle.) And even where A's general principle is true may it not be the case that A's belief in the principle is a *mere* true belief? Neither of these situations would seem sufficient to entail that A knows that p. Hence we now seem forced to add that A *knows* that the general principle of his reasoning is true. This condition makes redundant the condition that 'q' be in fact a conclusive reason for believing that p ('if q, then p'), because knowledge entails truth. So the suggested conditions for A's inferential knowledge that p become:

(i) A believes that p

(ii) A knows that q (non-inferentially)

(iii) A's belief that q actually functions in A's mind as a conclusive reason for believing that p

(iv) A knows the truth of the general principle of his reasoning.

(Condition (iv) does not make (iii) redundant because of the possibility of A's having the knowledge of the general proposition, but
failing to put this knowledge to work.)

But now, alas, we are once more threatened by an infinite regress.
The trouble lies within the fourth condition. It demands *knowledge*
of the truth of a general proposition. And what account are we
going to give of this knowledge? We have given an account of what
it is to *believe* such propositions, but what must be added, besides
truth, to make the belief into a case of knowledge?

This knowledge of general propositions must either be properly
based upon evidence, or must be non-inferential. If it is *always* based
upon evidence it seems clear that the regress will be vicious. So, after
a finite number of steps, we must base ourselves upon non-inferential
knowledge. It may be suggested that this non-inferential knowledge might be knowledge of particular matters of fact, and that
therefore we need not postulate any non-inferential knowledge of
general propositions. Thus, if it really is the case that we *know* that
arsenic is poisonous (I pass no opinion on this point) then this knowledge might be based upon knowledge of what happened on particular occasions on which arsenic was ingested under experimental
conditions. But the difficulty with this suggestion is that again we
will require knowledge of general propositions (whether necessary
or contingent is not a question here) in order for the particular
evidence to support in our mind the belief that arsenic is poisonous.
That is, we must *infer* from the particular evidence to the general
truth. The inference demands a general principle of inference and
this general principle must be *known* to A. And so it seems that,
if our four conditions for inferential knowledge are to be accepted,
we must allow that such knowledge always involves some *non-
inferential* knowledge of *general* propositions. (We have already
advanced other arguments for this conclusion in Chapter Thirteen,
Section Three.)

Now, as we have seen, our account of non-inferential knowledge in the two previous chapters could not be applied to knowledge of general propositions. So our first necessity seems to be

to give an account of non-inferential knowledge of general propositions.

II Non-inferential knowledge of general propositions

Let us suppose that A believes the general proposition (x)(if Fx, then Gx). Under what conditions can he be said to *know* this (non-inferentially)? We have seen that such a belief is a disposition of A's, and, as a disposition, a *state* of A. For all x, the initiating cause will be acquiring a belief, Fx, the manifestation (if it occurs) will be acquiring a belief, Gx, which continues to be sustained by the antecedent belief. (Unless Gx is already believed, when it simply acquires an additional sustainer.) Now suppose we subject this disposition to a further restriction, which will represent a further characterization of A's state. For all x, *if* the belief having the content Fx is a case of *knowledge*, then the manifestation (if it occurs) *viz.* acquiring a belief of the form Gx, will also be a case of knowledge, which continues to be sustained by the antecedent knowledge. Now it may be suggested, if this condition is added, A *knows* that (x)(if Fx, then Gx).

Putting the matter more formally:

(1) A believes that (x)(if Fx, then Gx) if, and only if:

A is so *disposed* that, for all x, if A believes that Fx, then this belief-state will both create (if necessary) and weakly causally sustain within A's mind the belief that Gx is true.

(In Chapter Six, Section Four (V) it was noticed that such a formula was strictly unsatisfactory, because x might be required to range over individuals which do not exist. But general lines along which the formula could be reconstructed were indicated.)

(2) A *knows* that (x)(if Fx, then Gx) if, and only if:

(i) A believes that (x)(if Fx, then Gx)
(ii) If this disposition (this general belief) is *manifested*, then (x)(if A *knows* that Fx, then A *knows* that Gx).

It is clear that the second condition ensures the *truth* of A's belief. For if there existed an F that was not a G, then, for that value of x, condition (ii) would fail to hold. So, once again, the truth-condition is a redundant one.

General beliefs were recursively defined in terms of causal relations between beliefs about particular matters of fact. And now it is suggested that knowledge of general truths (at any rate for non-inferential knowledge) be recursively defined in terms of causal relations between instances of knowledge of particular matters of fact.

To put the point in a further light. An account of what it is to *believe* a general proposition has been given in terms of a disposition to transmit belief about particular matters of fact. Now we attempt to give an account of what it is to have non-inferential *knowledge* of general propositions in terms of the transmission of knowledge from particular matters of fact to further matter of fact.

With the account just given, I was for a time content. However, Christopher Murphy has pointed out that the two conditions of our formula are insufficient for knowledge of general propositions. Consider the case where A believes that there is a law-like connection in nature which has the form $(x)(Fx \equiv Gx)$, and, furthermore, his belief is true. It is easy to show that in this situation the second condition of the formula must be satisfied. Suppose that A knows that b is F. In that case, given our account of knowledge of particular matters of fact, there exists a condition H, instantiated by A, such that Ha and BaFb together nomically necessitate Fb. But since $(x)(Fx \equiv Gx)$ is also a nomic connection, Ha and BaFb also nomically necessitate Gb. Now A may not believe that b is G, because the disposition that is A's general belief may fail to manifest itself despite the existence of the characteristic initiating cause (A's belief that b is F). But if the disposition does manifest itself, and A comes to believe that b is G, then this belief must also satisfy the condition for knowledge. For Ha and BaGb, which both obtain, nomically necessitate that b is G. This result seems unacceptable. Surely it must be possible for A to come to believe the true proposition '$(x)(Fx \equiv Gx)$' *by accident?*

What is to be done? I think it is clear that the second condition of the formula is a *necessary* condition. For suppose that the disposition that is a general belief manifests itself. Suppose further that the antecedent belief is a case of knowledge. Now apply the 'method of subtraction' and suppose that the *consequent* belief is *not* a case of knowledge. Would we not have to consider that the *general* belief is not a case of knowledge either? For surely *knowledge* of the general proposition thus applied to a *known* premiss must yield knowledge in the conclusion? So, given that the general proposition is known, and that the antecedent belief is also a case of knowledge, we must take it that the consequent belief is also known. But this is a statement of the second condition. It is therefore a necessary condition.

Our problem, then, is only that of finding some further condition to add to our formula to yield necessary and sufficient conditions.

The trouble seems to be that our second condition does not ensure that the general belief is 'controlled' by the facts in the way that beliefs about particular states of affairs are 'controlled' by those states of affairs in our account of non-inferential knowledge of these situations. One would like to say that a belief that arsenic is poisonous is a case of *knowledge* provided that this fact about arsenic is a necessary condition of the belief being held. But how can we say this? How can we connect a state of a man's mind with a fact about every piece of arsenic?

In fact there is something we can do. We can connect the belief-state *with the existence of arsenic*. Suppose that the knowledge-transmitting general belief nomically ensures the existence of arsenic. That is, suppose that the existence of arsenic is necessary for the knowledge-transmitting general belief. The nature of arsenic itself ensures that it is poisonous. So the belief ensures the existence of arsenic which ensures its own poisonousness. May this not be sufficient to turn the knowledge-transmitting belief into knowledge?

In practice, this will mean that the belief, to be knowledge, must have been brought into existence *by the action of individual samples of arsenic*. This action of individual samples of arsenic must be action in virtue of properties of arsenic which are, or which nomically necessitate, its being poisonous. The arsenic must act in virtue of its arsenious-poisonous properties. Then, perhaps, the knowledge-transmitting general belief is more than a mere true belief.

An obvious objection to this suggestion is that it is possible to hold true general beliefs of the form (x)(if Fx, then Gx), although nothing is F. Such a belief could not stand in a nomic relation to F's!

However, it seems that the difficulty can be rather easily provided for. It seems clear that in such cases (i) there will be another true proposition of the form $(x)(\text{if } F_1x, \text{ then } G_1x)$ where there are such things as F_1s and G_1s. (ii) It will be an *analytic* truth that Fs are F_1s, and that Gs are G_1s. *Knowledge* of (x)(if Fx, then Gx) will then demand 'control' of the corresponding belief-state by things of the sort $F_1 G_1$. (In the case of knowledge of analytic truths, it would seem that the appropriate 'control' would not be instances of things falling under antecedent and consequent, but rather the corresponding *concepts* in the mind of the believer. If it is correct to say that the truth of necessary truths generally is wholly determined by the concepts they involve, then the appropriate 'control' for knowledge of all such truths may be the concepts in the mind of the believer.)

So we now say:

A knows that (x)(if Fx, then Gx) if, and only if:

(i) A believes that (x)(if Fx, then Gx)
(ii) If this disposition (this general belief) is *manifested*, then (x)(if A *knows* that Fx, then A *knows* that Gx)
(iii) ($\exists$ J)[Ja and there is a law-like connection in nature such that (y)[if Jy, then {if conditions (i) and (ii) hold, then ($\exists$ z)(Fz)}]].

In the cases where there are no F's, the expression '($\exists$ z)(Fz)' becomes '($\exists$ z)(F$_1$z)' where F bears to F$_1$ the relation just discussed. The same sort of restrictions are placed upon J as were placed upon H in our account of non-inferential knowledge of particular matters of fact. In general, similar qualifying remarks about this condition are required as were required for the law-like connection for knowledge of particular matters of fact.

There remains, of course, the question exactly what general propositions are known non-inferentially. But that is not a question which a mere definition (which is all that we have offered) can be expected to provide, any more than our definition of non-inferential knowledge of particular matters of fact was able to tell us just what facts of this sort are known to us. *Prima facie*, it is a plausible hypothesis that in the case of human beings non-inferential knowledge of general propositions is restricted to relatively simple logical necessities and principles of scientific method. But there is no necessity in such an hypothesis. Chomsky has argued for innate knowledge in man of principles of linguistic functioning. Such principles, assuming them to be truths, will be *contingent* general truths. And if *known* they will, presumably, be known non-inferentially. There is nothing in what has been said to rule out such an hypothesis.

This brings up an interesting final point. Although condition (ii) in the definition ensures the truth of the general proposition believed, there seems no reason why the condition should not obtain even although A does not hold the corresponding belief. (I have stated it in such a way as to appear to presuppose (i), but it is easy to see that this presupposition can be eliminated. We can say 'If this belief is held, then, if it is manifested. . . .') Suppose, then, that conditions (ii) and (iii) hold of A, but (i) does not. What name should we give to the epistemic relation that A then stands in to the proposition which he does not believe?

We might say: A is wired for knowledge of that proposition but does not know it, because he does not believe it, though he may come to believe it. Is this one sort of cognitive state that Chomsky and others might call 'knowledge' by a certain extension of the term? In particular, it seems to fit in very well with what Leibniz says about his innate principles. Just after introducing that great image in his *New Essays* where he compares our innate knowledge to a statue of Hercules embedded deep within a block of marble, he goes on to say:

Thus it is that ideas and truths are for us innate, as inclinations, dispositions, habits, or natural potentialities, and not as actions; . . . (p. 46).

At other times he speaks of our innate knowledge as often being merely 'virtual'. The situation where it was not the case that A believed a certain general proposition, but did answer to conditions (ii) and (iii) with respect to that proposition, could naturally be called a case of 'virtual' knowledge.

III   Inferential Knowledge

The argument of the previous section has been presented somewhat dogmatically. I find it difficult to support what has been asserted except by going on to show its place in a total picture of the nature of knowledge, non-inferential and inferential. But even if my argument is at least provisionally accepted, it will be seen that it has not delivered us from the problem about inferential knowledge developed in Section I of this chapter.

We said there that for A to know that p on the basis of 'q' it was necessary that:

(i) A believes that p
(ii) A knows that q
(iii) A's belief that q actually functions in A's mind as a conclusive reason for believing that p

(iv) A knows the general principle of his reasoning.

A's knowledge of the general principles of his reasoning may be either inferential or non-inferential, but even if inferential it must, it was argued, ultimately involve non-inferential knowledge of general principles. An account of this sort of non-inferential knowledge was then given in the previous section. But, scrutinizing this account, we see that it does nothing to solve our current problem of defining inferential knowledge. For the account of non-inferential knowledge of general principles proceeds, in part, in terms of a causal relationship of a conditional sort between knowledge of the sort q, *and knowledge of the sort p*. But it is (inferential) knowledge that p which we are now trying to define. We are involved in circularity yet again.

What is to be done?

I think we must finally abandon the attempt to see inferential and non-inferential knowledge as different types of knowledge. We have seen reason to think that knowledge of particular matters of fact and knowledge of general popositions are different. A different account must be provided for each, the later being defined recursively by reference to the notion of the former. But *inferential* and *non-inferential* knowledge do not differ as knowledge, whether it is particular matters of fact or general principles which are in question. For we can in fact extend our account of non-inferential knowledge of particular matters of fact to cover *all* knowledge of particular matters of fact, and our account of non-inferential knowledge of general principles to cover *all* knowledge of general principles.

Consider the following simplified situation. A believes that p and knows non-inferentially that q. His belief that q causally sustains his belief that p in such a way that 'q' functions for him as a conclusive reason for believing that p. 'q' is the proposition 'Fb', and 'p' is the proposition 'Gb'. So 'q' sustains 'p' in A's mind on the basis of the general principle (x)(if Fx, then Gx). But A does not simply believe that (x)(if Fx, then Gx), he *knows* it (non-inferentially, let us say). Now our account of such knowledge of general propositions has been in terms of the transmission of reliability from belief to belief. If A knows that b is F, then he will know that b is G. But this knowledge that b is G (knowledge that p), will simply be that complex law-like connection between A's belief that b is G and the actual state of affairs of b's being G which was spelt out in connection with non-inferential knowledge of particular matters of fact. The whole state of affairs, A's knowing that b is F, which is a certain law-like connection between BaFb (Baq) and b's being F (q's being the case) ensures a certain law-like connection between BaGb (Bap) and b's being G (p's being the case). So non-inferential and inferential knowledge of particular matters of fact is, *qua* knowledge, exactly the same sort of thing.

Similarly, *all* knowledge of general propositions, non-inferential or inferential, must be conceived of as in the formula of the previous section. If A knows that (x)(if Fx, then Gx) then, even if his knowledge is inferential, it is nothing more than the corresponding general belief governed by two further conditions. First, if the disposition which is the general belief is manifested, then knowledge that something is F ensures knowledge that that thing is G. Second, the general belief and the knowledge-transmission condition themselves ensure the existence of things of the sort F. This complex state of A may itself be suitably sustained in existence by further pieces of knowledge. Then it is inferential knowledge of the general principle. Or it may have no further pieces of knowledge among its sustainers (it may just be wired-in). Then it is non-inferential knowledge of the general principle. But inferential and non-inferential knowledge of general principles is, *qua* knowledge, exactly the same sort of thing.

At this stage the reader is no doubt finding it difficult to gain an intuitive grasp of the whole analysis. Let us go back to our ever-useful model of the thermometer, but make an addition. Let us suppose that the thermometer is operating in circumstances in which *pressure* varies directly with temperature. If the temperature is T° then the pressure is P. Furthermore, if the thermometer registers 'T°' then this brings it about that an attached pressure-gauge registers 'P'.

Suppose, now, that this whole apparatus, thermometer operating a pressure-gauge, is in a certain state and circumstances. This condition (state and circumstances) is such that *if* the thermometer is giving, not merely a correct, but a reliable reading, *then* the pressure-gauge is giving, not merely a correct, but a reliable reading. The thermometer-reading may not be reliable. It may not even be correct. But the condition of the apparatus is such that *if* the first reading is reliable, so is the second.

Suppose, further, that this condition of the apparatus nomically ensures the existence of the phenomenon of *temperature in these circumstances* (circumstances in which it varies directly with pressure). That is to say, the phenomenon of temperature-in-the-circumstances is nomically necessary for this linking of reliabilities in the apparatus. (A condition that presumably is satisfied in well-constructed instruments.)

An apparatus that satisfies these conditions is in a state which serves as a model for knowledge of general principles. It serves best as a model for *non-inferential* knowledge. But imagine this state sustained by further conditions, in particular by further readings of other parameters of the environment, this sustaining having the same reliable character, *etc.* found in the original connection of the thermometer-reading and pressure-gauge. We then have a model for knowledge of general principles based upon further knowledge of general principles and/or knowledge of particular matters of fact.

It may be noted that the model has one defect. If the thermometer reads 'T°' then the pressure-gauge, as a matter of law-like necessity, has to read 'P'. But we can have a belief concerning some particular matter of fact, know an appropriate general principle, but, on occasion, fail to draw the appropriate conclusion. This is parallel to the defect noted in the thermometer model as a model for non-inferential knowledge. If the temperature is T, then a reliable thermometer has to register 'T°', but A's knowledge that p is not subject to the condition that, if p is the case, then, as a matter of law-like necessity, A believes that p. Unlike the thermometer, knowledge is not a matter of *two-way* reflection.

Inferential knowledge of a particular matter of fact may now be compared with the case where the pressure-gauge is giving a reading of 'P', a reading which is not only correct but reliable in the ways specified, and this reliable reading is the reliable result of a reliable temperature-reading. (The temperature-reading, once more, serving as a model for non-inferential knowledge of some particular matter of fact.)

At this point, our account of the nature of knowledge is finally before the reader.

IV   O'Hair's objection

Gregory O'Hair (private communication) has suggested the following counter-case to any account of knowledge in terms of a law-like connection between belief and the facts. A father believes that his son is innocent of a crime he is accused of. The father has no evidence, it is just a father's partiality. Later the father sees his son's innocence dramatically and unexpectedly proved in court. Beforehand the father merely believed that his son was innocent. Now he knows him to be innocent.

The suggested difficulty for our analysis is this. To be a case of knowledge, a belief must ensure (not, of course, causally ensure) its own truth. But it is clear from his original attitude that the father would have believed his son to be innocent even if the latter had in fact been guilty. So perhaps this belief does not meet our suggested conditions for knowledge. Yet, after the trial, does not the father know?

However, I think O'Hair's case can be dealt with without too much difficulty. Is not the situation one where, although the belief does not change, the further state of the man who has the belief does change? At first, it is clear, there is no empirically repeatable property (the property H in our definition of knowledge) characterizing the father and his situation such that, if anybody has those properties, then, if they further hold a belief of the sort the father holds, then, as a matter of law-like necessity, the belief is true. So the father believes, but does not know. But after the court-hearing the father is characterized in a new way. His mind is filled with evidence of a sort which ensures knowledge of the thing evidenced in any halfway rational person. And so his belief is now reliable in a way which previously it was not. He now instantiates some property H. He knows. If this is correct, O'Hair's case can simply be accepted. It does not falsify my account.

This solution may be illustrated by reference to our model. Suppose that the pressure-gauge can be in one of two conditions – either swinging at random, or under the reliable control of the thermometer. At first the pressure-gauge needle moves randomly. At time t it is registering 'P'. By a coincidence, the pressure *is* P. Suddenly the pressure-gauge needle comes under the control of the thermometer. But it continues to register 'P', but now *because* the pressure is P. In one way, the state of the pressure-gauge is unchanged. But, in another way, it is quite different because now its reading is *reliable*. I suggest that the father was 'firmed up' in the same way.

This solution may be thought to be too simple. Now when the

gauge is in working order again, it is true of it that, if the pressure were not P, then it would not be registering 'P'. But, it may be suggested, even if his son was guilty, and was proved to be guilty in court to the satisfaction of any rational man, perhaps the father would still believe his son to be innocent. O'Hair could, if he wished, write this extra condition into the case, and then it is clearly different from the suggested parallel with the pressure-gauge.

But is this extra condition compatible with saying that the father, after hearing the evidence, now *knows* his son to be innocent? The proof in court appears to have in no way changed his cognitive attitude to his son's innocence – from his point of view the vindication is unnecessary confirmation. But I think it is only if we believe that the new evidence has produced a new cognitive attitude in the father that we would accept that he now knows. If this is correct, O'Hair's case when altered still does not falsify our analysis, because in the altered case the father never achieves knowledge.

V Between inferential and non-inferential

Before ending this discussion of inferential knowledge it may be advisable to say something about knowledge which is not *clearly* inferential knowledge nor yet clearly non-inferential knowledge. The stock example in modern discussion is the knowledge which many of us have that the sun is about 93 million miles away from the earth. Many know this, but most of that many do not even know on whose expert knowledge they are relying. At the same time, it is not a natural case to call 'non-inferential' knowledge. We did have evidence for it once, even if only the evidence that it was asserted in such-and-such a reliable book.

The difficulty here is caused by our demand that reasons, really to be reasons, must continue to be at least weak sustainers of the further beliefs which they are reasons for. This has duplicated in the model just developed, where the temperature-reading causally sustains the pressure-gauge reading. But already in Chapter Six, Section Six, we recognized that there can be processes where belief gives rise to belief, processes subject to rational appraisal because they are manifestations of dispositions to move according to general patterns or principles, but where the first belief does not continue to sustain the second belief. We said that it seemed to be a verbal question whether such a process could be called 'inference' or not.

It is not inference in the full-blooded sense, because there is no possibility of a rational criticism of the person's 'inference' which will affect the person. Convince him that his 'premiss' was untrue, or that the general principle of his 'inference' was incorrect, and this will not affect his belief in the 'conclusion'.

This modified or 'weak' sense of inference would seem to be that required by the case in hand. Knowledge of the evidence showing that the sun is 93 million miles away gave rise to the knowledge of the fact. For a while, the knowledge of the evidence causally sustained the knowledge of the conclusion in the way requisite for inference in the fullest sense. Later the evidence was forgotten, but the belief in the conclusion was retained, and, it may be assumed, remained a reliable belief, that is, an instance of knowledge. It is accompanied, in the case considered at any rate, by the knowledge that it was reliably caused by a reliable belief. We can choose whether to call this inferential or non-inferential knowledge.

We may once again adapt our model to give an illustration. Suppose that the pressure-gauge reading takes the form of a print-out, which records on pieces of paper pressure-readings together with the times at which those pressures obtained. The *later* existence of those pieces of paper might then be reliable indications of what the actual pressure was at that time, even although the temperature-readings which brought the printed pieces of paper into existence did not any longer exist.

15

Further Considerations about Knowledge

In this chapter various topics will be treated in a rather miscellaneous way, with the object of rounding out our account of the nature of knowledge. In the last section it will be argued that not only does the concept of knowledge presuppose the concept of belief, but that the concept of belief presupposes the concept of knowledge.

I Knowledge of Knowledge

It is possible for A to know that p without knowing that he knows it (Kap & ~KaKap), and even for A to know that p and disbelieve that he knows it (Kap & Ba~Kap). Nevertheless, when we know we very often know that we know and, indeed, one who *says* 'I know that p' implicitly commits himself to the claim that he knows that he knows that p. What conditions have to be satisfied for such knowledge of knowledge?

'A knows that A knows that p' (KaKap) is simply a substitution-instance of 'A knows that A_1 knows that p' (KaKa$_1$p) for the special case where $a_1 = a$. In what follows I give an account of the general case which can then be applied without the slightest difficulty to the special case. In the case where A knows that he himself knows something this knowledge of knowledge will often be non-inferential, a situation which seldom if ever occurs in the third person case. But we have given the same account of both inferential and non-inferential knowledge of particular states of affairs.

There are two things to be noted about knowledge of knowledge. First, it is knowledge of a particular, spatio-temporally limited, state of affairs. But, second, if our account of knowledge has been correct, the state of affairs known is that further states of affairs (the original belief-state and the state of affairs that makes the belief true, in the case of knowledge of knowledge of particular matters of fact) are

212

connected together in a law-like way, although normally the exact nature of this law-like connection is not known. It is therefore to be dealt with in precisely the same way as other situations where we know *that* a law-like connection exists between states of affairs, but do not necessarily know what the connection is. (See Chapter Thirteen, Section Three.)

If somebody knows that some particular state of affairs obtains, then not only does he believe it obtains, but he is in a certain sort of state and situation such that, if anybody is in this state and situation and further holds a belief of this sort, then this belief is true. Given Ha (the state and situation) and Bap, then it is ensured that p is the case. So if somebody A_1 is to know that A knows that p, all that is necessary is that (i) A_1 *believes* that A knows that p; and that (ii) A_1 be in some state and situation, call it H_1, such that A_1's being H_1 together with A_1's belief that A knows that p, ensures, as a matter of natural law, that the conjunction of Ha and Bap obtains. $\{H_1a_1 \ \& \ Ba_1 \ (Kap)\}$ ensures that (Ha & Bap). And (Ha & Bap) ensures Kap. If a_1 is the same person as a, simply substitute a for a_1 in these formulae. (Even if $a_1 = a$, it does not follow that $H_1 = H$.)

The situation will be no different when the knowledge of knowledge is a case of knowing that somebody knows that a (specified) general proposition is true. We have argued that a belief that a general proposition is true is a disposition of the believer and that dispositions are states of the disposed objects. We have argued further, in the previous chapter, that *knowledge* of that general proposition is simply a further somewhat complex specification of the state which is the belief. And so to know that somebody knows a specified general proposition is, roughly, to believe that it is known, and, further, for the believer to be in some state and situation such that, if anybody is in this state and situation and has a belief of this sort, then the existence of the mental condition which constitutes knowledge of the general proposition is ensured.

So it turns out that knowledge of knowledge involves no especial difficulties but is (despite the apparent complexity of the statement in the previous two paragraphs) simply a routine application of our account of knowledge. We are thus enabled finally to answer the 'epistemological' objection to our analysis which was considered in Chapter Thirteen, Section Two. There the difficulty was raised that our account would never allow us to say that we know that we know certain things (as, quite obviously, we do). According to the thesis of this book we know when our beliefs are correlated with the world in a certain sort of way. But, it was asked, how could we ever know that such a correlation obtained? The answer now is clear. We know that we know that p when the belief that we know that p has the right sort of correlation with our knowledge that p. And this correlation between particular states of affairs of certain sorts involves no more difficulties than the original correlation between the belief that p and the situation that makes 'p' true. The same can be said of knowledge of knowledge of knowledge, and so on indefinitely. The objector has been guilty of begging the question by assuming that the account of knowledge of knowledge will be different from the account of knowledge *simpliciter*.

II   Knowledge of Probabilities

Like knowledge of knowledge, knowledge of probabilities seems to present few difficulties for our scheme. On the contrary, our analysis appears to cast light upon one type of judgement of probability. Suppose that somebody judges that it is more probable than not that there will be rain tomorrow. It is likely that somebody who believes this, will have evidence for his belief. And it seems that he should have evidence, because it is a commonplace of modern discussion of the subject that probability is *relative to evidence*. Relative to true evidence E, it may be more probable than not that there will be rain tomorrow. Relative to true evidence E_1, evidence which includes E as proper part, it may be certain that it will rain tomorrow.

But is it necessary that such a judgement of probability be backed by evidence? A man may 'feel it in his bones' that a certain event will occur. He has a belief for which, perhaps, he has no evidence. If the belief is correct, we may be prepared to concede that he *knew* that this event would occur. We have spelt out the conditions for such knowledge in this Part of this book. But is it not at least possible that A should believe it more probable than not that it will rain tomorrow, have no evidence for this belief, *and yet the belief be a case of knowledge*?

Our approach to the analysis of knowledge of particular facts enables us to give sense to this possibility. The point is that instead of speaking of the probability of a particular occurrence as relative to evidence, we can instead speak of it as relative to probabilifying conditions. Given certain particles in certain quantum states, a certain quantum-jump may have a certain probability. Now why should not A's belief-state, the belief that it is more probable than not that it will rain tomorrow, constitute such a probabilifying condition? Could it not be the case that, given a believer in the circumstances that A is in, and holding that belief, then as a matter of law-like necessity, it is more probable than not that it will rain tomorrow? If so, A's belief will be non-inferential knowledge of this probability. We should expect, in such a case, that there are meteorological conditions of a certain sort, C, that both (i) are causally responsible for A's belief and of which A's belief is a reliable sign, and (ii) make it more probable than not that it will rain tomorrow.

Normally, of course, A will have evidence (whether or not he can state this evidence) for believing that it is more probable than not that it will rain tomorrow. If A knows this evidence, and if this knowledge supports his belief that it is more probable than not that it will rain tomorrow in the proper way, then we have a straightforward case of inferential knowledge of a particular matter of fact.

I think that this is all that need be said here concerning knowledge of probabilities, except to reiterate an important point already made in Chapter Thirteen, Section One. We have rejected the notion that knowledge is nothing more than *very probable* true belief. We demanded the empirical *necessity* of truth, not simply high probability. But since there is no difficulty in bringing knowledge of probabilities within our scheme, we are in a position to soften the blow. Knowledge is a belief that *must* be true. But may it not be that on many occasions *what is known* is not always exactly what we *say* that we know? We hear a noise, and say that we know that there is a train within earshot. But, very often, should we not be a little more cautious and simply claim to know that *it is very probable that there is a train within earshot*, or, *barring something enormously improbable, there is a train within earshot*? For is it not *just* possible (*empirically* possible) that someone is simply playing a tape-recording outside our window? And if so, on our account of knowledge at any rate, we may not *know* that there is a train within earshot. But it seems clear that, in many such situations, the more cautious statement in terms of high probability *must* be true, and so is known.

III   Certainty

In Chapter Ten, Section Five, it was noted that there is some link between knowing that p is true and being certain (quite sure) that p is true. It is not the case that 'Kap' entails 'Cap'. But it is paradoxical to *say* 'I know that p is true, but it is not the case that I am certain that p is true'. The sentence can be turned round to give 'I am certain that p is true, but it is not the case that I know that p is true' and this sentence is still paradoxical, though perhaps it could be used by the speaker as a report on his (irrational) state of mind. The paradoxical nature of these sentences suggests the existence of some conceptual link between knowledge and certainty.

Now that we have given an account of the nature of knowledge we can understand the nature of this link. We have argued that knowledge of particular matters of fact is a belief that (as a matter of fact) has to be true. Suppose, then, that I claim to know such a particular matter of fact. My claim is that my belief is a belief which it is impossible should be wrong. I am claiming that there is literally no chance of its being incorrect. But if this is so, then I must regard any doubt about the proposition on my part as irrational. Certainty is the only attitude appropriate to the situation if the situation is as I claim it to be. So to claim to know, but simultaneously to admit that I lack certainty about the proposition I claim to know, must be an absurd performance.

What of claims to know that *general* propositions are true? Belief that such a proposition is true is a disposition to infer according to a pattern given by that proposition. The belief is a case of knowledge only if the antecedent belief being a case of knowledge ensures that the consequent belief is a case of knowledge. If a transmission of knowledge is thus *ensured*, the appropriate subjective attitude of the knower must again be certainty.

IV   Metaphysical implications of our account of Knowledge

If our analysis of knowledge has been on the right lines, then two conclusions of metaphysical interest can be drawn from it.

First, a formal limit is set to the possibility of knowledge. Knowledge is a law-like connection between belief-states and the world, or, in the case of unrestricted universally quantified propositions, a law-like connection of a conditional sort between belief-states. It follows, therefore, that if there is anything in the universe which completely lacks law-like connection with other things, it cannot be known. And to the extent that anything lacks such connections, to that extent it cannot be known, although some proposition about the probability of its occurrence might be known. But a thing which is quite outside the nexus of natural law is unknowable in principle. Such a conclusion does not seem counter-intuitive.

Second, the fact that the *epistemological* concept of knowledge presupposes the ontological concept of law-like connection seems to have some bearing on the 'problem of induction'. Philosophers have argued, or have been tempted to argue, in the following way. 'We can know the truth of certain particular matters of fact, *viz.* those which fall wholly within the scope of our senses, of our introspective awareness or of memory. These truths furnish us with our evidential base. But this evidential base is insufficient to yield knowledge of any universal connection in nature and, for all we *know*, there are no universal connections in nature.' But, on our account of knowledge, this line of thought involves a concealed contradiction. For if we know anything at all, even the existence of particular states of affairs, then it is entailed that there are at least some law-like connections in nature: those connecting our knowledgeable beliefs to the world. And once we are committed to these, it will be in the highest degree arbitrary to be sceptical about the existence of other law-like connections in nature.

I do not want to claim too much for this point. Perhaps the 'problem of induction' can be posed without initially claiming *knowledge* of any evidential base. But if the inductive sceptic is so incautious as to claim such knowledge, then, I claim, he covertly asserts the existence of some general connections while being overtly doubtful that we have knowledge of any.

V Scepticism

But what of a more thoroughgoing sceptic? What of the sceptic who argues that, if knowledge is a matter of law-like connection between belief-states and the world, then we have no good reason to think that our beliefs do ever answer the conditions for knowledge?

Such a sceptic is selective in his scepticism also. He admits the existence of beliefs (as he must if there is to be anything to be sceptical about), but asks what reason there is to account any of them knowledge. But has he any greater assurance of the existence of beliefs than he has assurance that some of these beliefs answer the conditions for knowledge? If he has not, his scepticism is selective, and, worse, arbitrarily and irrationally selective.

If the sceptic attributes beliefs to other people, then, presumably, he is making inferences and hence assuming the existence of general connections in the world. So he must set such beliefs aside. In the case of his own beliefs we may distinguish between his past and present belief-states. If he attributes beliefs to himself in the past, he is relying on memory. Now what reason can he offer for the reliability of his memory that in the past he existed and held certain beliefs? Presumably, he is claiming to *know* that he existed and held certain beliefs. But wherein lies the superiority of this claim to knowledge over any other claim about the past? What is the distinction in epistemological status between the claim to know that 'yesterday I believed it was raining', and the claim to know that 'it was raining yesterday'?

Perhaps the sceptic will try to base himself upon his *current* beliefs. Perhaps he can give these special epistemological warrant, by appealing to the doctrine of the infallibility of current consciousness. These beliefs will have then been selected in a non-arbitrary way. But if this doctrine is accepted (as I think it should not be) it limits the sceptic's epistemological base to the current *instant*. And so, as Russell has repeatedly emphasized, the sceptic will be reduced to putting his problem as the problem of extrapolating from the current instant of consciousness to everything else we claim to know. It is hard to take such a problem seriously.

But if the argument of this book is correct, the sceptic's position is even more arbitrary than this. In Chapter Five we argued that belief-states involve *Ideas*, which involve *concepts* which in turn involve *simple* concepts. And possession of the simple concept of X entails that its possessor has a *capacity* which, in suitable circumstances, issues in the forming of true beliefs about X's, as a result of the action of an X upon the possessor's mind. This true belief will therefore be a reliable true belief, it will be a case of *knowing* that something is X. It follows that in crediting somebody with a belief we are, implicitly, crediting him with an empirical capacity to *know* certain things (whether or not this capacity is ever exercised).

So beliefs entail a capacity for knowledge, a capacity for having beliefs that stand in law-like relations to the world. But if this is so, *knowledge* of our own beliefs, even beliefs which we currently hold, must be an extremely sophisticated sort of knowledge. It entails knowledge of our own *capacities*. So it certainly cannot be epistemologically prior to all knowledge of law-like connection in the world. Rather, it assumes that we have such knowledge. It *is* arbitrary, therefore, to admit the existence of such beliefs but raise questions about everything else.

But why should not the sceptic be arbitrarily selective in his scepticism, simply *choosing* to rest upon his own beliefs as his only epistemological base? I do not know how to answer such a desperate man. Do we need to?

Conclusion

The outline, if not the detail, of the conclusions reached in this essay may be summed up quite briefly.

Beliefs about particular matters of fact (including beliefs whose content is an unrestricted existentially quantified proposition) are structures in the mind of the believer which represent or 'map' reality, including the believer's own mind and belief-states. The fundamental representing elements and relations of the map represent the sorts of thing they represent because they spring from capacities of the believer to act selectively towards things of that sort. *General beliefs*, however, that is, beliefs in the truth of unrestricted universally quantified propositions, are dispositions, in the precise sense that brittleness is a disposition, to extend the 'map', or introduce relations of causal sustenance between portions of the map, according to general rules. It was argued that all propositions of logic and pure mathematics, whether true or false, and including apparently 'existential' claims in these fields, may be reduced to general propositions. If so, belief in the truth of such propositions reduces to general beliefs.

The *truth* of propositions, and so the truth of what is believed, is determined by the correspondence of actual or possible belief-states, thoughts or assertions to reality. But, unlike the classical correspondence theory, it is not demanded that the relation be one-one in every case.

Knowledge of the truth of particular matters of fact is a belief which must be true, where the 'must' is a matter of law-like necessity. Such knowledge is a reliable representation or 'mapping' of reality. *Knowledge of general propositions* are dispositions to extend the 'map', or introduce relations of sustenance between portions of the map, in such a way that not merely belief, but reliability of belief, is transmitted according to general rules. To be knowledge, such a disposition must further ensure, as a matter of law-like necessity, the existence of the sort of phenomenon that is the subject of the general proposition.

This account of the nature of belief, truth and knowledge is offered as a contribution to a naturalistic account of the nature of man.

Works referred to

Anderson, J. (1962) *Studies in Empirical Philosophy*, Angus and Robertson

Armstrong, D. M. (1968) *A Materialist Theory of the Mind*, Routledge
(1969) 'Does Knowledge entail Belief?', *Proc. Aristotelian Soc.*, 69 (1969–70)
(1971) 'Meaning and Communication', *Philosophical Review*, 80
(1972) 'Materialism, Properties and Predicates', *Monist*, 56

Austin, J. L. (1961) 'Other Minds' in *Philosophical Papers*, Oxford

Ayer, A. J. (1956) *The Problem of Knowledge*, Macmillan

Barnes, W. H. F. (1963) 'Knowing', *Philosophical Review*, 72

Berkeley, G. *The Principles of Human Knowledge*, Everyman

Black, M. (1952) 'The Identity of Indiscernibles', *Mind*, 61

Braithwaite, R. B. (1933) 'The Nature of Believing', *Proc. Aristotelian Soc.*, 33 (1932–3)
(1946) 'Belief and Action', *Proc. Aristotelian Soc.*, Supp. Vol. 20

Brentano, F. (1960) 'The Distinction between Mental and Physical Phenomena', trans. D. B. Terrell, in *Realism and the Background of Phenomenology*, ed. R. M. Chisholm, The Free Press

Chomsky, N. (1968) *Language and Mind*, Harcourt, Brace and World

Danto, A. (1968) *Analytical Philosophy of Knowledge*, Cambridge

Dretske, F. (1971) 'Conclusive Reasons', *Australasian Journal of Philosophy*, 49

Feinberg, G. (1970) 'Particles that travel faster than light', *Scientific American*, 222 (Feb.)

Geach, P. (1957) *Mental Acts*, Routledge

Gettier, E. L. (1963) 'Is Justified True Belief Knowledge?', *Analysis*, 23

Goldman, A. I. (1967) 'A Causal Theory of Knowing', *Journal of Philosophy*, 64

Harrison, J. (1957) 'Does Knowing imply Believing?', *Philosophical Quarterly*, 7
(1962) 'Knowing and Promising', *Mind*, 71

Heidelberger, H. (1963) 'Knowledge, Certainty and Probability', *Inquiry*, 6

Hochberg, H. (1967) 'Nominalism, Platonism and "Being True of"', *Noûs*, 1

Hume, D. *A Treatise of Human Nature*, Everyman 2 vols.

James, W. (1950) *Principles of Psychology*, Dover 1950

Kyburg, H. E. (1965) 'Probability, rationality and a rule of detachment' in *Proceedings of the 1964 International Congress for Logic, Methodology, and Philosophy of Science*, ed. Y. Bar-Hillel, North Holland

Leibniz, G. W. *New Essays concerning Human Understanding*, translated Alfred G. Langley, Open Court (1949)

Locke, J. *Essay concerning Human Understanding*, Everyman 2 vols.

MacIver, A. M. (1958) 'Knowledge', *Proc. Aristotelian Soc.*, Supp. Vol. 32

O'Connor, D. J. (1968) 'Beliefs, Dispositions and Actions', *Proc. Aristotelian Soc.*, 69 (1968–9)

Peirce, C. S. (1940) *The Philosophy of Peirce*, ed. J. Buchler, Routledge

Plato, *Meno*, translated by W. K. C. Guthrie,
Plato: Protagoras and Meno, Penguin, 1956; *Phaedrus, Republic, Theaetetus*

Quine, W. V. (1961) From a Logical Point of View, Harper & Row.

Radford, C. (1966) 'Knowledge – by examples', *Analysis* 27 (1966–7)

Ramsey, F. P. (1931) *The Foundations of Mathematics, and other Logical Essays*, Routledge

Russell, B. (1912) *The Problems of Philosophy*, Home University Library

Ryle, G. (1949) *The Concept of Mind*, Hutchinson

Skyrms, B. (1967) 'The Explication of "X knows that p"', *Journal of Philosophy*, 64

Squires, R. (1968) 'Are Dispositions Causes?', *Analysis* 29 (1968–9)

Stout, G. F. (1923) 'Are the Characteristics of Particular Things Universal or Particular?', *Proc. Aristotelian Soc.*, Supp. Vol. 3

Unger, P. (1968) 'An Analysis of Factual Knowledge', *Journal of Philosophy*, 65

Watling, J. (1954) 'Inference from the Known to the Unknown', *Proc. Aristotelian Soc.* 55 (1954–5)

Wittgenstein, L. (1953) *Philosophical Investigations*, Blackwell
(1961) *Tractatus Logico-Philosophicus* translated D. F. Pears and B. F. McGuiness, Routledge

Woozley, A. D. (1952) 'Knowing and not Knowing', *Proc. Aristotelian Soc.* 53 (1952–3)

Index